Ian Shaw is a former sch[...]...er, intelligence officer and security risk manager in both the aviation and insurance industries. With postgraduate qualifications from both Australian and American universities, he has divided his working life between the theoretical and the practical in two particular areas.

The first is the history and development of terrorism in Australia and the region, and he has written and presented widely on this area of expertise.

The second is Australian history, specifically our social history and those vents and influences that have shaped the Australian character. Ian's first book, *The Bloodbath* (Scribe, 2006) examined how one game of Australian rules football influenced both the code and the society around it, while *On Radji Beach* looks at another significant event, this one shaping Australian attitudes in the immediate postwar period.

Ian and his wife live in Canberra where he writes and designs, develops and delivers training packages across a range of disciplines.

ON RADJI BEACH

IAN W. SHAW

First published 2010 in Macmillan by Pan Macmillan Australia Pty Limited
1 Market Street, Sydney

Copyright © Ian Winton Shaw 2010

All rights reserved. No part of this book may be reproduced or transmitted in any form or by any means, electronic or mechanical, including photocopying, recording or by any information storage and retrieval system, without prior permission in writing from the publisher.

National Library of Australia
Cataloguing-in-Publication data:

Shaw, Ian Winton.
On Radji Beach.

ISBN 9781405040242 (pbk.)

Bullwinkel, Vivian, 1915–2000.
Australia.
Army.
Royal Australian Army Nursing Corps – Biography.
Nurses – Australia – Biography.
World War, 1939–1945 – Prisoners and prisons, Japanese.

940.547252

Every endeavour has been made to contact copyright holders to obtain the necessary permission for use of copyright material in this book. Any person who may have been inadvertently overlooked should contact the publisher.

Typeset by Post Pre-press Group
Printed in Australia by McPherson's Printing Group

Papers used by Pan Macmillan Australia Pty Ltd are natural, recyclable products made from wood grown in sustainable forests. The manufacturing processes conform to the environmental regulations of the country of origin.

*'Duty is weightier than a mountain while
death is lighter than a feather.'*
Imperial Rescript of the Emperor Meiji of Japan, 1882

CONTENTS

Prologue: Keppel Harbour, Singapore, February 1942 — 1

Part One: Rising Sun
1. Elbow Force — 9
2. 'The Land of Stinks, Chinks and Drinks' — 24
3. Reinforcements — 42
4. The Balloon Goes Up — 65
5. The Curtain Comes Down — 90
6. The Last Voyage of the *Vyner Brooke* — 120

Part Two: Banka
7. Banka Strait — 147
8. Adrift — 167
9. On Radji Beach — 197

Part Three: Setting Sun
10. Sumatra — 231
11. The Song of Death — 261
12. Homecoming — 280
13. All Their Tomorrows — 301

Postscript — 318
Endnotes — 329
Sources — 338
Bibliography — 341
Acknowledgements — 346
Index — 349

PROLOGUE
KEPPEL HARBOUR, SINGAPORE, FEBRUARY 1942

The little ship was painted battleship grey, she flew the white ensign and she had a four-inch cannon neatly mounted in her bow, and in some eyes that was enough to make her a warship. Appearances were not going to fool too many people though. Anyone who knew anything about the little ship also knew that the paint and the popgun – for that was all the cannon at the front really was – were just window-dressing, designed to trick both friend and foe that she was more than she really was, and could do more than she really could.

She may have been a support vessel, perhaps, or even one of the tenders that had bustled around the mighty *Prince of Wales* or *Repulse*, battleship and cruiser, and pride of the Royal Navy in the Far East, until they had gone to the bottom a few short weeks earlier, blown apart by Japanese bombs and torpedoes. She wasn't nearly that grand though, just a simple freighter, christened the *Vyner Brooke* after a local potentate, one of the White Rajahs of Borneo. Until two months ago she had worked

PROLOGUE

the route between Kuching and Singapore and sundry other ports, carrying lots of freight and sometimes a few passengers as well. She wasn't the largest, but she was one of the most reliable ships of the Sarawak Steamship Company.

And now she was about to run for her life.

The *Vyner Brooke* would carry no freight on this trip, and her cargo consisted solely of human beings. Those on board would be under Royal Navy leadership and Royal Navy discipline. The ship's captain was a newly minted officer of that navy, a middle-aged captain of the Sarawak Steamship Company, R.E. Borton, known to all as 'Tubby'. A Yorkshireman, Tubby had spent more than a decade in the Far East, living in a comfortable cottage in Orchard Road, Singapore, raising a family of four, and plying his trade while learning the ins and outs of sailing among the thousands of islands that comprised the Straits Settlements, the Netherlands East Indies, the Philippines and all the little sultanates that made up the region. Now he was saying goodbye to his home and his profession. He doubted whether he would be returning to either.

Tubby Borton also had a crew he could be truly proud of. The loss of the two capital ships in early December had been an unmitigated disaster, but perhaps a little bit of good had come of it, as it created a pool of professional sailors without ships to sail. The final evacuation of Singapore provided those ships.

Borton's first officer, Bill Sedgeman, and his second officer, the engineer Jimmy Miller, were both regular officers of the Royal Navy who had survived the loss of their ship, as indeed had most of the *Vyner Brooke*'s crew of 30. The remainder of the crew was Malay, professional sailors and members of the Straits Settlements Volunteer Naval Reserve. It was these Malays who would man the forward-facing cannon and the two elderly Lewis guns mounted on either side of the bridge, and who would direct

PROLOGUE

the passengers to their quarters, to their meal areas and, if necessary, to their lifeboat stations if the *Vyner Brooke* should need to be abandoned.

The passengers were also a mixed lot. Tubby Borton was told he would be taking aboard 200 passengers for this trip, but he was too busy to count them. What he did know, however, was that there were more people aboard than he had ever carried before. They were in groups stretched out on the decks, in clusters in the main saloon area just below the bridge, and in families in the ship's cabins, filling up those originally built for paying passengers in the past, and those officer and crew spaces that had been given up by the ship's complement.

Most of the passengers Tubby had seen were civilians, men and women and children fleeing Singapore before its inevitable surrender to the advancing Japanese forces. Some of the passengers were very young, and some quite old, but most were adults. From Singapore he recognised the redoubtable Mrs Brown, wife of one of that city's senior businessmen and arbiter of good taste in that colonial society. Mrs Brown, accompanied by her vivacious daughter Shelagh, was accustomed to deference and was not backward in letting those around her know that she was a person of both importance and substance.

There were many others from further north, people who had been displaced by the Japanese advance down the Malay Peninsula during the last ten weeks. Like the young and very pregnant Olga Neubrunner, wife of an up-country planter and reserve soldier, who had fled from the far north through Kuala Lumpur and the various states and principalities to ultimately arrive at Singapore's harbour. Some had run even further. Mr and Mrs Warman and their little boy Misha, Polish Jews, had first fled east ahead of the advancing German Army and, finding the Soviet Union only marginally more comfortable, had continued east through the

PROLOGUE

Urals, across Siberia to Manchuria and then south to Shanghai, where they paused for breath. The threat of Japanese aggression and further war sent them once more to the south and east, to Singapore, where the war they were running from finally caught up with them.

The *Vyner Brooke* was not just a passenger ship but an auxiliary vessel of the Royal Navy, and she carried representatives of several of the armed services currently engaged in the conflict with Japan. Because for Singapore there was only one possible outcome of that conflict, the Allied High Command there had finally authorised the evacuation of particular service personnel. That decision had been made just two days previously, and it was already starting to look like a case of both too little and too late. Some of these particular personnel were specialists with technical knowledge that made them simply too important to be allowed to fall into the hands of the Japanese – radar technicians, code breakers and cipher clerks, intelligence officers and the like. Their representative aboard the *Vyner Brooke* was the Australian major Bill Tebbutt, a staff officer with the 8th Division who had some intelligence responsibilities within the Australian command.

And then there were the nurses, 65 of them, clearly distinguishable in their light grey uniforms and armbands displaying the red cross of their profession. They were all members of the Australian Army Nursing Service, and they represented all three medical units dispatched to Malaya in 1941 – the 2/10th Australian General Hospital, the 2/13th Australian General Hospital and the 2/4th Casualty Clearing Station. They were led by two matrons – Olive Paschke of the 2/10th and Irene Drummond of the 2/13th – and they were just about the last Australian service personnel who would be authorised to evacuate the doomed city.

And Singapore was certainly doomed. Individually and in

PROLOGUE

their small groups, the nurses looked back across the water to a scene they would all remember to the day they died. Although the sun had set an hour earlier, the fires that lined the foreshore provided almost enough light to read by. Some of the fires came from godowns, harbourside warehouses stacked high with rubber, and others from various freight forwarders and provedores and from all those businesses that accumulate around the world's great port cities. The fires were started by bombs and shells and fallen wires, and they would continue until they burned themselves out.

For the Australian sisters, it was not even a bittersweet farewell. Not one of them had wanted to leave and, until the previous day they all believed they would remain on the island until the drama that was the Malayan Campaign played itself out. In their hearts they believed that their place was with the wounded Australian soldiers they had been nursing in ever-increasing numbers for the past month.

Somewhere below them, the engines started and the propeller slowly moved through the water, pushing the *Vyner Brooke* ahead and around. Up on the bridge deck a clearly Australian female voice began to sing, 'Wish Me Luck as You Wave Me Goodbye', and they all knew it was Jenny Greer because she would sing no matter what came along. But the voice faltered and then faded away as no-one joined in. They understood that something important in their lives had just ended and that they were moving into an unknown future. Tomorrow would be Friday the 13th, and Tubby Borton was well aware of sailors' superstitions about setting off on that date. He was also aware that Japanese ships controlled the seas and Japanese aircraft controlled the skies, and doubted that there was a Friday the 13th in their calendar.

'Half speed ahead,' he ordered.

PART ONE

Rising Sun

CHAPTER 1

Elbow Force

To all who were officially required to refer to her in their orders and their correspondence, she was the *QX*, and at the end of January 1941 she sat majestically at anchor off Bradley Head in Sydney Harbour. Even at that distance she dominated both the harbour and the city, and those who had no reason to call her the *QX* called her instead the name she was given at birth – the *Queen Mary*. She weighed 80,000 tonnes, had reputedly been the most luxurious ocean liner in the world and was the pride of the Cunard Line. While still holding the record for the fastest ever Atlantic crossing, she had been pressed into service when World War II broke out in September 1939. Eighteen months later, she had been converted into the world's largest and fastest troopship, painted battleship grey and remained the most impressive naval auxiliary vessel in the world.

The *Queen Mary* was clearly visible from Pyrmont Dock,

and it was here that most of the action was taking place in the days following her arrival. From late in the evening of 31 January, trains carrying large numbers of troops had been pulling into Pyrmont Station. Dozens and then hundreds of soldiers emerged from carriages emblazoned with chalk-written slogans on the doors. 'Look out Adolf' was a common theme, followed closely in popularity by 'Berlin or Bust'. Once unloaded, the soldiers would form into their platoons and companies and march down the hill to the dock.

Trucks carrying all shapes and sizes of boxes and cartons and crates also discharged their loads at the dock. All carried distinct writing in white paint – 'Elbow Force' – which was stencilled in large letters on each, and the soldiers joked about whether this was a designation, a description or an order. A few noticed that some had the word 'Singapore' stencilled in smaller letters below.

After a sit down and a smoke, the soldiers were placed into units, lines that shuffled across the dock slowly to the boarding stages, where they were directed to either lighters or ferries that slowly sailed down the harbour to the ship in the distance. Eventually, 5850 members of the 22nd Brigade of the 8th Division of the 2nd Australian Imperial Force (AIF) travelled that route. The overwhelming majority of them wore khaki but interspersed in the muddy green mass were occasional clusters of scarlet and grey uniforms.*

Those uniforms belonged to army nurses – specifically, to

---

* The 22nd Infantry Brigade Group was made up of three infantry battalions, the 2/18th, 2/19th and 2/20th, all of which were raised in New South Wales. The ancillary units were from all over Australia. The 2/9th Field Ambulance was a Victorian unit built around pre-war militia units in Melbourne but, like most other formations, included members from other states. The designations of those units commence with 2/ to signify they were the second unit to bear that designation. The first unit to be called the 18th Battalion was part of the First AIF and served in World War I. Keeping the original designations with the preface 2/ was seen as one way of continuing the traditions the original units had forged.

members of the Australian Army Nursing Service (AANS) who were now members of the 2/10th Australian General Hospital (AGH) or the 2/4th Casualty Clearing Station (CCS), two of the medical units selected to accompany the 8th Division as it went to war. The AANS had a history which predated many of the other elements in that division, and the nurses it contained were young women of considerable experience and expertise. To be eligible for service, they had to be at least 25 years old with qualifications well in advance of the basic training that all nurses received. Those nurses volunteering for overseas service also had to be under 35 years of age, and their matrons could not exceed 40 years; both figures were revised upward to 45 years later in the war. Upon enlistment, all nurses were given a medical examination and were X-rayed. They were inoculated against typhoid fever and smallpox, and took the pledge and signed an affirmation. They were then issued their uniforms, identity discs – that were to be worn at all times – and pay books, which would be the story of their service lives. Apart from these common features, the nurses were as individually different as the troops they would serve, and typical of the society from which they came.

There were 43 nurses attached to the 2/10th AGH and another eight attached to the 2/4th CCS, and they came from all over the east coast of Australia. There was about a fifty–fifty split between city and country in terms of where the girls had been born, but a clear majority had been nursing in a capital city when their call-up came. Most would be regarded as coming from the middle class, rather than from the industrial working class or the upper class of businessmen and farmers. Nursing was a caring profession, but it was a profession that had attracted some opprobrium as a career path until the early years of the 20th century. By 1941 it was an acceptable career and moreover a career that was attracting increasing numbers of girls who both wanted to make a contribution and to see something of the world; a trained nurse was a valuable commodity in most places.

The girls on the *Queen Mary* were more excited than apprehensive. They had mostly come from all over New South Wales and Queensland and a lot of time was spent in their first few hours aboard the vessel checking out just who the other nurses were. Theirs was a special world, but not a particularly large one. In each state there were only a limited number of training hospitals, and all the nurses were funnelled through these. As well as providing a standardised training regime, the system meant that nurses from one state often knew, either directly or indirectly, those they had trained with as well as many of the girls who had gone before them. Catching up with old friends was one of their first tasks, and talking excitedly among themselves about old friends and new prospects was the second. In their groups and clusters they resembled excited schoolgirls about to go on an excursion.

If the nurses were like schoolgirls, their matron was like a headmistress, and both groups of nurses were fortunate in who had been selected to lead them. Recently promoted, in January 1941 Matron Olive Paschke of the 2/10th AGH was very much one of a kind. She had been born to Australian parents of German extraction at Dimboola in Victoria's farming west on 19 July 1905, and was educated at the local state primary and secondary schools. She also started her working life in Dimboola as a trainee teacher, but in 1930 switched to another profession and commenced nursing training at the Queen Victoria Hospital in Melbourne. She gained her nursing certificate in 1934, and also qualified for certificates in midwifery and infectious disease treatment. She returned to Dimboola to nurse before relocating to Melbourne and the Airlie Private Hospital, where she was employed for four years.

Olive returned to public nursing when she was appointed assistant matron at the Jessie McPherson Community Hospital in Melbourne. A short time later, she became part of the great surge of enlistments that followed the German invasion of France and the Low Countries in May 1940. On 23 July, she joined the AANS as a staff nurse, but was soon promoted to sister and then, in January 1941, to matron of the 2/10th AGH nurses. Olive was an ideal choice for the position. A warm and compassionate woman, she was always on the go and when not on duty could usually be found on either a golf course or a tennis court. She was more than competent at both and enjoyed the outdoor life although, like many of her generation, she had never learned to swim. Within a few weeks of taking up her new position, the nurses were calling her 'Dashing Dot' in tribute to her enthusiasm and energy, and in recognition of her capacity to involve all medical staff at the AGH in her circle of friends. The nickname also reflected her appearance; the original 'Dashing Dot' was an American comic strip character who had first appeared a decade earlier, a 'curly haired girl with long legs and sweetness to her appearance'. All in all, it was a nickname that was totally appropriate.

The qualifications and nickname told only part of the Olive Paschke story, however, for in many ways she was a woman and a nurse ahead of her time. Like all matrons, she possessed an acute sense of responsibility towards her nurses and, through them, to the patients they ministered to. Olive Paschke was always looking for ways to make those ministrations more effective for the patients and more rewarding for the sisters and nurses who delivered them.

In charge of the small group of CCS nurses and second in seniority to Olive Paschke was Matron Irene Drummond, who had been born at Ashfield in Sydney's inner west in 1905, but who had been educated at Catholic girls' schools at Broken Hill and Adelaide, where the Drummond family had lived in the inner-city suburb of Millswood. After leaving school, Irene had trained as a nurse at Miss Laurence's Private Hospital in Adelaide. Following the completion of her initial training, Irene qualified in obstetrics at the Queen's Home Hospital and subsequently worked at Angaston. In 1936, she moved to the Broken Hill and District Hospital, where she was regarded as a kind and extremely competent nurse, well-liked and respected by colleagues and superiors alike. At Broken Hill, she served as a surgical sister and assistant matron before being appointed acting matron in 1940. Irene Drummond enlisted in the AANS in November 1940, and in January 1941 was called up to be matron of the 2/4th CCS.

Again, the qualifications and the travels tell little about the real person. Irene's 'style' as matron was more old-school than Olive Paschke's. She was in many respects more conservative and less likely to make a fuss about the terms and conditions under which she and her charges worked. A very compassionate woman, Irene's life was nursing and would be for as long as she could foresee. She was happy to do her bit and let others consider the big picture. While Olive Paschke could light up a room with her radiant energy, Irene was the quiet achiever. A little tubby and always wearing her trademark round glasses, Irene was like a mother hen fussing over her chicks and greeting all with a cheery smile and a friendly squeeze of the shoulder.

Most of the equipment and stores had been taken aboard the *Queen Mary* by 2 February, and the final troops for embarkation arrived during the next day. There was an air of excitement aboard the vessel that evening, which grew the next morning when the great ship weighed anchor and sailed majestically down the harbour towards the Heads. Hundreds of small craft played around the liner and thousands of spectators lined every vantage point the lower harbour offered, many hoping to catch a last glimpse of a loved one. As she sailed through the Heads, the *Queen Mary* turned to starboard and headed south. The last glimpse many of the spectators on land had of those aboard were spots of grey and scarlet among the sea of drab khaki that lined the rails. The soldiers were off to war and the nurses were going with them.

After clearing the Heads the *Queen Mary* picked up speed in an attempt to confuse any spies who watched her departure and to leave any surface raiders or submarines well behind in her wake. With a top speed in excess of 30 knots there was nothing the Axis powers possessed away from their home waters that could get anywhere near her. The plan was to sail directly south to a latitude well below Tasmania, then angle across the Australian Bight to meet up with a convoy that was to form off Fremantle in Western Australia. Aboard the surging ship, the nurses continued their exploration of the vessel before settling into a shipboard routine.

Despite its drab wartime paint, the ship really remained a luxury liner. As they held commissioned rank, all the nurses were given cabin accommodation. They may have had to share with up to three other nurses, but most cabins had their own bathrooms attached and were very spacious, even by contemporary standards. The nurses had access to the shipboard cinema, the swimming pool and a number of other recreation areas, some of which were out of bounds for Other Ranks and some of which were off limits for males. They had a choice of wet canteens, where drinks were very cheap indeed, they could join in most of the sporting events that were held somewhere on the ship every day, and received several invitations a day to performances by the concert parties of the various units aboard.

If escorted by an army officer, the girls could also attend the nightly cabarets in the ship's ballroom. Matrons Olive Paschke and Irene Drummond were very good about this, asking only that the nurses return to their own quarters 'at a reasonable hour'. From 8 February, a shipboard newspaper called the *X-Press* was published on a daily basis. Olive Paschke called her girls together and told them that she would rather *not* read about them in its pages.

Despite the excitement and the luxury, all the passengers aboard the ship were part of an Australian expeditionary force going to war, and success in war went more often than not to those who were best prepared for conflict. All the Australians aboard were to use part of their time in those preparations. Both the 2/10th AGH and the 2/4th CCS had established their first medical facilities by 2 February, well before they left Sydney, and could take patients from that day. The 2/10th established a ship's hospital, and established it in a way that reflected the realities of their environment. The hospital they put together could handle up to 150 patients, although those patients would be somewhat spread out. The operating theatre was situated in a former salon on one of the ship's lower decks, while a smoking room was converted into the hospital's major general ward. The 2/4th CCS supported the hospital by establishing a dressing station on the 16th deck.

Not that they had a lot to do. There were the usual minor sports injuries, cuts and bruises from overenthusiastic training and an occasional cough and runny nose. The nurses worked their shifts in their long-sleeved cesarine dresses with starched white collars and cuffs, which were fine in the temperate zones but increasingly oppressive as the tropics approached. Between shifts they attended lectures; the treatment of tropical diseases was followed by *The White Race's Responsibility to Native Peoples*, with dire warnings of what would happen if they let the white team down.

As soon as everyone aboard had settled into the shipboard routines and accepted the restraints and responsibilities that attach to active service in wartime, new friendships grew and old ties among colleagues were re-established. It was also the time when individual characteristics and idiosyncrasies began to emerge.

Among the nurses of the 2/10th, second in seniority to Olive Paschke was Sister Nesta James. The two were soon close friends as well as colleagues, and early in the voyage began to stamp their character on their nurses. Olive and Nesta were pretty much of an age – at 37 years, Nesta was one year older than Olive – and were also very attuned to the changed circumstances of their wartime profession. Both were also dark-haired and quite vivacious, but one would never be mistaken for the other. The athletic and effervescent Olive was of average height, but her energy somehow made her seem larger than life, and she often stood out in a crowd. In contrast, Nesta was small. The little sister from Shepparton Base Hospital stood just over 150 centimetres tall in her stockinged feet. She was small, but she smiled a lot.

Friendships also formed on the basis of shared accommodation and previous contacts. In the 2/10th, Marjorie Schuman and Dorothy Gwendoline Howard Elmes, now cabin mates, were as thick as thieves within a few days of sailing, and soon formed the core of a much larger group of friends. Both were extroverts. Marjorie was never called anything but 'Shuie' after an initial meeting, while Dorothy would never be called anything but 'Buddy' because that was who she was and what she was. Shuie was from New South Wales and Buddy was from Victoria, but both were in their late twenties and both were country girls at heart. Shuie was probably the more outgoing of the two, and Buddy liked to set aside a couple of hours several times a week to write letters to family and friends back home.

Twice a week, irrespective of weather, accommodation or any temporary inconvenience, Buddy wrote to a friend she called 'Dear Old Smithy', a young nurse at the Corowa Hospital where Buddy had last nursed. Dear Old Smithy was not particularly old – 24 years in 1941, and therefore not old enough to join the AANS – and was part of a group of young nurses Buddy was mentoring at Corowa.* While specifically addressed to Smithy, Buddy's letters were also for the wider group of young nurses, the 'Tripehounds', and were full of vivid descriptions of life as an army nurse as well as the distractions of sailing off to war in a luxury ocean liner.

One of these distractions was a highly organised and occasionally stratified social life aboard the ship, and it was in this milieu that other characters emerged from the ranks of the nurses. Of the two units in which the girls served, the 2/4th CCS was by far the smaller. The 2/10th AGH was in reality the equivalent of an Australian Base Hospital and was expected to handle up to 1200 patients in general and surgical wards with all the features of a major city hospital. The 2/4th CCS would only ever provide initial treatment to the wounded. Doctors and nurses there would diagnose and treat before sending the wounded on to an AGH for more specialised and detailed treatment.

Because he could do so, Colonel Tom Hamilton of the 2/4th had chosen his matron and his nurses very carefully. The girls in the larger unit, the 2/10th AGH, were from the larger states. The smaller unit recruited from the smaller, less populous states of

---

* Clarice Smithenbecker did eventually follow Buddy Elmes into the AANS, enlisting the day after her 25th birthday. Lieutenant Clarice Smithenbecker was discharged from the army on 13 June 1945.

South Australia, Western Australia and Tasmania. All were talented nurses and under Hamilton and Irene Drummond, the nurses soon established themselves as an extremely efficient and very popular team. Aboard the *Queen Mary*, none was probably more popular than Elaine Balfour-Ogilvy.

Known to family and friends as 'Lainie', hers was a prominent family around Renmark on the Murray River in what was already being called Sunraysia. Her father, Harry, was one of five brothers who had all served in the Boer War, and Harry Balfour-Ogilvy had returned as the most highly decorated South Australian soldier in that conflict. At the time of his enlistment, Harry and his brother Walter were managing one of the family's properties, a 2500 hectare station at Paringa. When they said they were riding to Adelaide to enlist, one of their stockmen asked if he could join up with them. As well as being a very good stockman, this man was also something of a bush poet, and was also named Harry. Most people, however, referred to him as either The Breaker, or as Breaker Morant. Less certain was a family story about a cousin named Clementine, an American who had years earlier married a young Englishman named Winston Churchill.

Lainie was the fourth of five children. Born in 1912, she attended the Woodlands School in Adelaide as a boarder in 1928–29, where she excelled. She was a member of both the dramatic and debating societies, and played in the senior hockey team. Additionally, Lainie was an excellent swimmer and tennis player and, not unsurprisingly, was elected to be a school prefect. In her final year, her singing ability was also considered to be at a level good enough for her to be invited to join the Adelaide Choral Society.

Lainie completed her nursing training at the Adelaide Children's Hospital in 1934 after three years of study, winning the hospital's silver medal for her final results. After graduation, she returned to the hospital as a staff nurse, but it was her personality as much as her professional skills that made her the most popular nurse at the hospital. She loved parties and singing, and was always ready to offer up her version of her favourite song, 'A Nightingale Sang in Berkeley Square'. She also loved the outdoors, camping and fishing, but was always down to earth and very solicitous of her friends. With her older brother Douglas and her younger brother Spencer, Lainie continued the family tradition and volunteered for service when war broke out.

At first, Lainie had to be coaxed to sing at one of the many cabaret evenings aboard the ship, but once she did she amazed those aboard with the clarity, strength and sheer beauty of her voice. Within a few days she was turning down invitations to sing at social nights because she was a nurse, not an entertainer, but those few she did grace with a performance left a lasting impression on all who were present. There were many who said that when she sang her favourite song you could have heard a pin drop.

And so the voyage went. It took just over three days to reach Fremantle. Once they'd docked, some passengers were disembarked for medical treatment or because they had been found unsuitable to remain with their units. Other soldiers, and one or two nurses, joined the *Queen Mary*, now part of a much larger convoy that had formed in Gage Roads just offshore from Fremantle. There was speculation about their future deployment, with most believing the situation in Europe and the Middle East meant that they would probably be deployed to one of those two theatres. For many, it meant that they would be able to duplicate the movements of their fathers and uncles in World War I, and visit the places they had learned about from a very early age.

Others took a different view. A number believed that the Japanese posed a growing threat, and believed their ultimate destination might have something to do with addressing that threat.

A few thought Hong Kong was likely, as it was an important British outpost and one that had Japanese troops literally on its doorstep. Many more thought India was a real possibility, as from India they could travel relatively rapidly to where they would be most useful, whether that was the Middle East or somewhere in Asia. Still others were convinced that Singapore would be their ultimate destination because Singapore and the Straits Settlements were as much a part of the British Empire as Australia or New Zealand. The smart ones also based their beliefs on what they had seen on some of the crates lined up at Pyrmont.

The voyage west from Fremantle was also interesting, primarily because the *Queen Mary* joined a convoy and was therefore compelled to travel at a carefully calibrated speed that reflected the top speed of the slowest ship. As their escort, nippy destroyers hurried from station to station and a lean cruiser sniffed the wind in the distance, while the transports – mostly converted liners of all sizes and breeds – maintained their slow but steady pace towards the horizon approximately in the place where the sun set. By this point in their journey, the girls were all on a first-name basis with each other. The exceptions were the two matrons. No matter how much they wanted to, none of the girls could call Olive or Irene anything other than 'Matron'.

The speed and the direction both changed around Valentine's Day, just as the daytime heat was beginning to take hold. It was around mid-morning when all aboard felt the increase in engine revolutions. Those who could went to the rails and watched in awe as the great ship built up her speed until the bow wave was as large as a tidal race. With her foghorn blasting intermittently, the *Queen Mary* circled the convoy, receiving salutes and signals from all the other vessels. She then turned towards the northwest – the crates on the docks at Pyrmont hadn't lied.

Three days later, the great ship approached Singapore, sailing past Keppel Harbour and entering the Straits of Johore before proceeding towards the British naval base there. Aboard ship, the nurses had been given a comprehensive series of lectures about the base. They had been told that Malaya was one of the most important jewels in the British crown, and that its 300 million rubber trees supplied more than half the world's rubber and its tin mines more than half the world's tin. They heard how this economic powerhouse was divided into federated and non-federated states and crown colonies, all of which were pretty much under the control of the British businessmen and colonial authorities who represented less than two per cent of the population. The rest were a mixture of Malays, Chinese and Tamils, although it was expected that the nurses would have only limited contact with them.

In an era when Brittania ruled the waves, the most important defence for such valuable assets was naval power. During the 1920s and '30s, the massive naval base had been built on Singapore Island, a crown colony, and enormous naval guns emplaced along its southern shores. These defences would keep any potential invaders at bay while the Royal Navy's main battle fleet assembled at Scapa Flow in Scotland and sailed to Singapore to crush the enemy at sea. The process was expected to take 90 days to complete.

There were some apparent flaws in the plan. The naval base was sited some 40 kilometres from Singapore's military headquarters at Fort Canning and was positioned on the opposite side of the island from Singapore City and Fort Canning because that was where the colonial authorities had wanted it put. Utilising the existing facilities in Keppel Harbour at the mouth of the Singapore River had the potential to interfere with trade and that simply could not be allowed. The second, and potentially fatal flaw, was that this 'Main Fleet to Singapore' strategy had fallen apart by February 1941. The Admiralty had already admitted that the situation in the Atlantic and the Mediterranean meant that the main battle fleet of the Royal Navy could not possibly reach Singapore in less than 180 days – six months – and would soon be forced to admit that the fleet would never actually be able to reach Singapore because it was needed elsewhere. The soldiers and the nurses knew lots about the region's rubber and tin, diseases and animals, risks and threats as they sailed slowly up the strait towards the naval base. They also knew there was a welcome awaiting them because they could hear snatches of music.

But they had no idea they were about to enter a house of cards.

CHAPTER 2

'The Land of Stinks, Chinks and Drinks'

Forever afterwards, the girls would recall the assault on their senses that the first few weeks in the Orient represented. There was a colour and a variety of sensory experiences that they would never know at home; sights, sounds and smells that they had not even imagined existed. At the forefront was the constant heat, humidity and otherness of living in a tropical climate, especially one that seemed divided between haves and have-nots, native and expatriate. Most of those expatriates welcomed them to 'the land of stinks, Chinks and drinks' without ever going beyond that glib and meaningless phrase, but in time the girls would come to know all the subtleties of colonial society.

The different smells represented the lush jungle and the humid mangroves as they sailed up the Johore Strait and disembarked, but they were then overlaid with the cooking smells from exotic spices and rich fruits of the region. Added to this was the rank smell of stagnant water that contained all kinds of effluent and waste. The worst of all were the parits, the deep monsoon drains dug in every village and town to prevent the annual inundations of the past. Within a short while – days for some and weeks for others – these smells all melded into one, and that one became a constant in the background, so pervasive that it was rarely noticed. It was the smell of the East and the girls became part of that environment.

It was not really a land of 'Chinks' either, for that was the name given by Australians to those of Chinese descent at least as far back as the gold rushes, and it was quite plain that it was an inaccurate description for the majority of the native people. That majority was Malay, the small, light-skinned occupants of much of the island empires of South East Asia. Generally Muslim and part of a rich historical and cultural tradition, Malays dominated the traditional village and town system of the Malay Peninsula, concentrating on their agricultural pursuits and the raising of families with many children, most of whom seemed attracted to the Australians.

There were Chinese around, especially in Singapore where they had come to dominate both the population and the economy, but elsewhere they were in the minority. They controlled business up and down the peninsula; for instance most shops were owned by Chinese, but they kept pretty much to themselves and their clans. Many had been brought into the area to work in the tin-mining operations, but others had simply seen and seized business opportunities first. The richest people in any village or town or city in Singapore were inevitably Chinese. Again, the Australians seemed to get on better with the Chinese than either of the other two main ethnic groups.

The third of these groups were Indians, overwhelmingly Tamils from the south of India who had been shipped in by British rubber plantation owners to work as indentured labourers. Most remained there, living in the small, self-contained communities that the larger plantations were, with their own schools, hospitals and shops. The labourers were paid a pittance, and this would cause serious problems in time, but when the nurses arrived they were simply another exotic splash of colour on a crowded palette.

'Drinks' were the preserve of the expatriate community, who lived a life that they could not have imagined at home, whether that home was the United Kingdom, Australia or elsewhere. Drinking, and the exaggerated social life that both underpinned and characterised it, was a daily habit. The most renowned establishments in Singapore and the Straits Settlements were based around this. In Singapore, Raffles and the Adelphi Hotel, in Penang, the Eastern and Oriental, and in Kuala Lumpur, the Selangor Club were all bastions of white privilege and white drinking. There were even particular drinks that reflected this obsession – the Singapore Sling and the Stengah existed because they were needed by those who had little else to occupy their leisure time.

The nurses' first impressions were of colours and sounds, smells and movement. Coins rained down from the *Queen Mary* as it tied up at the British Naval Base at Selatar. The wife of the governor of the Straits Settlements, Lady Daisy Thomas, came aboard to personally welcome them, but there were shouts and whistles and orders and, before they knew it, the girls were lined up in marching formation and heading across the vast dock area to railway sidings where a number of trains awaited them. In the gathering dusk, they took a cup of tea with volunteers at a Salvation Army tent where their names and home addresses were also taken so their families could be informed of their safe arrival.

British and Australian officers with notebooks and folders directed them towards the embarkation area for the trains, and most stopped at an Australian Army tent with a 'Canteen' sign in front. There they were issued with the army sandwiches they would forever refer to as 'doorstops', two enormous slices of bread with slabs of bully beef within. If they did not look particularly tasty there was some recompense in knowing they could probably be brought into action as a weapon if things grew desperate.

They all found their appropriate carriages and headed off into the gloom. They were vaguely aware of crossing the causeway onto the Malay Peninsula, but by then it was dark and an appreciation of the countryside would have to wait until the next day. But before that day dawned, their first stop occurred at a time most guessed was around 0530 hours. At a minor station the girls detrained and boarded army lorries lined up in the roadway outside the station. The 2/4th CCS was told they were to be taken to a small coastal town named Port Dickson. The 2/10th AGH was also directed to a coastal town, but the much larger port city of Malacca, which many of the girls had heard of. There was enough light as they boarded the lorries for the girls to make out the nature of the countryside. Pat Gunther of the 2/10th was 28 years of age, a country girl from northern New South Wales who left school at 12 to help out on the family farm before moving to Sydney to learn the profession of nursing at the Royal Prince Alfred. Pat had seen a lot in her lifetime, but the locals made an impression she would never forget: 'The Malayans, small-boned, with easy fluid movements, were a joy to see in their colourful sarongs and blouses . . .' Others were less poetic, and simply wanted to get to wherever they were going and have a sleep.

* * *

The 2/10th's accommodation at Malacca was actually quite spectacular. Known locally as 'The White Elephant' in tribute to its size, colour and almost complete lack of patients, the establishment's real title was the Colonial Service Hospital. It was a large, light and airy complex containing several blocks for surgical and medical procedures, general hospital wards and staff accommodation. The hospital was designed to cope comfortably with up to 1600 patients. One of the Australian nurses was instantly impressed:

> Each block consisted of five storeys; instead of glass windows, shutters which could be partly or completely closed or opened were installed, while broad balconies protected the wards from the sudden furious wind and rain of Sumatra; the intervening walls of the various bays, approximately seven feet high, allowed full ventilation.

Writing to 'Old Smithy' shortly after arriving in Malaya, Buddy Elmes was impressed with both the nurses' accommodation and the general countryside: 'Four of us in a cubicle which opens onto a sort of balcony affair', while, 'the country here is absolutely beautiful from an artistic point of view'. Expanding on this point, Buddy continued: 'The country around here is like a big park; although all the trees are native, they look very like English trees, and of course a few palm trees thrown in . . . The native huts are awfully picturesque, made out of palm trees made into flat slabs and tied onto the framework. They seem very solid and watertight; at least we hope so as they are making our men's huts out of them.' There were some early indications of boredom, though, with the ominous: 'If you ever want to send me anything, an occasional book or Reader's Digest would be very much appreciated.'

The eight wards of the hospital could each accommodate 200

'THE LAND OF STINKS, CHINKS AND DRINKS'

patients in those light and airy conditions, and the nurses had equally pleasant living quarters on the top floor of one of the wings. For their first week there, however, they were unable to do anything. Upon closer examination, the doctors and nurses of the 2/10th found that the facilities within the hospital were not anywhere near Australian standards. Also, none of their equipment had arrived, and it would only turn up in dribs and drabs in the coming weeks. The Australians had to borrow instruments from the civilian hospital administrators to initially equip their theatres.

The senior Australian medical officers and Matron Paschke were aware of Major General H. Gordon Bennett's instructions that all Australian units were to commence training within four days of their arrival on site in Malaya. The 2/10th nurses went straight onto shift work, covering either 0900–1730 hours or a split shift covering 0700–1300 hours and 1730–2100 hours. Their hospital, equipped for 400 beds after their equipment belatedly arrived, was soon expanded to a 600-bed capacity, but it was never near full and the nursing was relatively easy.

Whenever several thousand soldiers are engaged in training and recreation in a new country and a new climate there is bound to be a need for medical services, and Malaya in 1941 was no exception to this rule. In an army in the field there were always broken bones, cuts and bruises to attend, but the first patients to present in numbers were those who had contracted tropical skin disorders. The constant perspiration and spending long hours in wet clothes contributed to insect bites and abrasions that quickly became infected if not treated. There were also fungal and viral infections, the best known of which were 'Singapore Ear' and 'Dhobi Itch'; the latter was a kind of tinea, especially common in the groin and underarm, that was very hard to control. Its name came from the supposition that the Indian laundry boys – dhobis – used too much starch in their laundries, and it was this that was responsible for the initial infection. Singapore Ear was a generic name given to all ear infections, and was thought to be especially prevalent in swimming pools, such as the Olympic swimming pool at the Singapore Swimming Club.

All the nurses were given training in the treatment of tropical diseases soon after they arrived on station in Malaya, but real cases of those diseases were relatively rare. Like the medical units, many of the Australian Army formations were based in areas considered to be free of malaria. Those that weren't took a range of anti-malarial precautions, mosquito eradication and the like, and the soldiers were also issued with mosquito nets for their beds and bunks, and a peculiar net-like garment designed specifically to keep the mosquitoes away from bare skin that they unrolled over their uniforms when on guard duty at night. Parasites, especially hookworm, were a problem in many areas, so basic rules of hygiene in the tropics were established. All water had to be boiled and footwear was to be worn at all times.

The nurses were able to practise their more traditional nursing skills as many operations were performed at the hospital. In the first few months there was a steady succession of surgical patients, with tonsillectomies and circumcisions being by far the most common procedures. As the troops became more acclimatised they also became a little less cautious, and accidental injuries became more common. Not all had happy outcomes. One soldier died after falling onto his bayoneted rifle while climbing a fence during a training exercise. There was also at least one fatality and several serious injuries from motor vehicle accidents and one death after a soldier collapsed during a game of rugby. The dead were buried with due ceremony at an AIF cemetery established at Malacca; those too seriously injured to return to duty were eventually evacuated back to Australia.

* * *

It was not a bad existence for the nurses. Shortly after their arrival in Malacca, a sergeant major from one of the infantry battalions was asked to teach them how to march and perform army drill using the flat roof of their accommodation block as a parade ground. The training continued once or twice a week for almost two months and then just petered out; neither the instructor nor his pupils regarded it as a great success. Their quarters in that block were also quite domestic as the Red Cross had supplied the girls with sewing machines, dress material, a gramophone and records. They also had amahs – female house servants who did their cooking, cleaning, ironing and washing. When they played tennis or badminton – which they did regularly – any errant balls or shuttles would be retrieved by ball boys.

They were female, they were white and they were officers, and in colonial Malaya and Singapore this meant that they were thrice-blessed. These qualifications allowed them to become honorary members of the more salubrious European clubs on the peninsula and on the island. In Singapore, they could join the Europeans-only Tanglin Club, probably the most exclusive club in that part of the world. In Kuala Lumpur, the equivalent was the Selangor Club, known to the locals as 'The Spotted Dog' because its mock-Tudor features were painted black and white. At such clubs, the nurses met and mingled with the colonial gentry, planters, managers, advisers, bureaucrats and the like.

In Malacca itself, the nurses were in constant demand, drawn in to what must have been a new set of experiences for many that propelled them a long way up the social ladder. They attended sampan parties, chicken suppers at the famous and historic St John's Fort, and tennis parties on the courts next to their hospital. There were dances and dinners, and parties at pools and mansions. One of the girls wrote home that: 'The local residents were all anxious to entertain us, and did so liberally. We thoroughly enjoyed those festivities, which included curry tiffin, almost a rite on Sundays, at which one consumed the hottest of curries at midday, followed by a sweet "Guala Malacca" which by virtue of its icy coldness, formed a delicious contrast.'

In her regular letters to 'Old Smithy', Buddy Elmes continued to provide pen pictures of all that was strange and exotic to girls from the Australian bush. Touring old Malacca, she described how: '. . . we went over some of the old Portuguese buildings which date back to the fifteenth century. An old ruined chapel, the walls are still standing but the roof over most of it is gone; it stands on a hill and commands a most glorious view of the sea.' Buddy was also keenly aware of the different groups who shared Malaya: 'The Chinese particularly are frightfully proud of never having intermarried with the other races although most of them have been here for generations.' And she was also aware – and wanted the 'Tripehounds', her nursing friends to know – that: 'They say in this country that after a while the appetite goes, then the mind, followed shortly by the morals, so it looks as though I have started in the middle. Don't know what will come next.'

As well as the regular weekday and weekend leave, the Australian nurses would each be given a four-day leave at Frazer's Hill every two months. Regarded as a luxury resort, and located in the hills to the north of Kuala Lumpur, leave at Frazer's Hill left a lasting impression on the girls: 'Frazer's Hill . . . a delightful spot in the hills, where one sat before a fire at night, and slept under a blanket.' Just getting there could be an adventure, as Buddy related to Old Smithy: 'To reach Frazer's, we passed through Kuala Lumpur . . . a fairyland of beautiful buildings with a kinder climate than that of Singapore. Here we visited the museum with its amazing collections, grotesque and incredible specimens of sea life, intricate Malayan carving and weaving,

'THE LAND OF STINKS, CHINKS AND DRINKS'

and collections of butterflies resembling beds of delicately coloured pansies.' Pat Gunther, too, recalled Kuala Lumpur as: 'A delightful small city. It had an air of quiet affluence. Amongst its attractions was a racecourse surrounded by Casuarina trees . . . The Majestic Hotel and the Selangor Club were favourite rendezvous for dining and dancing.' She also loved Frazer's Hill, and the winding road that led to the highland retreats: 'It was said that the road maker was Chinese and that he had been paid by the mile . . . Frazer's Hill was lovely, mountain ranges disappearing into the distance, mists rising in the gullies. Oh, the joy of fresh, cool air on one's skin after months in the steamy humidity of the lower areas. We golfed, played tennis and generally relaxed.'

While the cool climate of the hill country was a relief, Singapore, the hub of Britain's Far East colonies and the region's premier port, was the major tourist attraction for nurses going on weekend leave. The trains that carried them to and from the city were air-conditioned, they were honorary members of the city's best clubs, the shopping was fine, and they could visit Raffles and the Adelphi Hotel, a privilege denied enlisted ranks. At Raffles, at that time possibly the most famous hotel in the world, the nurses could take high tea, stay on for dinner, and sample the drinks menu with its selection of exotically named and tasting variants of alcohol. They could, later in the evening, dance to the best bands and orchestras in Asia. At the hotel, as elsewhere throughout the Straits Settlements, the most popular dances were the slow foxtrots. Anything more up-tempo tended to cause excessive perspiration. As well as the social life, the girls found other things to admire. For Pat Gunther, it was the exotic sights: 'The Botanical Gardens were a joy, bright with colour, yet with plenty of lawns, which were beautifully maintained by gardeners using fine bladed scythes with a swinging, circular movement.'

For Buddy Elmes it was the sheer exoticism of what she saw around her: 'One sign in front of one of the shops amused us. Tamid Mohomat – Oculist. Eyes. Piles. Woman disease. He must have a wide range to cure.'

Not all the nurses found Singapore an attractive prospect for leave. Writing to a friend in Australia, Rene Singleton recalled: '... the narrow, smelly streets ... the native shops are awful. You would not like them.' Irene 'Rene' Singleton was also better qualified than most to comment on the ways of Asia. Born into a prominent pioneering family from Victoria's Gippsland region, Rene was raised by a single parent, her widower father, who had spent much of the early part of the 20th century living in Yokohama in Japan where he was a well-respected merchant. Hers was also a service family and when war broke out, Rene's two brothers, Ken and Doug, both joined the army while her sister Parthenia ('Pat') joined the Women's Auxiliary Australian Air Force (WAAAF). Rene had been raised on stories of Japanese cleanliness and Japanese industry, two things that she found distinctly lacking in what she was seeing in the East. She did say, though, that she was well and happy and putting on weight.

Most of the girls liked to visit the bright lights of Singapore and Kuala Lumpur on a regular basis, partly to socialise with new European faces, while the time they spent at Frazer's Hill was always recalled fondly. For many, however, one of the real pleasures in those first few months was simply being in a place that was so exotic, so different from anything they had known before: 'We had many long and lovely drives throughout that delightful countryside; the sky was always intriguing with its ever-changing cloud effects, and the varying greens of the jungle were a continual fascination. Throughout the year, we watched the progress of the growing rice in the paddy fields.'

* * *

The Australian nurses were not without complaints over issues they felt were either unnecessary impositions or things that interfered with their ability to undertake their duties properly. They were required to wear uniforms at all times, except when on leave, and they were only allowed out in pairs, or in foursomes with officers. The punishment for those who fraternised with enlisted men was being confined to barracks for two weeks. While matrons Olive Paschke and Irene Drummond were sympathetic, the male officers in 8th Division Headquarters were not, and indicated that if the rule were breached they would apply the punishment to the entire unit. It caused some bizarre situations. Jenny Greer, for instance, had a brother in the 2/10th Field Regiment, a unit that was stationed in Malacca at the same time as the nurses. The two could not officially be seen in public together as he was a gunner and not an officer. Jenny, who was never known by her given name, Jean, also had a beau in Singapore, a young Scotsman named Duncan Pemberton. The two had met shortly before Jenny enlisted, when Pemberton had been in Sydney on leave from his job in Singapore. Although they had known one another for just a few weeks, both felt that, if the circumstances were right, their friendship could grow into something more.

There were also tensions between members of the same unit, with the male medical orderlies being less than impressed at times with the superior conditions the nurses were granted. The men, often with almost the same qualifications and often the same competencies as the women, were medical orderlies and enlisted; the women were nurses and commissioned officers. The feelings of frustration were expressed in different and interesting ways, the most popular of which seemed to be a mix of denigration and ridicule. One of the orderlies would later explain, in all seriousness, how: 'The army, in the early stages of the war, favoured older, less attractive women, so as to avoid sexual distractions . . . Compared with the Chinese and Eurasian nurses, they looked like horses.'

It was the uniforms, though, that were the cause of many of the nurses' complaints. In the first instance, the issue was one of cost. The girls had all been given a clothing allowance of 50 Australian pounds upon enlistment. Prior to embarkation, they had themselves fitted for their distinctive uniform and then found, to their horror, that the allowance covered less than half of the expenses. They then found that the uniforms they had paid so much for were entirely unsuitable for service in a tropical climate. Many of the girls quickly removed the starched cuffs from their nursing attire, and many had also cut their sleeves off at the elbow. Olive Paschke shared her girls' concerns and took them forward, and within two months of their arrival, a new uniform was approved. Open-necked, with short sleeves and made of lighter cotton, the uniform was instantly popular with all the girls as well as the Indian tailors of Malacca who were to make dozens of them in the coming months. They also proved to be popular with the patients. The material proved to be translucent when backlit and, upon realising this, most of the nurses chose to wear petticoats underneath the uniform. Mavis Hannah, a 30-year-old who had been born in Perth but who was living and nursing in Adelaide when she enlisted in the AANS, was aware of the potential distractions. Writing about the uniforms, she observed: 'We didn't think it would be fair on the boys otherwise.'

The other Australian nurses in Malaya, those of the 2/4th CCS, shared most of the experiences of the girls of the 2/10th – amahs, cooks and the like – albeit in a different location. The 2/4th had originally been based at a small, 50-bed hospital on the coast at

Port Dickson, headquarters of the locally raised Malay Regiment, composed almost exclusively of native Malay volunteer regular soldiers, but within weeks was posted to Kajang, outside Kuala Lumpur, where they were based at the Kajang High School. Under Colonel Tom Hamilton and Irene Drummond, the unit gained a reputation for professional efficiency. At Kajang, the nurses also worked shifts, nursing the same types of patients as those at Malacca, teaching medical orderlies, making dressings and undertaking all the other tasks associated with nursing in a small hospital. With one exception. The 2/4th housed a section for patients with venereal diseases, staffed by specialist personnel from the 2/10th.*

The nurses in both units wrote home regularly and their family and friends no doubt shared the nurses' news with others, so the details of the girls' lives in Malaya were known to a relatively small group of Australians. All this changed dramatically in May 1941 when the *Australian Women's Weekly* sent its best reporter, Adele Shelton Smith, and a photographer to both Singapore and Malaya to report on the circumstances of the servicemen and servicewomen stationed there. Smith's gossipy reports filled pages of prime space in several editions of the popular publication and caused a sensation in Australia.

Her articles, and the accompanying photographs, detailed what seemed to be a dizzy round of social activities – parties, swimming and picnicking on unspoilt tropical beaches – and showed the Australian soldiers chatting with the 'taxi dancers', the often beautiful hostesses who worked at the cabarets and

---

* In various lectures aboard the *Queen Mary* en route, the troops – and the nurses – had been told that VD was at epidemic proportions in Singapore and Malaya and that some health experts calculated that up to 90 per cent of the local female population had VD. There was nothing to base such statistics on, but one of Bennett's first medical requests back to Headquarters was for a specialist VD treatment unit for his command.

clubs in towns and cities all over colonial Malaya and Singapore. The photographs usually showed numbers of fine-looking, sun-bronzed soldiers. Many of them also included attractive Eurasian women, bottles and glasses of beer, or a combination of both. There were photos of Australian soldiers holding rickshaw races in Singapore, or wearing sarongs as they slept through their daily siesta. More often than not, they were sharing the bed with a large bolster, designed to absorb perspiration rather than letting the sheets become wet; the Australian soldiers called the bolster a 'Dutch wife'.

It was unfortunate that the articles appeared at the same time as the fortunes of war appeared to be turning against other Australian forces overseas. At Tobruk and in Greece, soldiers were either besieged or were in retreat, and were suffering increasing numbers of casualties. Accordingly, there was an immediate and somewhat vitriolic response to the articles in both public and private Australia. Newspaper lead writers vied with each other over coming up with the most caustic title for the troops in Malaya: 'The Glamour Boys' was one, but it was nowhere near as popular as 'Menzies' Mannequins'. Most people felt that the name was appropriate. The soldiers were in Malaya because Prime Minister Menzies had agreed with Churchill that they should be there. And they appeared as mannequins, models who were wearing uniforms without ever really being soldiers. Wives and girlfriends wrote fiery letters to the soldiers suggesting that they, too, knew how to have a good time. Others accused them of shirking their duty. As a result, a raft of requests for transfers out was made from the ranks of the 8th Division.

One edition of the *Weekly* devoted most of its Malayan coverage to the nurses. While the article and accompanying photographs did not generate the same level of anger as those reports on the soldiers – most of the nurses were resigned to spinsterhood for the duration – it did paint an interesting, if slanted, picture of the girls' lives in Malaya. The article opened with the observation that:

> The people of Malaya cannot do enough for the Australian nurses. Off duty could be whirls of gaiety were the girls not interested in their work and in sightseeing. 'Some days we feel like film stars,' said Matron Pascke [sic]. 'The local residents send us huge baskets of orchids, presents of fruit, and invitations to their homes or clubs.'

One of the nurses, who is not identified in the story, recalled their arrival in the Far East: 'We left Singapore in the evening and were handed our first army rations – two doorstop sandwiches and an apple. We were glad to eat the doorstops though, before the night was very old.'

Adele Smith then went on to describe the nurses' living and mess conditions:

> The nurses' quarters are plain but comfortable. Some have rooms to themselves, others share in groups of four. They are furnished with a metal bed, table, easy chair and small wardrobe. Some of the rooms look out through wide windows on marvellous views of deep green and blue hills. On every table there are framed family photographs and photographs of boyfriends . . . The nurses' mess is a lofty attap palm-thatched hut built in the shade of two wings of the hospital. Their dining room is at one end and their recreation room at the other.

She moved on to describe the kind of life the girls were leading, again quoting an unidentified nurse: 'Some of us are playing golf, and whenever transport is available, a party of us goes to the swimming club. Others play tennis. We are feeling very proud because an AIF sister, partnered by one of our officers, won the club tennis tournament.' Smith added: 'They told me about visits to rubber plantations, and where to shop for souvenirs, how to stop my makeup sliding off in the heat, and in exchange I told them all the gossip I could think of from home.'

Another unidentified sister told the reporter: 'Nursing makes one a realist. I used to think the glamour of the tropics was a lot of "hooey", but the colour of this country gets you. We are all so touched by the kindness of the people and the warm welcome they gave us.' And Adele Smith herself had the final word: 'Many of the boys over here are putting on weight, a doctor told me. He said there was very little illness and not much work for the AIF hospital.'

The *Women's Weekly* articles were light and frothy, easy to read and accompanied by well-balanced and constructed photographs. Buddy Elmes told her friend Smithy: '. . . you will think everything in the *Women's Weekly* is true; it's not, because we are working pretty hard at the moment, and don't have time for much social activity.' But the articles told a story that was read widely and generally accepted as accurate. And while it was only accurate up to a point, it generally did all the Australians serving in Malaya a disservice. It characterised them all as 'Menzies' Mannequins', a description that would re-emerge much later in an attempt to explain what subsequently occurred.

Around that time, in May 1941, while some Australians waited for the next edition of the *Weekly* to discover what else the troops were getting up to in Malaya, the first reinforcements for the troops were already on their way, including a small group of nurses who were excited about their new adventure. They travelled aboard the *Zealandia*, and departed Australia in early May. The oldest in the group of five reinforcement nurses was one of the real characters in the AANS, a staff nurse named Betty Jeffrey.

Agnes Betty Jeffrey was called either Betty or, more often, 'Jeff' by those who knew her well. She had been born in Hobart but moved to Melbourne as a small child when her father's work with the Postmaster General's Department saw him posted to the General Post Office there. After a stint of school teaching, and at 29 years of age, Betty enrolled in nursing studies at Melbourne's Alfred Hospital. Four years later, she had completed her training, turned 33, joined the AANS and was on her way to her first posting, with the 2/10th AGH at Malacca. It all felt appropriate; Betty's main aim when she entered nursing was to ultimately win a job aboard an ocean-going passenger liner. Uncertain about her ability to cope with seasickness, Betty had embarked on the *Zealandia* with a pot plant she had named 'Agatha'. Whenever she felt slightly nauseous, Betty would sniff the soil in Agatha's pot. She was not sick at any time on the voyage.

The voyage from Sydney aboard the *Zealandia* followed fairly closely the route of the *Queen Mary*, although with neither the speed nor the luxury. There were no surface raider or submarine scares, and there were no vice-regal welcoming parties or regimental bands to welcome them to Singapore. They disembarked onto small ferries at Keppel Harbour rather than at the naval base to the north, as had been the case with the *Queen Mary*, but thereafter their voyage again paralleled that of their sister nurses four months earlier. A short journey to the railway station and then an overnight trip in an air-conditioned train, another short trip in a staff car and they were at the 2/10th AGH, the hospital on the hill in Malacca. There was someone there to meet them. 'Welcome to the 2/10th girls,' said Olive Paschke, 'and welcome to Malaya.'

CHAPTER 3

Reinforcements

The declining fortunes of the Allies, including the Australians, in the North African and Balkan campaigns that erupted in mid-1941 could not have come at a more inopportune time for Australia. Political instability at home had seen Prime Minister Menzies dumped by his coalition partners and, after some quiet negotiations, the installation of John Curtin as Labor leader and Prime Minister. Australian eyes were becoming increasingly focused on the northwestern horizons, beyond the Netherlands East Indies and Singapore as nervous politicians, soldiers and the general populace pondered Japanese intentions in the region. Little by little, Japanese forces had been creeping closer. Their 1941 pact with Germany and Italy had suggested their political preferences, while their non-aggression treaty with the Soviet Union both guaranteed their northern defences and indicated where their strategic interests were heading. Any doubts about their intentions were removed when several divisions of battle-hardened troops, with their transport, were relocated to bases in southern China and the Vichy French territories of Indochina.

Curtin's War Cabinet responded to the increasing threat from the Japanese advance during the latter half of 1941 in two ways. They firstly asked and later demanded that British Prime Minister Winston Churchill authorise the return to Australia of the AIF divisions either serving or forming in the Middle East. Churchill was loath to accede to the Australian request – his electorate was British, not Australian – and when he eventually did authorise the recall, it was far too late for the troops to have anything beyond a cameo role in the opening stages of the Pacific War.

Both Curtin and Churchill recognised that the British forces in Malaya and Singapore could well be inadequate to face the Japanese divisions being assembled in Indochina. Churchill's response was to publicly belittle the Japanese forces as a credible threat, reorganise the command structure in the Far East, and promise substantial reinforcements at an appropriate time. Curtin's second response was to ask the War Cabinet to reinforce Major General Bennett's forces in Malaya. The obvious move was to add one of the 8th Division's other brigades; the War Cabinet approved the move and authorised the 27th Infantry Brigade and its ancillary units to relocate to Singapore and Malaya. Among those ancillary units were several medical establishments, one of which was the 2/13th Australian General Hospital, with its complement of 40 plus nurses.

There were both similarities and differences between the movements of the 2/13th AGH and that of their friends and peers in the 2/10th AGH and 2/4th CCS. Both groups travelled from

Australia to Singapore by sea but, while the first group travelled in the relative luxury of the *Queen Mary*, the second travelled in the relatively spartan and functional circumstances of a hospital ship, HMAHS *Wanganella*. The *Wanganella* had a top speed less than half that of the *Queen Mary*, and had further to travel as well; the bulk of its journey would also be as part of a convoy. Irrespective of which trip they made, however, the nurses all shared one common characteristic – the excitement of young women heading off on an adventure.

The journey began in Brisbane on 25 August 1941 when six AANS nurses boarded the *Wanganella* shortly before it weighed anchor and sailed south to Sydney. There the Queensland nurses were joined by 28 other nurses drawn from all over Sydney and rural and regional New South Wales. Like the nurses they now met, the New South Wales girls represented a cross-section of their profession and age, although one or two were quite notable through either their character or personal circumstances.

One of the nurses who boarded in Sydney was Mary Eleanor McGlade. Educated at St Ursula's Convent in Armidale, she was known throughout her life as 'Ellie'. Born at Armidale in northern New South Wales in 1903, her mother had died shortly after her birth and her father, a successful New England lawyer, died just two years later. An aunt, Mrs Walter Scott of Wallalong, near Maitland, became Ellie's guardian, and from preschool she was enrolled as a boarder at St Ursula's where the writer Dymphna Cusack was one of her classmates.

After finishing her secondary education, Ellie visited relatives in Scotland and Ireland with her cousin, Eleanor Scott. Returning to Australia after her grand tour, she commenced nursing studies at the Royal Prince Alfred Hospital in Sydney in May 1923 and graduated in June 1927 with certificates in General Nursing, Cooking and Dispensing. Ellie was always determined to make her own way in life and, instead of settling into a general nursing career, she decided to specialise in an area that would perhaps allow her to help young mothers in a way that her mother had not been helped. Following her graduation, Ellie became a Mothercraft Nurse in the lower Hunter Valley. When called up for service with the 2/13th, Ellie was the second most experienced nurse in the unit.

The *Wanganella* did not tarry long in Sydney, and two days after arriving it departed, again heading south, this time to Melbourne where it was to collect another tranche of nurses who had assembled there from the southern states of South Australia, Victoria and Tasmania. They had come together at a hostel in suburban Armadale named Lady Duggan's Hostel after its patron, the wife of the Governor of Victoria. Two of the waiting nurses were already fast friends with a habit of looking at life through somewhat unconventional eyes; to them, their accommodation would always be 'Duggan's Dugout'. They were Mona Wilton and Wilma Oram.

Mona Margaret Wilton was born in 1913 at Willara in western Victoria and three years later Wilma Oram was born a short distance to the north in the Wimmera region. The girls met in 1934 when Wilma commenced training as a nurse at the Warrnambool Base Hospital in the Western District. Mona was as outgoing as Wilma was reserved, but they enjoyed each other's company and soon became firm friends. Although they went their separate ways upon graduation, the girls remained in touch. Wilma moved to Melbourne in 1938, to the Jessie McPherson Hospital where she met another young nurse who had also moved around a bit. Her name was Vivian Bullwinkel and she was from Adelaide via Broken Hill.

While Wilma was in Melbourne, Mona was nursing at Allansford in the west of the state. They wrote and telephoned one another regularly, and caught up with each other whenever they could. When news of the fall of France reached Australia in May 1940, the girls decided to volunteer for service. Until then, Wilma had given no thought to volunteering for war service, but when the Germans reached the Channel and looked across at England, she felt a surge of patriotic feeling. Both girls decided to serve their country. Mona completed the army application form but Wilma felt drawn to the air force, and filled out two application forms, one for each service. The girls walked together to a post office to send off their applications. As they walked, Mona chanted, 'Post the army. Post the army.' Wilma did just that.

Both girls registered for service with the army and then waited almost a year before they were called up for service. Wilma was posted firstly to the new Heidelberg Military Hospital, where she met Katherine Kinsella. At 37 years, 'Kit' Kinsella was a decade older than Mona and was a very experienced and highly regarded sister. They, too, became friendly when both were sent to the Alfred Hospital for training in brain surgery theatre support. Wilma was then notified that she had been posted to the 2/13th; her best friend Mona was already there.

Being together again not only thrilled both girls, it stimulated a veritable orgy of letter writing to family and mutual friends.

> Mona: *'You'll never guess who's been posted to the same AGH – Oram . . .'*
> Wilma: *'Mona and I are together, which is absolutely marvellous . . .'*

Best friends forever, and soon to be posted overseas. When Wilma learned that she and Mona and the other girls were to be posted on active service overseas, her excitement knew no bounds. The nurses' allowance for overseas service was 30 pounds, and while it was never going to cover all their expenses, it was a start.

Wilma, for one, was prepared to spend some of the amount on underwear, a small luxury that both she and Mona felt they deserved. Unfortunately, they were also told they would need to buy their own rugs or eiderdowns, and this created something of a quandary. The underwear won.

The Victorian girls at the Lady Duggan Hostel sat and talked and awaited the arrival of their country and interstate colleagues. Vivian Bullwinkel was one of the first to arrive, sent down to Melbourne from the army hospital at Puckapunyal. Vivian had been born at Kapunda in South Australia but had grown up and completed her nursing training at Broken Hill, where her late father had worked for a mining company. A tall and fair young woman, Vivian had excelled at basketball and tennis at school and at one stage had thought of becoming a school sports mistress. Nursing exercised a stronger attraction, however, and Vivian enrolled as a trainee nurse at the Broken Hill Hospital. There she had reported to a sister in charge named Irene Drummond who, at 29 years of age, was ten years Vivian's senior.

After nursing at Broken Hill, Vivian worked as a staff nurse at a private hospital in western Victoria before moving to the Queen Victoria Hospital in Melbourne where her senior sister was a fascinating young woman named Olive Paschke. In 1940–41, Vivian worked as a staff nurse at the Jessie McPherson Hospital, also in Melbourne. There she met Wilma Oram and, like her, was keen to become an RAAF nurse. She failed the medical because of flat feet, however, and so followed Wilma into the AANS.

There were a number of administrative tasks that had to be completed by all the girls at the embarkation ports before they could depart. Uniforms, pay books and identity discs had to be collected, vaccinations and inoculations administered as well as a final series of medical checks. In Melbourne there was an additional requirement: Army headquarters had organised a march past for the Victorian Governor on 31 August, and asked for some of the 2/13th nurses to add some colour to the occasion.

The *Wanganella* was scheduled to depart Port Melbourne on 2 September, almost exactly two years to the day after war had broken out in Europe. Before they departed, though, they were addressed by a Major General McGuire, Chairman of the Army's Central Medical Co-ordination Committee, who told them, among other things: '. . . you are going to nurse the brothers, sons, sweethearts and husbands of the people of Australia. You are very dear to them.' The girls agreed it was a good talk and that the 9500-tonne *Wanganella* was a very comfortable ship, and then they were on their way.

They sailed out of Port Phillip Bay and into one of the worst crossings of the Great Australian Bight anyone aboard could remember. Before then, however, there was a formal introduction to life at sea. Ship's orders on their first full day out of Melbourne included: 'No written messages to be placed in bottles and thrown overboard. The hairdressing salon is open for two hours in the mornings and afternoons. ORs [Other Ranks] Free. 9 pence for officers and nurses.' Two days later, the orders reminded those aboard that: 'Library open between 1615–1700 hours each day.'

Both the salon and the library were probably of only minimal interest by then, as monster waves were constantly rocking the ship. For those girls brave enough, the rough crossing presented an unbelievable opportunity. The *Wanganella* had a glassed-in bow, and there were lifelines leading to it. A thorough soaking was guaranteed but for those girls brave enough, a once in a lifetime opportunity awaited. Huddled together, and perhaps even screaming a little, they held on to a rail as the bow plunged down and, as it started to rise again, speared into the heart of another monster wave that was hovering almost directly above. There

REINFORCEMENTS

was a rush and a roar and then the glass cleared to show the sky before the whole process started again.

Just a couple of days later the *Wanganella* anchored in Gage Roads off Fremantle. Leave ashore was granted to most and they took the opportunity to visit Perth, telephone family and friends back east, or visit old friends or relatives. The stopover also allowed the 2/13th to bring its nursing numbers up to their authorised strength. Four nurses joined the unit in Perth. The final member of the unit was also the smallest. Standing at barely 150 centimetres, Staff Nurse Iole Harper had been born at Guildford in Perth, the oldest of nine children and the daughter of a state cricketer. Iole stayed at school until she was 18 and then helped her mother at home until, aged 22, she started as a trainee nurse at the Royal Perth Hospital. After completing her training, Iole travelled to Sydney where she worked at several large private hospitals. After three years she returned to Perth. Iole was living at home and working at a private hospital when she was summoned to the AANS in August.

If the weather in the Bight had been terrible, the travellers were more than compensated for their discomfort by what awaited them in the Indian Ocean. The days were at first balmy and then hot, and there were many new sights and sounds from the sea that did not involve mountains of cold water, violent movement and seasickness. They also did not have a lot to do in the way of practising their profession. While the permanent medical staff attached to the vessel looked after that side of things, the 2/13th girls attended a series of lectures on tropical medicine and helped to look after the sisters' sick bay on a roster basis. When time permitted and they could be bothered to organise it, most of the sisters also taught some basic nursing to the medical orderlies and stretcher bearers who travelled with them.

There were also a couple of non-nursing highlights during

the trip. One was when the *Wanganella* crossed the equator and King Neptune, assisted by a group of mermaids who looked suspiciously like the ship's nurses, dunked all those aboard who were crossing the equator for the first time. Another highlight was seeing an eruption of the volcanic island of Krakatoa, in the Sunda Strait between Sumatra and Java. For several days they watched the smoke and ash climb into the sky, while at night the glow from the lava made almost enough light to read by. They were also entertained by the flying fish that at times seemed to be escorting their ship: 'At night . . . the reflections on the water made the flying fish appear like silver arrows.'

There was a serious side to their travel, however, and as Singapore approached they had many lectures on life in the tropics, tropical diseases and what was expected from them across a whole range of circumstances. Many of the girls found the dangers, as described to them, quite confronting and wondered whether they would be able to eat and drink in the tropics without coming down with a potentially fatal disease. Some even became wary of drinking the ship's water, and for weeks none could eat any fruit that had a broken skin. A couple of days out of Singapore there was a compulsory church parade, an opportunity for the chaplains aboard to make one more plea for the girls to resist the many and varied temptations of the flesh that they would soon be facing. The first chaplain warned them at great length of the wickedness of Singapore, his audience slowly wilting in the heat of the ship's salon. They perked up a bit when the second chaplain commenced. Yes, he said, Singapore was indeed a wicked city but, he added, they were all big girls, adults entitled to live life to the full. Go ahead with the courage of your convictions. They weren't exactly sure what he meant, but were pretty certain he was encouraging them to do *something*.

* * *

The Singapore that greeted the disembarking nurses of the 2/13th appeared unchanged to the one that had greeted the earlier arrivals, but that was only on the surface. At the various colonial and military headquarters in the city were some very worried men, in a quandary about what they could do to alleviate their concerns. On the island, the British Army and Royal Air Force headquarters were eight kilometres apart, with the Royal Navy headquarters a further 25 kilometres from both. Even when the three services were talking, which seemed to be the exception rather than the rule, this did not automatically lead to cooperation. The RAF had built airfields up and down the Malay Peninsula to defend against the Japanese forces they knew were coming. When dry, they were ideal for landings and take-offs. The features that made them ideal for aircraft also made them indefensible against ground troops, however. The army, which was responsible for defending them, had not been consulted about where the airfields would be sited.

Senior figures from all three arms of the British military followed Churchill's lead and publicly denigrated the Japanese as soldiers, as people and as a threat to Malaya and Singapore. They told their troops and the people of the Settlements that the Japanese soldiers were both short and short-sighted, and that their rifles were of such a low velocity and small calibre that any wounds they inflicted could literally be treated with a bandaid after the bullet was squeezed out like a blackhead. Their pilots were incapable of both aerobatics and night-flying; the one because they were swaddled so tightly as babies that their neck muscles never developed, and the other because they didn't eat vegetables in what was exclusively a fish and rice diet and therefore suffered from myopia and other sight deficiencies.

While such observations may have offered some comfort to the population at large, and certainly did pander to their prejudices, in their quiet and private moments those senior commanders also wished for more experienced soldiers, more modern aircraft and for a modern battle fleet that would not take six months to sail out from Britain. The senior colonial authorities do not seem to have ever shared these misgivings. Governor of the Straits Settlements, Sir Shenton Thomas, was even more dismissive of potential Japanese threats and point blank refused to institute the civil defence measures that were helping Britain through the Blitz. Slit trenches were not only bad for civilian morale, he declared, but would become filled with water and turn into breeding grounds for mosquitoes.

Some wise military decisions were being made at times. Malaya Command decided that the arrival of the 27th Brigade would allow it to group all the Australian land forces together as a kind of strategic reserve. General Bennett was also to be given, from October, responsibility for the southernmost Malay state of Johore. If the Japanese were coming, they would most likely land on the east coast of the Malay Peninsula, with Johore the best tactical place to land. They would not attack Singapore frontally as the big British guns would blast them out of the water. And neither would they invade in the north, as the jungle would trap them there. Bennett and his Australians were to be given the hot spot and they made their plans accordingly.

The *Wanganella* did not follow the route of the *Queen Mary* around to the naval base but instead anchored in Keppel Harbour off Singapore City, and the passengers and equipment were ferried to the main dock area. The medical units were met by Colonel Wilfred Kent-Hughes, the Deputy Quartermaster General, who explained that he had organised buses to take the 2/13th to their new abode, the St Patrick's School on the East Coast Road at

Katong, halfway between the city and the large British fortress and barracks at Changi. Many on the dock were impressed by the organisational qualities on display, but others found different things interesting, one nurse recalling: 'I was most impressed as we docked in Singapore harbour with the appearance on the wharf of the most handsome and finest fighter in the world. I saw this Sikh in all his magnificence, six feet tall, turbaned, with the classical features of his race, standing with the proud bearing of his famous Indian regiment.'

All too quickly for some, they were aboard the buses and skirting through the city and along the coast. St Patrick's School occupied 6 hectares of prime land on the island's east coast. To the nurses, the place looked smart and clean. The complex consisted of three large buildings with many outhouses. The two main buildings were each three storeys high, built of brick and containing all modern conveniences. Throughout the school grounds there were monsoon drains over a metre deep, with many noting their potential danger during blackouts. To the south of the school and across the road, the foreshore and the beach were out of bounds. The nurses were informed that the area was mined, covered with barbed wire and signposted 'Danger Keep Away!' The nurses' quarters were in the south wing of one of the main buildings with panoramic views over what was suddenly quite a scary landscape.

After the girls had unpacked and settled in came the realisation that there was very little for them to do. The first generally leisurely days were spent in acclimatisation and introductory lessons in tropical medicine, with the occasional excitement of an air raid or a gas attack training drill. There were trips to Singapore, but for some the extreme change of lifestyle was almost overwhelming. Said Phyllis Pugh, one of the Queensland nurses:

I shall never forget the first week in Singapore mainly because I lost my appetite. The canals of Singapore's streets smelt dreadful as did most of their markets. As Singapore sat almost on the equator, the heat was at first unbearable and any worthwhile sleep was impossible. Then for breakfast the army served us goldfish – herrings in tomato sauce – morning after morning . . .

Part of the problem was that the bulk of the Australian forces were some distance to the north in the Malay states of Selangor and Negri Sembilan. The only substantial bodies of Australian servicemen on the island were the three squadrons of the RAAF, who had their own, separate medical arrangements. To assist in the acclimatisation of the new nurses, Irene Drummond from the 2/4th CCS was appointed to matron in August 1941 and took up her position as soon as the *Wanganella* arrived. Replacing her as senior nurse at the 2/4th was Kit Kinsella of the 2/13th. Colonel Pigdon and Matron Drummond set about finding gainful employment for their charges. For Irene Drummond, it was an opportunity to give her new nurses the benefit of the experience of those who had already spent several months in the country. A series of attachments to other units was quickly organised; to the 2/10th, the Singapore General Hospital and several other units, and the nurses of the 2/13th were rostered for a series of rolling deployments. The general rotation was three weeks at another unit before returning to St Patrick's, but there were no hard and fast rules, and the practice was broadened to include postings across the length and breadth of the 8th Division. For instance, Pat Gunther and Winnie May Davis, a petite, vivacious girl from the Big Rivers country of northern New South Wales, both from the 2/10th, were posted to the 2/4th CCS, meeting up with Mona Wilton and Wilma Oram who were also undertaking an attachment there, while a tall Tasmanian, Jessie Simons, had her eyes opened when posted to the 2/10th AGH: 'It was a surprise to me to find modern trains in Malaya, and even more to find the hospital in Malacca housed in a fine modern building.' The 30-year-old had really only known her home town, a small settlement on the Tasmanian north coast, and the larger cities of Launceston and Hobart, before travelling to Melbourne for embarkation. It was a new world, a big world, and she was loving every bit of it.

All the nurses sooner or later returned to St Patrick's, and there the hospital was quickly organised as though it would be undertaking a normal workload. During their first week, the nurses listened to lectures on local conditions and were given lists of detailed instructions about what to do during emergencies and air raids. All ranks were warned against signing chits for food, drink or gifts in shops as they were told this was a method of obtaining information frequently used by enemy agents. Visits were arranged to the Alexandria Hospital to view the malaria films – microscope slides showing malaria-infected blood samples – and treatments there, and also to the Tan Tock Sang Hospital for clinics on tropical diseases conducted by Dr Wallace and Professor Ransom. The senior officers also arranged for the nurses to visit the Singapore General Hospital to acquaint themselves with beriberi and typhoid fever patients.

Within a few days, staggered nursing shifts had been introduced: 0700–1600 hours, or 0700–1300 and 1600–2000 hours. Night duty ran from 2000 to 0700 hours. Those on morning shifts gave lessons to medical orderlies: for instance, Phyllis Pugh lectured on correct bandaging and how to test urine. Between 1100 hours and lunch at midday, one of the senior doctors would usually deliver some form of medical presentation, of which the most popular were Dr Bruce Hunt's presentations on tropical medicine. Major Hunt of the 2/13th AGH, a senior surgeon and originally from Perth, emerged as one of the hardest working of all the medical staff and soon became a popular figure with the nurses. Occasionally there would be small exercises to prepare the hospital for possible action. To make the simulation as realistic as possible, ghastly-looking 'wounds' were made out of papier-mâché and tied onto the volunteer victims. There was not a lot to do, however, and in their off-duty hours boredom was a constant threat as the hospital was supplied with Chinese amahs to undertake all the nurses' domestic tasks.

After the initial settling in period of four days, the nurses were given free time on alternating nights, commencing at 1400 hours in the afternoon and continuing until midnight. The girls took the opportunity to do what anyone else would do in the same situation; they went out to enjoy the sights and sounds of a whole new world. Raffles for high tea, cocktails and dancing was a popular destination, probably just ahead of the Adelphi and Airport hotels as the premier meeting, greeting and dancing venue. The regimental dinners held at the legendary hotel were something to be especially savoured: '. . . very formal affairs with beautiful women of all nationalities, magnificent decor, an abundance of tropical flowers and playing background music was the kilted band of the Argyll and Sutherland Highlanders'.

Wilma and Mona decided early that they were in a place that most people only ever dreamed of visiting, and furthermore, that they were being served low-class food in a high-class environment. They considered regular servings of herring in tomato sauce to be both boring and unattractive, and took the opportunity to travel into Singapore when they could to eat at one of the better eateries. Raffles, the Adelphi and the Seaview hotels were their favourites, although just a little too expensive to patronise regularly.

Robinson's, a department store, was both *the* place to shop and to meet for coffee; it also boasted the only air-conditioned restaurant in Singapore. The Cathay Building was another magnet. The largest building in Singapore, the Cathay contained the city's largest cinema, showing *New Moon* with Nelson Eddy and Jeanette McDonald when the 2/13th nurses first arrived. There were plenty of shops and bartering was encouraged, and for a little bit of excitement, the girls would occasionally stroll past Lavender Street, Singapore's famed red-light district.

The scarcity of single European women in Singapore meant the nurses were an instant success and a welcome addition to the social life of the colony. The initial sightseeing tours were followed by invitations to tennis parties and then dinner parties, and ultimately to the whole gamut of socialising that seemed to play such an important part in the life of Singapore's expatriate community. Finally, they were given the keys to the kingdom, honorary membership of the Singapore Swimming Club, home of the eponymous ear infection and social scene par excellence. Many years later, Jessie Simons still waxed lyrical about the place:

> I'll never forget the Singapore Swimming Club – out of this world. A big tiled pool surrounded by tables under beach umbrellas was only the beginning. Showers, post office, electric irons, dining room and dance floor, in fact almost everything we could wish for was there. Good food, immaculate Chinese waiters and a hearty welcome made our visit most enjoyable.

It was a scene and a crowd that Mona and Wilma thought may have been scripted just for them. On duty, both were regarded as being better than most in their theatre nursing specialisation, but away from duty they were a two-woman social movement. Predictably, they shared a room at St Patrick's. Mona wrote home that: '"We" means Wilma and me, as we go places together always and without any of the other girls, as we don't like them very much . . .' The others were sometimes too serious for these young women out for adventure. Despite their love of a good time, both Wilma and Mona were teetotallers, never taking anything stronger than lemonade; life was enough.

Inevitably, they attracted male admirers, and seemed quite adept at promising a bit and delivering a bit less. Each found a beau within weeks of arriving in Singapore. Mona's was an Englishman who managed a tea plantation in the highlands, while Wilma's preferred partner was a newspaper reporter. They met when and where they could, and enjoyed one another's company in one of the many exotic locations in their new world.

There were some minor distractions. One afternoon tea, Major Bruce Hunt spoke to the on-duty nurses in a way that caused one of those present to later record his thoughts: 'There will be a war with the Japanese. They will come in through the back door and advance down the peninsula. Our troops will most likely retreat to Singapore Island, trapped like rats. The Japanese, then, will control our Singapore reservoirs and we would then be under extreme stress. At the worst, none would get home to Australia.' It was a sobering moment, but any such outcomes seemed a long, long way into the future. For the here and now, there was Singapore and all the excitement that the city contained. Even those condemned to night shift while their sisters were out dining and dancing had something to look forward to. In the cool of the morning, just as the sun climbed above the horizon, the sheer beauty of their situation was revealed, the coconut palms and the blue sea and islands beyond, and the grounds of the school itself: 'hibiscus, bouvardia and the sweet, sweet smell of frangipani'. For two months, the 2/13th enjoyed the variety and the opportunities that Singapore offered, then it was their turn to move north.

* * *

The arrival of the 2/13th nurses in September dovetailed nicely with some restructuring of the medical arrangements for the AIF in Malaya, of which Irene Drummond's appointment as matron and Kit Kinsella's promotion were a part.

The 2/10th AGH was to remain at Malacca while the 2/4th would temporarily relocate from Kajang to a new site, a former mental hospital on the top of Tampoi Hill, a prominent feature just outside Johore Bahru, capital of the Sultanate of Johore and not far from the causeway linking Singapore and the Malay Peninsula. The large hospital contained 22 incomplete wards and enormous grounds, and had just been purchased from the sultan by the Australian government for the knockdown price of 25,000 pounds. Plans were also put in place for the 2/13th to relocate from St Patrick's to Tampoi when their acclimatisation and detached duties had been completed. When they did so, the 2/4th CCS would move again, this time to Kluang, a small town in Johore which had both an airfield and a railway station. Moreover, Kluang was almost exactly halfway between the two larger general hospitals.

Accordingly, between 21 and 23 November, the 2/13th, its staff and over 800 tonnes of equipment and supplies were relocated from St Patrick's to the mental hospital. The hospital itself was also a relatively long way from the nearest community of any size and was surrounded by thick jungle. While this was a bit exciting it was also quite daunting, and some of the more outgoing nurses took to playing hide and seek when not on duty, appearing and disappearing at will and scaring the life out of their colleagues. In the hospital complex there were over 10 kilometres of corridors running between the wards and the various orderly rooms, and the nurses would eventually be given bicycles to help them get from one ward to another. Within the grounds the nurses' quarters were almost two kilometres from the wards and travel between the two was by ambulance.

There were other issues at the hospital beyond its size and isolation. It had been designed as a mental hospital and it had not been completed, so there were a number of surprises for the Australians. The windows in all the buildings were barred, and the girls borrowed sledgehammers to knock them out. The operating theatre was an ordinary room, and the instrument room was at the opposite end of the building. Instruments were a problem, and most surgeons elected to buy and supply their own, which had to be sterilised over primus stoves. The girls had to make most of their own theatre linen. Even after a long day putting the hospital into shape, the nurses felt let down. All their food supplies were provided by the British Army, and the Australians almost gagged at the sight of their old friends, the goldfish. Most of the meals consisted of tinned herrings in tomato sauce with mashed potatoes while, on those few occasions when they were supplied meat, the consensus was that they were dining on the constituent parts of a horse.

The situation was rectified a little by the man whose reputation was growing as something of a benefactor to the Australians – Sir Ibrahim, the Sultan of Johore. Most of the girls knew who he was and would have recognised him from the photographs published earlier that year in *Women's Weekly*. An older, stouter and more heavily tattooed man than most they had seen in Malaya, Sir Ibrahim was referred to by many of the Australians as 'an Oriental gentleman with Eastern values and Western wives', a jibe about his very young and very attractive wife, a Romanian model he had met in an air-raid shelter in London. Rumours abounded that the sultan and his wife dined off plates of solid gold and that, staunch Anglophile that he was, he had presented a warship to the Royal Navy. At least two of the nurses, the friends Mona Wilton and Wilma Oram, attended a ball he gave at his Johore Bahru palace during the first week of October.

Their story, which Wilma recorded in some detail in a letter to her family in late October, is almost like something out of a fairytale. The two Australian girls had actually met the sultan by chance as they headed into Johore Bahru on leave. The ambulance that they had hitched a ride in had not been going all the way to the state capital and had dropped them off at a club between Singapore and Johore. There, they waited inside the front door of the club as they debated how to find a taxi to take them the rest of the way. An older man, sitting in the lounge of the club, sent a staff member to ask them if he could be of assistance. The girls explained their predicament and joined him for a lemon squash. Without divulging his identity, the older man said his car was at their convenience and, within minutes, they were sitting in the back seat of a limousine, heading into Johore Bahru.

Two days later, both girls received formal invitations – in crisp white envelopes – to attend a ball to be hosted by His Royal Highness, Sir Ibrahim, Sultan of Johore. It then became a little complicated. The decision to allow Mona and Wilma to attend had to be made at senior levels at AIF Headquarters. While they were officers, the girls were only the equivalent of lieutenants and in normal circumstances were far too junior to be allowed to attend such an event. However, both had been personally invited by the sultan and to forbid them to go could possibly involve a breach of protocol. A compromise was reached: Mona and Wilma could attend, but they would be escorted by AIF colonels.

For the girls, the night was an unqualified success. They were taken to and from the ball in one of the sultan's private vehicles, complete with uniformed Indian syce (driver). Wilma later described the evening in some detail:

What a night we had. We danced from 9 p.m. until 3 a.m. with nothing below a major in rank. The Sultan is supposed to be a bad old thing but we were so surrounded by AIF of high rank that we were never safer . . . The Sultan's wife was there, of course, and is the loveliest woman I have ever seen. She is a Rumanian. Her clothes and jewellery left us spellbound. We were dressed up for the occasion in our silk uniforms, red capes and cap tail caused many comments I think.

It was also during that week that the sultan became aware of some of the issues at the hospital at Tampoi Hill and moved to do something about them. Using his own resources and contacts, he found and donated several items of vital medical equipment, including a portable X-ray machine and diathermy apparatus. By 8 December, the hospital was almost completely operational, although it hadn't yet treated anything more significant than fungal infections and abrasions. With the help of a few of its former inmates who had opted to stay behind, staff from the 2/13th had also completed all the approach roads to the hospital. All was in readiness for what was coming their way.

Pushed out by the 2/13th at Tampoi, the 2/4th fell on its feet in its new location at Kluang. The nurses were accommodated in the modern new hospital complex in the town itself while, a reasonable walk away, their tents were erected alongside the airfield. Tom Hamilton mused upon his unit's new circumstances:

> Below our tent lines stretched the lawns of the civil hospital, girded by a double line of stately casuarina trees. To the north west swept the wide expanse of aerodrome from which training planes were able to take off on three or four days a week, provided it didn't rain any more than usual . . . Work was easy, and amusements consisted of an occasional walk to the native

shopping centre in Kluang, a round of golf on the little course behind the aerodrome, or the hilarious interlude of a noisy Tamil funeral from the hospital morgue.

As the 2/13th settled into life in the Far East, firstly at St Patrick's and latterly at Tampoi Hill, events in the wider world started to gather pace. Japan was on the move, but was taking small, almost hesitant steps, as if testing the water. Japan's war cabinet had decided on a southern strategy, expansion to and through South East Asia, seizing the tin and rubber that they were currently being denied because of Western sanctions. Their preparations were well advanced. Battle-hardened divisions were withdrawn from mainland China and sent south, to Hainan Island and Cam Ranh Bay and Saigon. There, they were practising landing on both defended and undefended beaches, and spending long hours in cramped ships' holds to toughen them up for what lay ahead.* Army and navy aviators were practising a number of tactics. The bombers concentrated on high-level pattern bombing and low-level attacks on capital ships. The fighters focused on bomber escort and ground support.

The psychological aspects of being a member of the Japanese Imperial Forces were also addressed as part of their war planning. They were fighting to free Asia from the Western colonial powers, to end the domination of the underprivileged majority by a pampered minority. Theirs was a holy mission, a crusade to liberate those too weak to liberate themselves, to make an Asia for Asians and, under Japanese guidance, to create an economic and political powerhouse to be called the Greater East Asia Co-Prosperity Sphere. They were fighting in the name of, and as

---

* The Japanese called these ships 'banana boats', not because of what they had formerly carried or what they were given to eat aboard, but because they were being used to 'ripen' the troops for whatever lay ahead.

representatives of, the Japanese Emperor Hirohito, descended from the gods themselves and representing an unbroken hereditary line that stretched over 2000 years. To fight and to die for him was the supreme honour, and surrender therefore was never an option. Those who surrendered were like ghosts upon the earth, casting no shadows and leaving no traces.

Until the end of November there was still a faint chance that war could be avoided, that the negotiations under way with the Americans in Washington would achieve some kind of breakthrough. But the Americans offered no concessions and the die was cast. At the start of December, the various Japanese task forces set sail from their ports and, once at sea, opened their sealed orders. It was 6 December in the eastern Pacific and 7 December in the west. At Kajang and Malacca and Tampoi, the Australian nurses were at parties or dinners or, for those unlucky enough to be rostered on a weekend, on duty. In the early hours of the next morning, as most of them slept, Japanese aircraft were being launched from aircraft carriers and taking off from airfields across South East Asia and the central Pacific. The Pacific War was about to begin.

CHAPTER 4

The Balloon Goes Up

Most of the Australians in Malaya and Singapore knew what was coming and who it was coming from. There were only two questions they were uncertain about: where the Japanese would attack, and when? They were also quietly confident about the outcome, and it was this confidence that allowed them to concentrate on what was in front of them rather than on what might come to pass.

From the middle of 1941, Japan had been making moves suggesting that if war was to come, it would involve a strike against the European colonies to her south: French Indo China, British Malaya and the Netherlands East Indies. An alliance with Germany ultimately led to Japanese forces occupying bases in Indo China while a non-aggression pact with the Soviet Union released tens of thousands of troops stationed in Manchuria for active service elsewhere. On-again and off-again negotiations with the United States provided occasional respite from the ongoing threat of war, but that threat – increasing as the year wound down – provided a constant background to the more mundane activities that occupied the nurses.

In their writings home and in their diaries, those girls who mentioned the threat of war did so in terms of it being a short and victorious conflict, but many simply discounted the possibility, perhaps to reassure family and friends at home. Buddy Elmes simply refused to acknowledge any threats in her instructions to her Tripehounds. After thanking Smithy for the gift of a new suspender belt, '. . . my old one was getting very pongy owing to the constant heat . . .' she continued her musings and observations about nursing life in the tropics in her twice-weekly letters: 'Just fed my face on a Violet Crumble. They get very sticky in this climate and almost pull your teeth out . . . am getting quite old, can produce a few grey hairs, so when I come back expect something fat, grey and forty.'

In September, she informed Smithy that she and Shuie were going to study Malay for at least 30 minutes every day, and in October detailed how invisible friends and invisible dogs were now all the rage. As November unfolded, Buddy urged her friends to send clothes as hers were becoming worn out rapidly in the heat and humidity of Malaya, and she advised her young protégés that, if they were considering service in the tropics: 'I would get plenty of voile underwear, even bloomers, if you have to wear them as they don't wear out nearly so much as the cotton and Milanese ones do.'

In late November, Buddy and the other nurses were advised that all Japanese-owned businesses were now out of bounds, with photography studios being specifically singled out as places to be avoided. They were also warned that hostilities could be expected to commence at any time in the near future and, when they did, the nurses would be required to wear suitable attire when travelling, including tin helmets and gas masks.

War, when it came, came suddenly. At around the same time in the western and central Pacific Ocean, Japanese forces attacked at Pearl Harbor, the Philippines, Hong Kong and Malaya. At Kota Bahru, in the north of Malaya, Japanese forces stormed ashore well before dawn while, to the south, Japanese bombers flew over Australian positions at Kluang and Tampoi en route to Singapore where their bombs landed on the brightly lit city, killing dozens of civilians. The first bomb to land destroyed the air-conditioned restaurant at Robinson's in the heart of the city.

Shortly after the outbreak of hostilities, a stream of messages and instructions flowed from General Bennett's Australian headquarters to all his units in the field, ordering some to pre-planned positions and instructing others to assume formations and commence work programs that had also been pre-planned. One of these orders directed all medical personnel to wear brassards featuring a red cross and forbade all combatant units to either bivouac or manoeuvre within one kilometre of a hospital or a casualty clearing station. The nurses were also required to carry their gas masks and tin hats, and to carry emergency kits. It was a message reinforced to the nurses of the 2/13th by their commanding officer, Colonel Pigdon, who called them together in their mess at Tampoi and told them: 'You will wear these Red Cross armbands at all times, that is an order. Do not put too much faith in them though, as the enemy we are fighting does not play cricket.'

Pigdon added some personal observations about what was to come, and he stressed that war was about conflict and danger and that they should be prepared for both. He said that the strength of the Japanese should not be underestimated, noting that they had paratroops and that a facility such as the Tampoi complex could easily be isolated by such troops. He also told them that if

Tampoi was at risk of capture, they were to take their emergency kits and iron rations, head into the surrounding jungle and make their own way, individually or in small groups, to the coast. To prepare for such an eventuality, all nurses should begin to devote time to studying maps of the area. And, Pigdon added, he was now putting a curfew on the nurses and they would no longer be allowed outside the hospital compound after dark. Nor would they be allowed visitors.

The specific medical directives differed somewhat from the instructions issued to combat units. For example, fighting formations contained both medical vehicles and medical personnel, but neither would wear or display the Red Cross as they had been told that these would be used as targets by Japanese soldiers and aircraft. Also, as the medical vehicles were usually parked near unit headquarters, they could easily give away the location of those headquarters to enemy spotters. The medical and hospital units also made some concessions to the realities of battle, and their ambulances were left 1500 metres from the front lines. Casualties from the front would be placed in utility vehicles for the trip back to the nearest ambulance.

As well as these personnel and security measures, a number of changes were made to the structure and organisation of the medical units. One of the first decisions was to increase the capacity of the 2/13th from 600 to 1200 beds, to bring it up to the same capacity as the 2/10th at Malacca. This also involved some rotation of nursing staff between the various units, and some reassignment of responsibilities within those units. For instance, Wilma Oram and Mona Wilton were both transferred from general duties to the fractures ward, before Wilma was sent back to her area of specialisation, the operating theatre. The 2/13th was also authorised to take and treat casualties from Singapore, and there was soon a steady trickle of them.

For the first weeks of the war, however, the two Australian hospitals continued to treat patients who presented primarily with skin and stomach disorders, and those injured in accidents. Apart from some bomb splinter patients at Tampoi, the war seemed to be only a slightly different version of the peace that preceded it. The girls' diary entries and letters home suggest no sense of impending doom, or even of heightened danger. Irene Drummond continued writing her regular letters to her sister in Glen Osmond on the fringes of Adelaide. The first one she wrote after the Japanese invasion opened with: '. . . your parcel of books arrived and I am very pleased to have them now when we are so isolated.' Like all others writing around the same time, she noted the outbreak of hostilities but observed that the main problem the war had brought was: '. . . the blackouts are the bane of my existence at present. I dislike not having proper light at night.'

The larger hospitals at Malacca and Tampoi were clearly identified with red crosses and were nowhere near any legitimate military targets, but the smaller clearing station at Kluang was located alongside the town's airfield, and Tom Hamilton was concerned about the likelihood of his facility being hit by misdirected bombs. The entire CCS was therefore moved to a predetermined location in a rubber estate some four kilometres away. This was a major logistical exercise, as 35 army lorries were normally required to transport the unit and all its equipment and supplies. That equipment alone weighed 135 tonnes, while the tents and marquees were big and bulky, and required a real effort to either erect or dismantle. At the new location the tents and stores were positioned according to plan, with two rows of tents and marquees with a broad roadway between them. The thoroughfare was christened 'Kinsella Avenue' in honour of the unit's senior sister. It resembled a little village; and when they moved, the 2/4th was always accompanied by their Chinese amahs, chickens, cookboys and assistants.

The period up to Christmas and the New Year was one of great uncertainty for the Australian forces. The British and Indian Army divisions continued to retreat south while Singapore was being bombed several times a day. No-one seemed to either know or want to share what the short to medium outlooks might be. All were confident about the long-term outlook, believing that Allied troops, generally Australian or American, were preparing to land behind the advancing Japanese who would then be crushed in a pincer movement. Apart from the RAAF, who had suffered a number of casualties and were struggling to find serviceable aircraft, Australian forces were not directly engaged with the Japanese. The airfield at Kluang had been bombed and the nurses at Tampoi watched the Japanese flying overhead en route to and from Singapore. Apart from that, the Australians felt they were contributing little to the war effort in Malaya, as the mainland battles were being fought far to the north of the Australian positions.

For some, the outbreak of hostilities was pretty much just a hiccup in their ongoing social life; Mona Wilton and Wilma Oram saw it as a kind of punctuation mark offering a minor and temporary impediment to their plan to become the social lionesses of the lower Malay Peninsula. Both were extremely dedicated and competent nurses, but Mona could not help detailing the important things in their service to a friend back home in Victoria: 'We went dancing with two nice British officers – one my tea planter man – Friday night and on Saturday afternoon they took us for a long drive. My tea planter is going to India for a couple of months shortly – to look after his estate – and is going to bring me back a tiger skin.' The following week, the girls saw their nice British officers off at the railway station and then met up with two Australian majors they had met at the sultan's ball: 'They took us to the nicest place we've ever been to – a swimming club with a scrumptious swimming pool, verandas, ballrooms and things.' The war was treated with the contempt it deserved, if it was ever mentioned at all, and on 20 December Mona could write: '. . . I gave my tea planter a little bit of cake, and he is quite sure he will come home with me after the war.'

At Tampoi, as at St Patrick's and Duggan's Dugout back in Armadale, Mona and Wilma made certain that not only were they billeted together but they also arranged to have the same shifts on and the same time off. During that time off, they would beg, borrow and sometimes contemplate stealing a lift into Johore Bahru at least and Singapore at best. If it could be wangled, they would also overnight at Raffles because that was where their contacts and beaus congregated. Shortly before the Japanese attacked, Raffles had constructed a large underground car park which was being used as a bomb shelter during the daily air raids. It was also a good place for a kiss and cuddle.

There were some forceful reminders though that not everything was what it had been just weeks earlier. When the nurses went into town – whether to Johore Bahru or Singapore – they were accompanied by an armed guard and whenever they left their hospitals they would be confronted by the sight of army lorries heading south to Singapore with full loads of British and Indian Army wounded en route to their own hospitals on the island. Australian troops were not yet engaged with the enemy, and so there was still relatively little for the nurses to do beyond basic nursing, letter writing and preparing to celebrate what was for most their first Christmas and New Year away from home.

That festive season was celebrated in Malaya as elsewhere, although in more restrained circumstances. General Bennett hosted a quiet cocktail hour for a group of nurses in Malacca shortly before Christmas. During the event, he made a short speech about their safety, saying that he thought they were in more danger than the Australian nurses had been during the ill-fated Greek campaign earlier in the year. At both hospitals, and at the CCS, Christmas was celebrated in traditional army style. Despite the heat, a large roast dinner was consumed and, again sticking with tradition, the meal was served up to the enlisted men by their officers. At Kluang, Tom Hamilton's men brightened up the day for anyone who chanced by. On that day, the password was 'Coolabah'. Anyone who could not pronounce the word correctly – generally British soldiers and expatriate plantation managers – was taken under escort to the sergeants' mess and there invited to drink a pint of beer as punishment for not having been born an Australian.

Being furthest from the fighting, the celebrations at Tampoi were a little grander than those at Malacca or Kluang. The wards of the old mental hospital were decorated and the Red Cross and Salvation Army provided some additional foodstuffs for both staff and patients. The unit's male officers carved the chicken and ham and served it to the patients in their beds, and the medical orderlies in their mess. The mobile patients and the nurses were also seated and served in the nurses' mess. The Sultan of Johore made a surprise appearance during the afternoon to wish his guests the compliments of the season. On Boxing Day, the nurses reciprocated, hosting a party for the officers in the nurses' mess and a Christmas party for all the orderlies who had been required to work the previous day. To top off the celebrations, the sultan invited Colonel Pigdon and Matron Drummond, plus any officers who could be spared, to a formal dinner at his palace. Those who went recalled fondly how they actually did eat off golden plates and moreover used golden cutlery to do so.

A number of functions were planned to welcome in the New Year of 1942. At Malacca, the officers of the 2/10th hosted a New Year's Eve party in their mess as did the officers of the 2/13th across the peninsula at Tampoi. They were happy to do so, they said, as it partially repaid the kindness shown by the nurses in hosting a Christmas dinner for them. At Kluang, the nurses of the 2/4th hosted a much less formal celebration. After decorating the main bungalow at the civilian hospital quarters they occupied, Kit Kinsella, the other nurses, and the select group of officers they had invited all danced to gramophone music. The party was interrupted by air-raid sirens that sounded as waves of Japanese aircraft flew overhead on their way to bomb Singapore into the New Year. The party resumed with the all clear, and in fact gained a second wind around midnight with the arrival of four RAAF officers who brought both good cheer and, more importantly, additional supplies of beer and gin.

Mona and Wilma had New Year's Day off and decided to continue their personal festive season by visiting Singapore to see how their luck held up. It did, as they were able to meet Mona's major at Raffles, where they also had tea, and still found time to do some shopping. Apart from regular air raids during the day, and the inconvenience caused by bomb craters in all manner of places, it was a day like many others they had enjoyed in the past three months.

As well as the rumours about Allied landings behind the Japanese lines, the period between Christmas and New Year also saw the emergence of a number of new and very disturbing rumours about the behaviour of the Japanese forces. The first of these rumours circulated on Christmas Day when the nurses in Malacca were told that Japanese forces were now advancing through Burma. It was also reported that a number of hospitals had been overrun there by Japanese troops who then proceeded to murder the patients and rape the nurses. By New Year's Eve, it was common knowledge that Hong Kong had fallen to the Japanese a few days previously, and lurid stories about their behaviour there were beginning to circulate. These included accounts of British and Asian civilian nurses being forced into a small room before being taken out one at a time to be gang-raped by Japanese soldiers. Two who resisted were beheaded on a nearby tennis court.

Such rumours were very alarming and senior Allied officers felt they were part of a plan by fifth columnists to break the morale of the Allied forces. Most, though, including the nurses, felt that while they were only rumours they probably contained an element of truth. They did, and that truth was even worse than the rumours suggested.

Far East Command had known that Hong Kong was practically indefensible, but insisted it be defended because of reasons of appearance and prestige. When Japanese forces stormed into the New Territories on 8 December, the British and Canadian forces stationed there fought a series of rearguard and delaying actions as they fell back towards Hong Kong Island. There they set up final defences but soon realised that it was only a matter of time before they would be overrun. To cope with the ever-increasing number of casualties, local command took over St Stephen's Boys' School at Stanley on the south coast of the island and converted it into a makeshift hospital. They did the same at the Hong Kong Jockey Club.

By Christmas Eve the Japanese had gained control of most of the island, and that night their soldiers began breaking into shops, warehouses and private homes. By the morning of Christmas Day, effective resistance had all but ceased and drunken bands of Japanese soldiers roamed at will across the island. One such band entered the grounds of St Stephen's at 0600 hours on Christmas morning. In a drunken frenzy, they shot down the doctors who attempted to surrender the hospital to them and, once inside the buildings, embarked on an orgy of murder and rape. Doctors and patients alike were bayoneted and the nurses, all of whom were Chinese or Eurasian, were confined to a room before being taken out one at a time and gang-raped. One nurse later testified that she was forced to lie on the bodies of two of her dead colleagues before being assaulted. Several were executed after being raped. By lunchtime, 56 medical staff and patients had been murdered and a dozen nurses repeatedly raped. Similar scenes, but on a smaller scale, were repeated at the makeshift hospital at the Jockey Club.

The atrocities were committed by soldiers from the 38th Division of the Imperial Japanese Army. By way of explanation, one of the perpetrators told the nurse he had just raped that a very popular member of his unit had been killed in street fighting on Christmas Eve. The St Stephen's massacre was how the Japanese soldiers exacted their revenge.

From the time of the early British reverses in the north of the country, the Commanding Officer of the 2/10th, Colonel Albert Coates, pointed out to both Far East Command and Australian Headquarters that the Japanese appeared to have adopted a west coast strategy that, if continued, meant that his hospital at Malacca would probably be in their direct line of advance. At first Far East Command suggested that Coates was wrong and that it was too early to tell; Singapore itself was the most likely target for the next landing. Within two weeks, however, they had changed their mind and General Bennett was given discretion to relocate the hospital at an appropriate time. On 26 December, a third of the 2/10th transferred to Tampoi to join the hospital there, while the remainder of the unit followed in dribs and drabs over the next few days. By 2 January 1942, the White Elephant, all of Malacca and all of the state of Negri Sembilan had been evacuated.

During their 200-kilometre retreat to Tampoi, the 2/10th stopped several times to help establish field hospitals to treat the increasing numbers of wounded coming from the north, and to shelter from the bombing and strafing attacks on all the main roads through the area. All this took time, but the process was helped by the fact that the hospital had already evacuated its patients to Kluang and Tampoi. Olive Paschke and 20 of her nurses stopped at the 2/4th's facilities in the rubber plantation at Kluang and were given a large bungalow to occupy while accommodation further to the south was prepared for them. Tom Hamilton apologised for not being able to do more for the 2/10th nurses, who had left their amahs and cook-boys behind. Still bubbling with enthusiasm for her work, Olive told him: 'If twenty strong, healthy women can't look after themselves in a place like this, I'll eat my tin hat.' Men from a nearby signals unit came over to check out the new nurses within minutes of their arrival, explaining that they were there to show them the lay of the land. The matron explained that she doubted that would be necessary and sent them on their way.

By 10 January, all the elements of the 2/10th were at Tampoi and there the hospital paused. The 2/13th made them welcome and welcomed too their assistance. Ordered to double its capacity and then add some more, the 2/13th had grown from 350 beds on 11 December to 945 beds on 18 December, with another 300 to be added by the middle of January. Not all the beds were occupied, but the number of admissions was growing. Australia's infantry battalions were expected to be in the front line by mid to late January, and when they clashed with the advancing Japanese, casualties were expected to be heavy.

To deal with this anticipated change of circumstances, a number of additional duties were identified and introduced at Tampoi. To cope with a possible gas attack, a decontamination squad was formed, while another group of nurses became the signals squad, chosen because theirs was the only hut equipped with a telephone. The Army Signals Corps would call them at any hour of the day or night and if the message they delivered was 'Air Raid Red', a large brass bell would be rung continuously. At this signal, off-duty nurses and amahs would seek refuge in the jungle; those on duty had their own set of instructions. Most of the nights at Tampoi were now interrupted by some form of air-raid warning, as wave after wave of Japanese bombers flew over on their way to attack targets on Singapore Island, softening up the defences and trying to break the will of the defenders.

Even at this late date, the full experience of war was something the girls read about rather than lived through. For many of them, their first vision of war wounded was when they were in Johore Bahru on leave, and ambulances and trucks rolled through the city carrying British and Indian Army soldiers wounded in the fighting in the north to their own hospitals in Singapore. They were allowed leave in Johore Bahru during the daytime right up until the end of January, and for all the girls at Tampoi, the war was more an occasional inconvenience than the life and death struggle it was for others. They could still entertain visitors in their mess after 2100 hours, and go shopping in the shops and bazaars of old Johore.

As the tired and dispirited British and Indian troops continued to fall back onto and through the Australian defensive positions in northern Johore, preparations were being made well behind those positions for the kind of last-ditch effort that many in command thought might become necessary. In order to free up more beds in the hospitals of Singapore, the first evacuations of convalescent patients – mainly those with tropical diseases – had taken place on New Year's Eve, when 114 Australian patients had sailed for home accompanied by several AANS nurses. Plans were made for other, more seriously injured Australians to be relocated to the 2/12th AGH, based at Colombo in Ceylon (Sri Lanka). Despite a constant and recurring rumour that at least one Australian hospital ship was on its way, the only actual 'hospital' ship to operate was a converted riverboat named the *Wah Sui* which began to ferry parties of Allied wounded to Batavia (Jakarta) in the Netherlands East Indies. Convalescent depots were also set up across the island to relieve pressure on the civilian and military hospitals there.

The Australian medical units were also involved in the reorganisation that accompanied the plans for a final stand on the impregnable fortress of Singapore. The 2/10th medical staff at Tampoi were held there temporarily while their stores and equipment were sent across the causeway to Singapore, where they would be unpacked and the unit reconstituted as a working hospital there, awaiting only its staff and patients. The bulk of the hospital was to be based at the Oldham Hall Mission Boarding House, part of the Anglo-Chinese School located on the main road north from Singapore to the causeway, the Bukit Timah Road, a little over three kilometres from the heart of the city.*
The Oldham Hall complex was not large enough on its own, so

---

* The Anglo-Chinese School at Oldham Hall was a Methodist school founded in 1886 with just 13 students. Its name came from the fact that lessons there were conducted in English during the morning and Chinese during the afternoon. The school still exists, and still continues to turn out well-rounded students who have a record of success in business and government.

a guesthouse known as the 'Manor House' and located several hundred metres away was also taken over for the overflow from Oldham Hall. The entire move, which in peacetime could take anything up to six weeks, was completed in less than two.

The month from mid-December to mid-January was the calm before the storm, and all the Australians sensed this. They knew that their family and friends at home would be anxious, especially as the war news from Malaya was not good. Their diaries and letters and stories from this time have a hint of uncertainty, of a desire to assuage worries at home, but also to calm their own increasing concerns. Many of the girls seem to have tried to write home at least once a week, and their letters are peppered with exhortations to not worry, as well as descriptions about just how far out of harm's way they were. Writing to her sister, Irene Drummond explained: '. . . we have hurricane lamps with blue paper as our usual light . . . we don't go beyond the precincts of the hospitals and our quarters so it is nothing but work and sleep with food whenever', as if the banality of her existence was somehow reassuring. She went on to describe how large the hospital was and how they were all working together, before allowing herself a moment of levity that might have surprised some of her nurses: 'I heard a good story the other day. Have you heard it? What did the brassiere say to the top hat? You go on a head, and I'll give the other two suckers a lift.'

What Irene didn't say was that she, too, was beginning to share some of the fears that all her girls were now starting to harbour deep inside, too afraid to bring them to light in case they be considered 'windy', or in case their patients picked up some hint that not all was as well as the nurses kept telling them. Irene did not really know how to share these feelings with the girls, or even how to raise them. She did not have the way with words or with people that Olive Paschke had; all she knew was that these were her girls, and she loved each and every one of them. So every day, and every shift, she either rode or walked or hitched a ride to every one of the wards being used in the vast hospital at Malacca. She called in to all the nurses' rooms and invited those girls available to share a cup of tea with her. What's more, she usually both made and poured the tea. And then she asked her girls how they were going.

Nell Keats of the 2/10th was another of the girls whose letters were positively upbeat. Writing to her mother in Adelaide on 20 December, she recorded: 'Each night we have community singing in the Mess, which I enjoy very much, and tonight I am going to the pictures to see *Waterloo Bridge* . . . We are still not very busy as we haven't started receiving casualties.'

Some took advantage of the hiatus to indulge in one of the traditional practices of the Australian soldier on active duty – devising practical jokes. At Tampoi, one of the toilet blocks was built on a slight slope, and the sanitary arrangements included a drain flowing beneath the cubicles filled with running water from a spring which carried all the effluent into a large settlement pond downhill. The block was assigned to the nurses but a number of medical orderlies recognised the potential of the situation. At odd times, but most often shortly after reveille in the morning, one of the orderlies would occupy the cubicle at the 'top' of the block. When he judged that several of the other cubicles were occupied, he would take a shoebox which had previously been filled with cotton wool soaked in cigarette lighter fluid, light the device and allow it to slowly float downstream. There may have been bets on who could produce the most squeals. No matter how many times they tried it, the trick still reduced the orderlies hiding in the foliage to tears.

* * *

The general mood among all AIF units remained positive and the nurses in particular were thrilled to learn that Principal Matron Olive Paschke had been awarded the second highest award for service in nursing, the Royal Red Cross, First Class, in the Australian New Year's Honours List. Paschke had been nominated for the award in October, and General Bennett had added his own endorsement to the recommendation:

> Matron Paschke has, by her enthusiasm and by her unfailing attention to duty, given exceptionally good service to the AIF in Malaya. On the arrival of the first contingent of troops, a large number of cases of sickness had to be handled. She, with her nursing staff, facilitated the establishment of a hospital and provided the necessary comforts for the patients. Her work was above average in its efficiency. Her unflagging zeal and cheerfulness and long hours of duty have been an inspiration to the nursing staff and have been particularly valuable under the difficult conditions of the tropics.

Apart from celebrating Olive Paschke's award, the nurses spent the first half of January making certain the medical and hospital facilities at Kluang and Tampoi were in readiness for the casualties they knew they would soon be required to receive. In their spare time, they sometimes watched and wondered and later wrote about the flights of Japanese bombers that came over several times a day. They always appeared in groups that were multiples of nine, with 27, 54 and even 81 aircraft going over and back, over and back. They generally flew without fighter escort as there was nothing for that escort to do on most days. The majority of the Japanese fighters were flying close combat support missions for the advancing troops. The nurses knew the lead aircraft would release its bombs somewhere over Singapore, and those following would then release theirs simultaneously. They also knew that this pattern bombing had a devastating effect on both land and on the shipping in Keppel Harbour. But they were not without hope: early in the New Year the *Straits Times* announced that Robinson's restaurant had reopened in the basement of the department store.

Clashes between Australian troops and the advancing Japanese commenced on 15 January, when a company of the 2/30th battalion ambushed a column of Japanese bicyclists at the small town of Gemas and killed several hundred before withdrawing successfully. The bicyclists were almost a secret weapon for the Japanese, enabling them to move – at speed – in numbers and directions the Allies thought impossible. The Japanese absorbed the blow and continued to do what they had been doing so successfully for much of the previous six weeks – they regrouped, advanced, and simply flowed around or bypassed obstacles put in their path. Within days, all Australian front line units, infantry and artillery were engaged. While the main thrust by the Japanese continued to be along the west coast where the Australians fought major battles at the Muar River and the Bakri crossroads, the changing nature of the terrain as the war moved south allowed the Japanese forces to advance inland as well. In addition, a secondary thrust down the east coast threatened the weakened Australian positions there in turn.

Just as the British and Indian troops before them had done, the Australians retreated rather than be surrounded or overrun. The Japanese seemed to specialise in infiltrating small units and snipers behind the Australian positions where they created havoc. Officers were particular targets for snipers, and they soon learned to both remove their badges of rank and carry rifles rather than revolvers. There was nowhere that was really safe; Japanese control of the air meant any daytime movement by Australian troops was almost certain to attract artillery fire, bombs or both. In the close-quarter fighting that was characteristic of the campaign, Australian casualties mounted. This, coupled with the constant withdrawals to prepared positions, increased the pressure on the medical units. One of the front line doctors later described the work under these conditions:

> We commandeered big brass trays from some of the deserted bungalows in that region and each medical officer had two teams of orderlies attached to him. One pair, called the 'dirty pair', had scissors, jacknife, soapy water, washers and towels, so that a wound could be quickly exposed, boots cut off, clothes cut off and a quick cleaning made. Then the other two men with the so-called 'clean tray' would move in and their tray was like an ordinary hospital ward dressing tray, with sterile forceps, dressings, antiseptic in bowls, etc. Artery forceps and ties to arrest major bleeding and needle holders and suture material for special cases, although we expected to transport most patients quickly back to our main dressing station.

Increasingly, that main dressing station was the 2/4th CCS at Kluang. As the wounded were sent back, they would have either a red card (seriously injured) or a white card (less seriously injured) tied to their shirts. Descriptions of the wounds were written on the reverse side of the card. Those who required resuscitation before further examination or treatment would first be separated from the others, while those who had been given morphia at any stage of their treatment would have the letter 'M' written on their foreheads in indelible pencil.

The scenes in the dressing and clearing stations were

Dante-esque. Because movement on the main roads during the day was fraught with danger, the ambulances and lorries travelled mainly at night. At the medical stations, the examination rooms and operating theatres were brightly lit, and the combination of bright lights and enclosed spaces generated great heat. Perspiring doctors probed and cut and stitched while the nurses, their dresses soaked, passed instruments and mopped both brows and wounds. The cooler mornings brought some temporary relief but, more often than not, also brought orders for the station to pack up and move another 20 or so kilometres closer to Singapore.

If anyone had been keeping a careful tally, new records in patient management would have been set on a regular basis; one night at Kluang, the 2/4th treated over 2000 casualties. But no-one was keeping a tally, and much of the paperwork was being burnt anyway as the units maintained their steady retreat southwards. While they were doing so, circumstances changed and a number of key decisions were made. At Tampoi, the changes were most evident. In the presumed normal course of events, an Australian soldier wounded in action would be given immediate treatment on or near the battlefield by medical orderlies, who would organise stretcher bearers if necessary to take the wounded soldier back to an advanced or mobile dressing station for initial diagnosis and treatment.

After this reception the soldier would then be transported by field ambulance to a casualty clearing station, where emergency surgery could and would be performed if necessary. Wounds would be cleaned, stitched and bandaged, and broken limbs set. From there, the wounded would be taken, again by ambulance, to a General Hospital for additional treatment, higher-level and more delicate surgery, and initial recuperation. Once stabilised and recovering satisfactorily, the soldier would be sent to a convalescent depot before eventual return to either his unit or to Australia for further treatment or perhaps discharge.

That was the theory, and the theory that had proved so successful on the Western Front during World War I. For the best part of four years, the front lines there did not move by more than a few hundred metres, so systems assumed an air of permanency. Malaya in 1942 was very different and the reality was that the wounded were given the best treatment possible wherever and whenever it could be given. Because of its size and location, the 2/13th treated most of the casualties from the AIF's battles in Johore, and as the fighting moved ever closer to Tampoi, the hospital was forced to operate as if it were a large-scale casualty clearing station. Its staff was also forced to deal with situations that had not been previously imagined, as wounded arrived from units other than those of the AIF. All were told briefly of the differences between the various religions and castes in the Indian Army and instructed not to attempt to remove a kukri – a wicked-looking knife – from a wounded Gurkha or a turban from a wounded Sikh unless the owner was conscious and gave approval.

The decisions that would shape how the campaign played out were not made in the medical units, though. Towards the end of January, Churchill's choice to head up Malaya Command, Lieutenant General Arthur Percival, and his senior commanders in the British Army accepted that they could no longer hold the Malay Peninsula and made plans for a final retreat to Singapore Island. Independent of that decision-making, General Bennett and his senior commanders had determined that the Australian medical units would be evacuated from the peninsula back to the island. The 2/4th simply continued their gypsy existence, moving from Kluang to Tampoi, where it paused with the others before crossing the straits to the Bukit Panjang English School on the island before making a final move to the Swiss Club, just north of Singapore City, on 6 February.*

The brief stop at Tampoi was just long enough for some lasting memories to be created. In one of the medical wards a number of wounded soldiers were trying to come to terms with both their injuries and the shock of the ongoing retreat. The men were particularly fearful of what might happen to them, fears that were exacerbated at night by both the blackout and the background noise of distant battle and bombers overhead. When the hum of voices started to build up as the soldiers talked about their injuries and their fears, Lainie Balfour-Ogilvy would often start singing. Among the wounded was Private John Carey of the 2/30th battalion: '. . . [Lainie] won the hearts of all the men with her lovely personality, dedication to work, and the fact that she was a breath of home to one thousand men. None of those men will ever forget her lovely singing voice, particularly in her singing of "The Last Time I Saw Paris".'

On 24 January, the 2/13th commenced its evacuation of Tampoi. The previous day, Nancy Harris, a 28-year-old Sydneysider from a medical family, had been listening to her wireless in her room between shifts when Tokyo Rose came on and spoke to the Allied troops in Malaya. Among her usual greetings she sent her special regards to 'the 2/13th Australian General Hospital at Tampoi', suggesting that they should be thinking about moving as the entire area they occupied was scheduled to be occupied by Japanese forces on 25 January. That didn't happen but by 26 January, the hospital was elsewhere anyway. It was reassigned to its original quarters at St Patrick's School in Katong, and by the date that the Japanese were supposed to occupy Tampoi it was ready

---

* The Swiss Rifle Club had been established the previous century by Swiss expatriates who were required to keep their marksmanship up to a reasonably high level. The club still exists, although its main functions today are social rather than martial.

to accept casualties at that site. Along with her staff Jean Ashton, an Adelaide girl now second in charge of the 2/13th nurses, had set up a 100-bed medical ward in the school's concert hall, while the dormitories were reorganised with the patients upstairs, and all surgical, medical and messing facilities downstairs. The operating theatre was established in a large room in the basement, which, the last time the 2/13th had been there, had served very well as an officers' mess. The school chapel was then converted into a smaller, second surgery to deal with any overflow.

Before the patients arrived, Major Hunt insisted that every possible receptacle – baths and buckets, spare pots and pans – be filled with water, as he believed the Japanese would cut the supply to the island as a matter of priority. The nurses were also rostered to clean up the abandoned homes around the school preparatory to these being taken over as accommodation for the medical staff, including the nurses. They anticipated there would be too many wounded for them to occupy any of the space available at the school.

In the assembly hall, beds were made up, and on each were placed pyjamas and towels. There was a cool logic to all the preparations. Along one side, the surgical trolleys were lined up and a large notice outlined the shifts and the duties of both nurses and orderlies. The first row of beds was specifically for the very seriously wounded, and an intravenous drip was attached to each bed. The second row was for the seriously wounded, the third for the less seriously wounded, and so on. Cold drinks were prepared and refrigerated and a large supply of sandwiches was made and put aside. Teapots were filled with tea, cups and milk and sugar placed at the ready. The experience of the past few weeks had proved invaluable.

At Oldham Hall, the 2/10th also used the last days of January to consolidate its facilities. It was decided that the school's main building would hold the medical section of the hospital, while the surgical section would be located at Manor House. A large Red Cross was laid out on the lawn alongside Oldham Hall. Between their two primary locations, the 2/10th also occupied some private homes that had been abandoned by their owners. They even set up six marquees on a tennis court attached to one of these homes to take the overload of wounded they expected they would be required to treat. The senior officers commandeered equipment to replace the losses they had incurred during the long retreat from Malacca and, when it became obvious that still more room would probably be needed to house casualties, the hospital also took over the nearby Methodist girls' school. Even at this late stage of the conflict there was an air of unreality about what was needed. After learning that there were issues with civil authorities over the requisitioning of the houses around the hospital, General Bennett noted in his diary: 'I rang General Percival, told him I was going to use an armed party if necessary to get possession of suitable homes . . . I am sorry to say I was very rude.'

With all the decisions made, their implementation then began with British, Indian and Australian units leapfrogging each other back towards the causeway that connected Singapore island to the Malay Peninsula. While they tried to destroy anything they thought might be of value to the Japanese – the retreat was marked by the thick black smoke of burning rubber stockpiles – the things that should have been destroyed earlier remained largely intact. The Japanese had hundreds of boats of all sizes and configurations, seized from fishermen and ferry companies up and down the east and west coasts where they had been left sitting by the retreating Allied forces.

On the last day of January 1942, the remaining British soldiers not under Japanese confinement in Malaya marched across the causeway. Fittingly, they were the remnants of a battalion of the Argyll and Sutherland Highlanders, a unit that had first engaged the Japanese on 8 December, the day the Pacific War began. They were piped across the causeway by a lone kilted piper. As the final notes of his tune faded away, a massive explosion rocked both sides of the Straits of Johore. When the dust cleared, it revealed a 60-metre gap in the causeway with the water rushing through the breach. Singapore, with its thousands of soldiers and millions of civilians, would now face the Japanese alone.

While there were many decisions that were made in Singapore and Malaya during the last two weeks of January 1942, there was one that actually wasn't made. On 20 January, Colonel Alfred Derham, senior medical officer in the 8th Division, formally asked Major General Gordon Bennett to authorise the evacuation of all Australian nurses from the Malayan theatre of operations. Derham was aware of the rumours of Japanese atrocities, and while they were of some concern, of greater concern was the fact that as the area held by the Allies became more and more concentrated because of the continuing retreats, there would be fewer and fewer areas that were not part of a battle zone. While there had been no casualties among the nurses as yet, Derham believed it was only a matter of time before they occurred. Bennett considered the request briefly before rejecting it outright. He would not evacuate the nurses, he told Derham, because their departure would have a profound and negative effect on the morale of the Australian troops as well as on the nurses themselves.

CHAPTER 5

The Curtain Comes Down

For a week after the causeway was blown nothing much seemed to happen. The Japanese bombers still flew over to deposit their loads on Singapore City and various Allied strongpoints, and the hastily constructed defences around the island's northern coastline were increasingly subjected to artillery fire. But otherwise, it was a time when both sides paused to take stock before the final assault that both knew was necessary to end the campaign one way or another.

For the nurses and their hospitals, it was a time to both catch up and consolidate. Those of them who were able to may have read the editorial in the last edition of *The Bulletin* published on the last day of 1941: '. . . but the invasion has not yet reached a point where it may be described as dangerous . . .' Those on the ground in Singapore viewed events differently. During the night of 31 January a bomb hit the southwest corner of the main hospital building at St Patrick's, and blew a hole in the roof of a recovery ward containing 75 wounded Australians. Apart from some minor panic among the soldiers there were no significant injuries. The incident reminded the girls of just how serious their circumstances were and, if they needed any further reminder, from mid-January, all the Chinese merchants and shopkeepers on Singapore island started to phase out the use of the chit system and would only accept cash for purchases.

From 1 February, the island held 16 field ambulance units, two of which were Australian, three casualty clearing stations, including the 2/4th, and seven general hospitals, two of which were Australian. The Alexandra Hospital, a permanently built pre-war British Army establishment, was now full and would only admit British officers, with their enlisted men being sent to the Gillman Hospital. Indian and Malay Army wounded were sent to the 17th Combined General Hospital, which had taken over the Union Jack Club, the club established before the conflict for British Army soldiers on leave in Singapore. Of the other hospitals, No. 1 Malayan General Hospital had been relocated to Selarang Barracks in the Changi complex, but was equally quickly relocated again when Japanese bombers plastered the entire area.

The locations and circumstances of the two Australian hospitals were static and remained more or less the same until the final hours of the fighting. The 2/4th CCS, however, was never quite certain of where it should be. When Tom Hamilton led his unit onto the island, their first resting place was the small village of Bukit Panjang in the north centre of the island. There they established a 200-bed facility, with the nurses still being headed with vigour and compassion by Kit Kinsella. Because Hamilton was led to believe they may remain at Bukit Panjang for the long haul, he recalled the staff he had loaned to the 2/13th to help them establish themselves at St Patrick's. Mavis Hannah, Shirley Gardam, Jess Dorsch and Mina Raymont were more than happy to be back with their friends.*

For a couple of days at least there was a possibility of pretending that things were almost normal. On 1 February, the 2/4th CCS officers' mess rules were relaxed to allow the nurses to attend the luncheon the unit put on for the visit of the 2/30th Battalion's commanding officer, Lieutenant Colonel Frederick 'Black Jack' Galleghan. Galleghan's men had inflicted the first setback to the Japanese at Gemas, and he was widely regarded as Australia's premier fighting soldier in Malaya. After the meal, the renowned warrior and disciplinarian regaled the doctors and nurses with war stories based on his experiences in the two great conflicts of the century. It was also during this brief interlude that Tom Hamilton confided to a friend that, when the dust had settled on the campaign, he proposed to recommend Kit Kinsella for the Royal Red Cross for her outstanding leadership under pressure at Kluang. She was, he said, '. . . possessed of a splendid nursing technique based on equal parts of straight talking and compassion'. He also said that he would be recommending to AIF command that she be both recognised for her work with a decoration, and promoted to matron and given responsibility for a larger group of nurses.

The Australians established an effective routine during those first few days of February. After the near carnage of the last days in Johore, casualties on Singapore were relatively light and

---

* Shirley Gardam was another Tasmanian personally selected by Tom Hamilton. From Port Sorrell on the north coast, Shirley's matron thought she might be 'too nervous' to work in a casualty clearing station. 'Jess' Dorsch was from Adelaide where her family was prominent in educational and religious affairs, while Wilhelmina 'Mina' Raymont was also from South Australia, but had been nursing in Hobart when Tom Hamilton came recruiting.

were mainly shrapnel wounds from Japanese bombs or from the artillery shells the Japanese gunners fired into the Australian defensive positions established in the northwest of the island. Those casualties were forwarded to the 2/4th at Bukit Panjang who sent them on, after treatment, to either of the two main Australian hospitals. On odd days of the month, they were sent to the 2/13th, and to the 2/10th on even days. Considering the debacle that had occurred in Malaya morale was extremely high, and this was reflected in the nurses' attitudes. One later recalled: 'Our morale had never fallen, but now we were really optimistic. We were quite confident of our ability to stand a siege indefinitely, and spoke proudly of the achievements of the AIF in Tobruk.'

Writing to her sister in Adelaide, Irene Drummond described proudly: 'Our hospital grows bigger daily and a tremendous amount of work has been done during the last ten days.' She was especially proud of how competent her sisters had become, and how they had learned to cope with just about anything fate had thrown their way. At a quiet moment during the evening of 1 February, 20 patients suddenly arrived in ambulances, diagnosed as suffering from a variety of fevers and infections caught in the swamps and jungles they had been living and fighting in during the previous two weeks. A quiet Queenslander, Blanche Hempsted, wasn't the most senior nurse in the unit, but she immediately took charge, directing the application of the prescribed medicines and then speaking to each of the patients about their situation and what they could do to help the medical staff treat them and make them well. It was what Irene herself would have done.

But the artillery fire continued to build during that first week of February and the bombers and fighters appeared from first light to last and beyond. At the end of that week, Bukit Panjang village burned to the ground after a particularly heavy artillery barrage, and the 2/4th was pulled back to the Swiss Club on the outskirts of Singapore City. Tom Hamilton was, as usual, impressed by the opportunities the new situation offered:

> Deviating from the entrance to Singapore's palatial racetrack . . . a gravelled road led up the hill past groups of handsome bungalows, occupied either by civilians or Indian Army transport units. At the top of the rise the road passed through an ornate gateway into a beautifully wooded glade, then curved in a graceful circuit through the porch of a pleasant two storeyed clubhouse, built in the style of an Alpine chalet . . . Alighting from the car, a sweeping glance embraced the luxury of well-kept lawns, tennis courts, bowling alley, secluded rifle range in a glade of its own and – wonder of wonders – the shining gleam of clear water in a green-tiled swimming pool.

The Australian infantry positions in the northwest – and their reserve positions immediately behind – came under steadily increasing artillery barrages until the afternoon of 8 February, when the barrage reached an intensity that many who survived it said was the equivalent of anything they had experienced on the Western Front during World War I. The reason for this was soon obvious; later that night, wave after wave of Japanese troops stormed ashore in the Australian sector of the island, pushing through determined resistance towards Bukit Timah Road, which was to be their main axis of advance.

While much of the next week was chaos there were elements of consistency. The 2/10th, in its complex of buildings around Oldham Hall, found itself targeted by Japanese artillery and bombs, despite the large Red Cross displayed next door. Their trials started on 30 January when a stray Japanese shell destroyed the hospital's kitchen, which was fortunately vacant at the time. As the fighting in the north of the island intensified, so did the bombing and shelling. Shrapnel shredded the marquees that had been erected on the tennis courts and the rain swept straight in. Eventually the patients' beds sank slowly through the surface of the courts until the bottom of the mattress and frame were resting on the grass. During air raids, the nurses would wear tin hats, while most of their patients donned bedpans. Their commanding officer, Colonel Glyn 'Ted' White, had established his office on the balcony of Oldham Hall. He, too, continued working through the air raids, his tin hat on his head as he typed out yet another request for more assistance.

At the Methodist girls' school hospital annex nearby, the nurses could not go outside without an escort to protect them from both the enemy and the friendly fire that any movement seemed to attract. For instance, on 7 February, long-range Japanese artillery appeared to deliberately target the school. During that barrage, one medical orderly and one patient were killed, while Dot Freeman, a junior staff nurse from Melbourne, was lucky to escape unscathed, emerging from a demolished building covered in dust and scratches.* Two more medical orderlies were killed when the Manor House was shelled, while at Oldham Hall, the plaster in the walls and ceilings started to crack and flake from the concussion of the shells. A number of patients there suffered additional wounds from the shrapnel, while one was killed and several others injured in one incident when 15 Japanese shells bracketed the complex.

Attempts were made to alleviate the situation, and Betty Jeffrey later wrote about one occasion when Olive Paschke tried to assist the girls and patients at the Methodist school:

---

* One of the unit's diarists would later recall how: 'a shell landed on the veranda of another section of the hospital, killing one patient and wounding others. Sr. Dot Freeman and orderlies carried the injured men into wards on stretchers.' (From the papers of Veronica Clancy, Australian War Memorial MSS 1086.)

Later in the week there was worse to come. Matron Paschke drove Sisters Halligan, Cuthbertson, Blanch, Davis, Freeman and myself over to our other hospital on the next hill. There were wounded men everywhere – in beds, on stretchers, on the floors, in garages, tents and dug-outs. Low flying planes were machine-gunning all around us. They just cleared the roof and trees, but did turn off their guns while passing over us, starting to fire again immediately they left us behind. We . . . rigged up a large Red Cross on the front lawn with white sheets and yards of red material matron had obtained.*

The 2/4th was also at risk because of the proximity of several British artillery units to their tents and marquees, so there was a constant danger of counter-battery fire hitting their complex. Tom Hamilton went through the appropriate channels and was urged to write a formal letter of protest to the artillery commander. Instead, he chose to use a combination of bluster and charm to convince the artilleryman to relocate his guns to a more appropriate distance away from the CCS. Only the 2/13th, in relative isolation on the east coast at Katong, escaped the daily threat of shelling.

They did not, however, escape the consequences of the Japanese assault on the island. The morning after they landed, ambulances in long convoys arrived bearing hundreds of wounded soldiers. The surgery teams would perform 65 major operations in the next 24 hours. All staff were rostered on 12-hour shifts

---

* Born in South Australia, Mary Cuthbertson was living with her family and nursing in Ballarat in Victoria when she enlisted. The 37-year-old Clare (Clarice) Halligan had been born in Ballarat but was living in Kew, Melbourne, with her parents when she joined the AANS. Jessie Blanch was from northern New South Wales but was nursing in Brisbane upon enlistment, while Winnie May Davis, attractive, petite and just 25 years old, was also from northern New South Wales, but had joined the AANS in Sydney where she was nursing.

except for the theatre staff, blood bank, X-ray and physiotherapists, who pretty much worked until they could work no longer. The blood bank was run with singular efficiency by Captain Dreverman, known forever after as 'Dracula' Dreverman because of his efficiency rather than his appearance. Because of blackout requirements, many of the windows were covered with blankets at night, causing the air in the wards and surgeries to become humid and tainted by a lingering smell made up of a combination of antiseptic, sweat and fresh blood. By day, windows and doors were thrown open to catch the breeze off the sea.

Many of the nurses wept openly on that and subsequent days, but the extreme circumstances brought out the best in most people, and the situation was deteriorating by the day. Meals for staff and patients had become a problem since the Australians were evacuated to Singapore. The two hospitals occupied schools where the facilities had never been designed for the numbers or the circumstances, while the 2/4th was never quite certain where its next destination would be, let alone its next meal. Local Red Cross volunteers stepped into the breach, delivering as many meals as they could to the Australian facilities, and risking their lives every time they did so. At the 2/4th, Mavis Hannah struck up a friendship with one of the Red Cross volunteers, the young wife of an up-country plantation manager named Allgrove.

The medical staff was also constantly surprised by the number of Australian soldiers who would turn up at odd hours to visit and check on the progress of their wounded mates. Most would try, at the very least, to bring cigarettes – and beer if they thought they could get away with it. A few also brought food to try to relieve the monotony of the bully beef that remained the staple both in and behind the lines. Many also offered to donate blood if the doctors thought it would help. Usually, this was a generous but futile gesture. The fighting had taken them away from the mosquito-free zones and many were beginning to experience the effects of malaria, which disqualified them from donating blood.

Among the nursing staff, selflessness was the order of the day. If there was one feature that was characteristic of the AANS in Singapore shortly before the fall, it was the leadership of the service. Olive Paschke, Irene Drummond and Kit Kinsella were inspirational in their work ethos, good humour and obvious concern for their nurses and patients alike. Their attitudes and behaviour filtered down to what had by now become a very close-knit group of workmates and friends. It was an infectious attitude that was reciprocated. At the height of the onslaught after the Japanese assault on Singapore island, Phyllis Pugh was under real stress at the 2/13th: '. . . I knelt beside a stretcher on which lay a soldier whose face was deathly white and not appearing to be breathing. I lifted the blanket to take his pulse and the stretcher was full of blood. Yes, he did have a pulse but very feeble. I looked at his face and he opened his eyes and winked at me. I nearly died of shock. This brave man did recover.'

Among an outstanding group of nurses, all those who worked at the 2/10th remember the performance of Jessie Blanch, 'Blanchie'. Her peers regarded Jessie as the finest operating theatre nurse they had ever seen, a quality first revealed in the relatively relaxed circumstances of the White Elephant at Malacca, and later in the hurly-burly and pressure that was Singapore in February 1942. 'I shall never forget seeing how calm she was while we were being shelled one morning in Singapore. She refused to stop working and more or less made everybody around her feel quite calm too.' Jessie was a young woman who rose to the challenge of the conditions, which was no surprise to those who knew her. Thirty years old, the tall and dark-haired nurse joined the unit on the same day as Olive Paschke and adored her new matron from the start.

THE CURTAIN COMES DOWN

The friendships and relationships between peers and superiors in both Australia and Malaya, both in peacetime and during war were providing the emotional underpinning for the young women who saw and faced death every day and who also saw things that were perhaps worse than death. It was not just the wounds, as they all had seen the results of motor vehicle and industrial accidents in their hospitals in Australia; it was the sheer number of wounded they were required to treat. Likewise it wasn't just the deaths they witnessed on a daily basis — they had seen death before and knew that it came to all sooner or later — but the number of deaths, the occasional one every few months in the pre-war period becoming one a week, then one a day and then several a day. All young Australians who, like themselves, were a long way from home. But above all, it was the fear that sooner or later one of the broken bodies they were called upon to treat would be someone they knew and, perhaps, someone they loved. Some of the girls had brothers in the army and in Malaya, while all had special friends they had met or made in the months since they left Australia. Each hoped they would be strong enough to cope if that feared moment ever came.

Each of the nursing groups had its own characters that helped to pull them through the trying times. Olive Paschke, Irene Drummond and Kit Kinsella provided the leadership and the inspiration, while the humour and the humanity came spontaneously from the natural leaders and bonders in the group. Rene Singleton in the 2/10th had a great sense of humour as well as a profound sense of the ridiculous, and could always be relied upon to raise the spirits of those around her – patients, nurses and surgeons. Betty Jeffrey – known to all as 'Jeff' – shared Rene's sense of humour but also possessed a very keen sense of responsibility. Jeff was one of the older nurses and felt she needed to not only set an example as a nurse but also be a buffer between the more unpleasant realities of their situation and the relative naivety of some of the younger girls. The 2/13th was blessed with Mona and Wilma, two of the best and most professional nurses anyone had seen and whose social escapades continued to provide light entertainment for all their colleagues. They might have believed they were a team of two, but the reality was a number of other girls lived their lives vicariously through the adventures of the dashing duo. A harder edge was supplied by Val Smith, a no-nonsense and laconic 29-year-old from far north Queensland. Like Rene Singleton, Val had a superb sense of irony; when a number of Sydneysiders in the unit referred to their training at 'the PA', meaning the Prince Alfred, Val took to referring to the hospital as 'the PBA', and threatened to add further letters if the practice didn't cease.

The 2/4th CCS was also doubly blessed. The AIF leadership regarded it as the most efficient medical unit then operational in Singapore or Malaya, a testament to the drive and vision of both Tom Hamilton and Kit Kinsella. Kit had grown into the senior nurse's position, displaying that rare gift of natural leadership and a genuine love for those she led. The unit also contained Lainie Balfour-Ogilvy, who continued to sing as she worked and who – if her contemporaries are to be believed – was loved by almost 2000 Australian soldiers, that number representing all whose lives she had touched either as a nurse or as a friend who would sing to them of better days to come.

By now the girls knew their position was serious, if not hopeless. The exhortations and platitudes issued on a daily basis by Government House and the Army Headquarters at Fort Canning carried far less weight than the evidence before their own eyes. But they still tried to minimise their peril to those back home who cared and would be worried. In her last full letter to her parents before the Japanese forces shut down any regular mail runs, Mona Wilton wrote:

> . . . You must have guessed by my letters that we have made a 'strategic withdrawal' – how I hate the words – and are now comfortably (more or less) established on Singapore island again, right back where we started at St Patrick's College . . . We might, if forced to, take ourselves off to Java, or some people say India . . . we will have lots of experiences before we get home again Duckies – plenty of hard work and plenty of fun and will have such grand things to tell you.

Buddy Elmes followed a similar path, ignoring the circumstances around her by and large to tell Old Smithy and the Tripehounds that: 'Our quarters are only a flat, but we have a wireless and Frigidaire, amahs to do our washing and cleaning, etc., which makes a lot of difference to our personal comfort.' And young South Australian Nell Keats chose to ignore the dangers she confronted on an hourly basis and instead describe her circumstances: 'The nurses' quarters are excellent, with an iron bench just outside the door and shower next door, and an electric fan in the room.' She went on to reassure her mother and other readers by telling her: '. . . don't worry because there is no need to and don't listen to rumours because most of them are false.'

The girls' last letters suggested a different reality. While still not wanting to cause unnecessary concern to loved ones, their future was clouded and they struggled to contain their fears. But they still would not admit how frightened they really were. Writing on memo paper with a St Patrick's letterhead, Mona Wilton informed her parents: 'Darlings, in a terrible hurry to get the boys on a ship to home and safety. Goodness knows when we will follow. Don't worry will you, we are dodging bombs with the best of them. Love always, Mona.' And Irene Drummond wrote to her sister in Adelaide: 'There is nothing to write about as usual, except bombs and more bombs, which is not a particularly cheerful subject. The new hospital is taking shape well and I am beginning to think it looks like me now . . . A good many of the officers I knew at Port Dickson have been killed or are wounded. The two Scotchmen who taught us to do the eightsome [sic] reel on the *Queen Mary* have both been killed.' All Buddy Elmes could find to write to Old Smithy on 8 February was: 'No news. Cheerio. Bud.'

The nurses' time in Singapore was almost over. Both General Percival and General Bennett were concerned about their safety. Although the British censors ensured that many of the more speculative and sensationalist stories about the behaviour of the Japanese troops were not reported, enough was known to suggest that the nurses could be at risk in the event of a Japanese victory. Both generals were aware of the latest rumours, that British officers had been held at bayonet point and forced to witness the rape of the nurses in Hong Kong, while other captured nurses had been prodded at bayonet point to walk in front of advancing Japanese troops as protection against snipers, ambushes and booby traps. The Japanese advances on the island meant that the hospitals and casualty clearing stations were increasingly in the front line. Although all such facilities were clearly marked, their safety could no longer be guaranteed. The Australian medical staff had been lucky not to suffer casualties, but others had not shared their good fortune. Wounded personnel from the several Indian Army divisions were evacuated to and treated at the Tyersall Park Hospital. There, many of them died when the hospital was bombed and set on fire by Japanese aircraft. Set up in tents and huts, the hospital was initially located next to a brigade headquarters.

The generals were caught in a bind. They personally believed, and they argued, that evacuating the nurses would have a serious negative effect on the morale of the defending troops. The treatment of the wounded would suffer, and their morale would also plummet along with that of their colleagues in the firing line. As morale declined, so would the capacity of the troops to withstand the Japanese pressure. Evacuating the nurses could easily lead to the capitulation of Singapore. At this distance in time it is impossible to know whether or not Percival or Bennett actually believed their own arguments. Both were regularly given alternative viewpoints – Colonel Derham both formally and informally asked every day for the nurses to be evacuated – but the tipping point was the actual situation on the island. Percival's plans for Singapore's defence had been predicated on the idea that his forces would smash the Japanese as they attempted to land. By 9 February, the Japanese were ashore and advancing. Within two or three days they would control all of the island's water supplies and the battle would be over, even if the fighting continued. Sometime during the night of 9 February, Percival and Bennett authorised the evacuation of the nurses.

The nurses were well aware of all the rumours then swirling around Singapore. They knew that Colonel Derham had been asking for at least a month for a hospital ship to be despatched to Singapore. As the battle for Singapore headed towards its logical conclusion, the nurses heard firstly that the ship had been despatched from Australia, then that it had been seen off Java, and finally that it had entered Keppel Harbour. Unfortunately, the ship didn't exist. The nurses had also heard about what was believed to have taken place in Hong Kong, and that was a concern for them. Of more immediate concern, though, were the reported thoughts and statements of their own officers, several of whom were believed to have said that they would shoot their nurses rather than let them fall into the hands of the Japanese. Wilma Oram heard all the reports and later recalled in an interview: 'We were conscious of the danger we were in. We knew. Some of our officers said they'd never let us fall into the hands of the Japanese; they'd shoot us first. I thought, hang on, I'm 25 years old. I'll take my chances please.' Pat Gunther was offered a phial of morphia by a friendly pharmacist in her unit, 'just in case'. There was more than enough for a painless death if she considered any of the alternatives unacceptable, but she declined, as she was not ready to consider that death may ever be preferable to life.*

Even before formal and official approval to evacuate the nurses had been given, Derham was working on ways to circumvent the blanket ban. The rumours about the arrival of a hospital ship had not been completely without foundation, as sitting in Keppel Harbour was the converted riverboat *Wah Sui,* which had already made one run to Java with wounded Australians. There were beds aboard and the vessel was painted white with a large Red Cross on both sides. The Japanese even recognised the *Wah Sui* as a hospital ship and had asked for it to be moved away from the proximity of legitimate shipping targets. But that was where any similarity with hospital ships like the *Wanganella* ended. Derham's first nurse evacuees would not be pure evacuees as such, as they would be on duty, nursing the 120 wounded soldiers the *Wah Sui* would be taking to safety.

The *Wah Sui* was to depart on Tuesday, 10 February, and all

---

* Facing a similar situation in the Philippines, all United States Army and Navy nurses were issued enough morphia to give themselves a fatal injection should the need ever arise. None of the morphia was ever used for that purpose.

patients and nurses were to be taken from the 2/10th AGH. Olive Paschke selected those nurses 'very reluctantly', but all, including Olive, were under orders and the nurses were leaving to accompany wounded soldiers who they were already treating. The girls were given only one hour's notice of their impending move, so things started to happen in a bit of a rush. Mona Wilton took the opportunity to scribble a note to her parents in western Victoria, and gave it to one of the wounded soldiers to post when he returned to Australia. It was her note about dodging bombs that was carried safely back to Australia and posted a month later from Sydney, and it was the last communication her parents ever received from her. Veronica Clancy, a tall and delightfully cynical observer of life, recorded the scene: 'The girls who had to go begged to be allowed to remain, but the orders had to be obeyed. Tearful farewells and last minute messages and they were gone.'

There were also some moving scenes as close friends realised they were to be separated and were possibly facing very different fates. Pearl Mittelheuser, 'Mitz', another Queenslander from a large Bundaberg family, was originally selected to be one of those to accompany the wounded aboard the *Wah Sui*, which meant she would be leaving behind her close friends from the Brisbane Hospital. Thelma McEachern and Molly Campbell, two long-term friends from pre-war days, were also going to be separated, with Molly leaving and Thelma staying. Thelma and Mitz agreed to toss a coin for the spot on the *Wah Sui*. No-one was really certain of the result as Mitz picked the coin up before they could see which side it had come down on. Mitz said she'd lost, and told Thelma to hurry off to join Molly and the soldiers. She gave Thelma a hug, wished her good luck, and returned to work.

The wounded and their six nurses were collected from the Oldham Hall complex by a fleet of ambulances that drove them down into old Singapore and to the docks and godowns (warehouses) that lined Keppel Harbour. From there they were ferried by launches and lighters out to where the *Wah Sui* sat at anchor, well away from all the other ships in the harbour. Once all were aboard, the anchor was weighed, and the little hospital ship steamed down the main channel through the harbour's minefields and out to sea. Two days later, after an uneventful journey, the *Wah Sui* tied up at Tanjung Priok, the port for Batavia (Jakarta). It had been buzzed by Japanese aircraft, but its Red Cross had been respected. From Batavia the nurses and wounded were taken inland to Bandung, where they were joined by the nurses from the 2/2nd CCS who were en route to Australia from the Middle East. The two groups joined up and travelled together back to Australia aboard the *Orcades*. By the time they arrived at their first Australian port of call, Adelaide, it was 15 March and Singapore had been in Japanese hands for exactly one month.

While the *Wah Sui* was steaming towards Java, the decision to evacuate all the Allied nurses was implemented. That decision was both difficult to make and to enforce, as the nurses simply did not want to leave their patients. There was also a major concern for some of the senior nurses. The possibility of an evacuation had been discussed at formal and informal levels by the nurses at the two hospitals and the clearing station. Each time it was broached it became apparent that none of the Australian nurses would leave voluntarily. The nurses spoke about the issue individually and in small groups, and they by and large shared the same opinion; they were nurses, they had taken an oath of service as nurses, as army officers and as Australians, and they were prepared to honour everything that those qualifications implied. They would stay with the men who relied so much on them.

The two matrons, Drummond and Paschke, had a slight difference of opinion on the matter. Irene Drummond believed that the nurses should stay with their patients under all circumstances. Olive Paschke tended to agree as a matter of honour, but also felt the nurses should be loyal to the service and the country and comply with any orders that were issued. When Olive asked Colonel Derham what would happen to any nurses who refused to be evacuated, she was told they would be court-martialled. While volunteers might be sought, if necessary, orders would be issued and those orders would be enforced.

At 1700 hours on Tuesday, 10 February, Olive Paschke started issuing those orders. At that point there were 130 nurses attached to the 2/10th and 2/13th AGHs and the 2/4th CCS. Six from the 2/10th had departed aboard the *Wah Sui* and Paschke ordered that the remaining nurses be divided into one group of 59, who would probably depart the next day and a second group of 65, who would probably depart the day after that.

At 1000 hours the next morning, the formation of the first party began. At Oldham Hall, Olive Paschke called the nurses together and asked for volunteers for an immediate evacuation aboard the *Empire Star* waiting in Keppel Harbour. There were none, so Paschke started to select those who would go. Three nurses were specifically chosen for evacuation because they were ill – two were recovering from dengue fever, while the third had an abscessed tooth. One not selected in this group was Betty Jeffrey who, suspecting what was about to happen, had chosen not to attend the meeting, remaining in one of the wards to change a poultice on a patient.

The nurses selected by Paschke were given a few minutes to collect their personal belongings – each was allowed to take a small haversack and an even smaller kitbag – and then they reassembled in front of Oldham Hall where they were given a tin of bully beef or a tin of baked beans. The group was then formally farewelled by Derham and Ted White, their commanding officers. They were permitted an additional few minutes to farewell Olive Paschke and the remaining nurses before climbing into waiting ambulances. It was a traumatic experience for everyone involved. One of those selected for the *Empire Star* later recalled: 'At the time we felt ghastly. It was like giving up all our nursing principles. There were so many wounded . . .' Her friend: 'When we were told to leave, most of us were crying.'

It was a funny thing, but at both major hospitals – Oldham Hall and St Patrick's – it seemed that most of those selected in the first tranche of nurses were the younger girls, the 25- and 26-year-olds who had worked so hard and been so confronted by many of the things they had seen. Jean Floyd, with the 2/10th at Oldham Hall, was selected for evacuation, and realised that she may never seen Matron Paschke and Jeff and the others again, but she was not given the option of staying. Phyllis Pugh, at the 2/13th, was also selected and felt very sad. Her letters and recollections described the adventures of a young woman abroad and, moreover, a young woman who had worked at Brisbane Hospital with nurses who were both friends and role models. She had turned 26 the week before, and she joined the 25-year-old Jean Floyd in farewelling her sisters.

The ambulances took the girls to the Adelphi Hotel in the heart of Singapore City, where all the nurses selected for evacuation came together. While those from Oldham Hall told of the sadness that infused Matron Paschke's very being as she identified who would go and who would stay, those who had come in from St Patrick's spoke of the scenes at Katong when the nurses there were divided into two groups. Irene Drummond farewelled all her girls individually, tears streaming down her cheeks. From the Adelphi, the combined group was again ferried by ambulance to the Keppel Harbour docks where some were given baby rusks to eat. The scene that confronted them when they arrived was way beyond anything they had prepared for: 'The situation we met when we arrived at the wharves was just like a nightmare, and we were living it . . . Storage tanks were going up in flames all around us. The whole sky was illuminated and there were thick plumes of smoke.' Another: 'There was a big crate of Christmas toys on the wharf. While we were taking shelter from the bombing, troops broke open the crate and threw teddy bears down to us.'

In batches, little boats – junks and lighters – ferried them out to the *Empire Star*. Fifty-two Australian nurses and seven masseuses went aboard.* *Empire Star* was one of the fleet that made up the Blue Star Line. She was familiar to many Australians and had arrived in Singapore on 27 January bringing a range of vital supplies. As well as prime Australian beef in her refrigerated holds, before the war she had also carried up to 20 passengers in relative comfort. Under Captain Selwyn Capon, her Royal Navy Reservist master, on this voyage her cargo and passenger mix would be very different. Around 2150 people were eventually crammed aboard the vessel. As well as the nurses, both Australian and British, there were a number of government officials and key military and civilian technicians who were felt to be too valuable to be allowed to fall into Japanese hands. The majority of the passengers were civilians, however, men, women and children, many of whom did not feel the need to leave a month ago but who were now prepared to abandon their estates and leave their cars on the docks. There were also some unwanted passengers – Australian Army deserters. A few had snuck aboard dressed as civilians but most boarded the vessel in a rush, armed

---

* The masseuses, whose role and functions would today be those of a physiotherapist, were called and considered nurses throughout the campaign.

and with bayonets fixed and led by an officer. Capon was unable to do anything about this group, who took over part of the forecastle and kept very much to themselves.

There had originally been night buoys to mark the passage through the minefields that protected Keppel Harbour, but these had all but disappeared by the second week of February and Capon was not prepared to risk his ship at night. Accordingly, he delayed the *Empire Star*'s departure until first light on the morning of Thursday, 12 February. The Australian nurses had already made themselves comfortable: 'We were to travel in the hold and were grateful for the convenient hooks on which to hang such luggage as we had. Usually those hooks carried frozen meat. We were joined in the hold by evacuating British sisters and Indian nurses.'

Several hours into the voyage, with Singapore well astern and nothing but blue sea all around, the *Empire Star* was spotted by a Japanese scout aircraft which called up the bombers that were scouring the seas around Singapore. Over the next four hours, the *Empire Star* was attacked by wave after wave of bombers; the crew later estimated that 57 different aircraft had been involved in the attacks. Capon threw his vessel around, zigzagging and making increasingly tight and irregular changes of direction. The nurses felt helpless, but found a surprising way to relieve the tension: 'Most of us were in the hold and several RAF gallantly came down to entertain us – we held an impromptu concert, while a scout above would call "heads down" as each wave of planes came towards us.'

The *Empire Star*'s luck ran out. In all, the vessel was hit by seven bombs which reduced her speed and made her a much easier target for the strafing runs the bombers made when they had no more bombs to drop. As the casualties started to mount, the nurses aboard set up sick bays in three different locations around the ship. Two of the Australian nurses were caught on deck, treating the wounded, when a Japanese aircraft swept in, spraying the *Empire Star* with machine-gun fire. Both nurses threw themselves on top of their patients in an instinctive gesture of protection. One would later be awarded an MBE, the other received the George Cross.

Eventually, the last Japanese aircraft flew off to the northwest. The *Empire Star* was still afloat and making towards Batavia, a destination it would reach due in large part to Capon's seamanship. There the dead and wounded were removed and the deserters who had forced their way onboard placed under guard. There were calls for them to be court-martialled for deserting their comrades and, if found guilty, executed. But cooler heads prevailed, and the men were given the alternative of joining the Australian forces in Java preparing to face the anticipated Japanese invasion. All the men took this option and joined the Allied forces, and within two weeks were surrendered to the Japanese. Some months later they were reunited with the comrades they had deserted at the Changi POW camp.*

At Batavia, the *Empire Star* was given temporary repairs and sent on her way. Two weeks later, she limped into Fremantle, described by those who saw her as a 'miracle ship' to have made it that far. The *Empire Star* was given comprehensive repairs at Fremantle and, when these were complete, she sailed to the United Kingdom where she was put on the North Atlantic convoy run. Capon was awarded the OBE for his efforts in bringing his ship to safety. Six months later, on a run to South Africa,

---

* For many months the *Empire Star* deserters were treated with thinly veiled contempt by the other Australian POWs. Many of the deserters were petty criminals who were to continue their activities in camps in Java, Changi, and along the Burma-Siam Railway. However, those of the deserters who were prepared to work as hard as their comrades, sharing in the difficulties all faced, were welcomed back into the fold.

the *Empire Star* was torpedoed and sunk by a U-boat. Captain Capon and all his crew went down with their ship.

With the departure of the *Empire Star*, 65 Australian nurses remained in Singapore. At breakfast on Thursday, 12 February, Olive Paschke was informed that 'for all intents and purposes' the hospital complex was almost surrounded by Japanese forces. At 1000 hours, Olive called the nurses together, stated that the time had come to leave and gave them a few minutes to collect their personal belongings. Like all the other sisters, Olive's girls had collected a lot of material, gifts and the like, in their months in Singapore and Malaya. This had been put into storage with all non-essential items on 9 December 1941, and they all wondered if they would ever see their fine and pretty things again.* By then, elements of the 2/10th, mainly orderlies and doctors, were in the process of relocating from the Oldham Hall complex back to the Cathay Building in the heart of the city, and there they were setting up for the wounded, with tents on the pavement outside for the overflow. There was a steady shuttle of ambulances heading into the city, and the nurses were formed up and rostered into these. Their route into the city was circuitous as no-one was exactly certain where the Japanese were, and travelling on any of the main roads guaranteed both artillery fire and attacks by the Japanese aircraft that swooped over any significant movement. All nurses already at the Cathay could walk to the rendezvous point at St Andrew's Cathedral, the others

---

* After the nurses left St Patrick's, and before the facility was surrendered to the Japanese, nursing orderlies from the 2/13th buried the nurses' trunks to avoid them falling into the hands of the Japanese. Unfortunately, before all the exact details of locations could be determined, new buildings had been erected on the school grounds.

still at Oldham Hall and the Manor House had to be driven there in the ambulances.

By now, the 2/4th CCS had joined the 2/13th AGH at St Patrick's in Katong. Life there had been quite different from that experienced by the other nurses on the island. St Patrick's was not in the line of any Japanese attack, it was not located near legitimate military targets, and it was far enough away from Singapore City to be unlikely to suffer from misdirected shells and bombs. At night, the staff and patients were able to read by the light of the burning oil tanks across the harbour on Singapore and on several small islands close offshore. Knowing they were to be evacuated, the Australian nurses had spent their spare moments in the preceding 24 hours making Red Cross armbands for the medical orderlies, using red threads picked from British and Australian flags.

There were a number of emotional farewells between wounded soldiers and tearful nurses, and the usual flurry of last-minute exchanges and instructions. Tom Hamilton gave Shirley Gardam a letter to take back to his wife in Australia, while a South Australian medical orderly named Juttner asked Mavis Hannah to let his wife know how and where he was when she returned to Australia. And then, before they were really ready, it was 1400 hours and time to go. As they walked to the waiting ambulances most of the nurses held their heads high but they had tears streaming down their faces. Officers and orderlies lined the main drive into St Patrick's, and as the ambulances carried the nurses past they came to attention and saluted. From the open windows and rear doors of the ambulances came a flutter of white handkerchiefs as the nurses returned the salute.

All the nurses came together at St Andrew's, where they were to depart for the docks in a convoy. Air-raid sirens sounded just as the St Patrick's nurses arrived so they all hurried inside. The cathedral was being used as a hospital but the nurses found a space around the altar and gathered there. Colonel White and Matron Paschke counted those present and checked their names off against a list that White was carrying. Olive Paschke then gave all the nurses a Red Cross armband. They were told that all their belongings had to fit into one small kitbag, including their tins of baked beans and bully beef, and then they were to sit down and wait for the all clear. Numbers of Australian soldiers, learning that the nurses were at the church, made their way there to farewell them and to give them letters to be taken back to loved ones in Australia.

The sirens sounded the all clear 45 minutes after the original alert. The nurses filed into the ambulances that took them the short distance to the docks. The last few hundred metres had to be covered on foot because of the general congestion in the docks area, including large numbers of abandoned cars, simply left where their owners had got out of them.* Betty Jeffrey's memory of the ride and what awaited them was stark:

> When the all clear sounded, we were driven to the wharf. Singapore seemed to be ablaze. There were fires burning everywhere behind and around us and on the wharf hundreds of people trying to get away, long queues of civilian men and women, and a long grey line – us. Masts of sunken ships were sticking up out of the water, but no ships in sight other than forlorn-looking barges.

The harbour and docklands had been the main targets of the recent raid, and as they disembarked from their ambulances

---

* As well as all the cars abandoned in the vicinity of the docks, many more had actually been driven onto the wharves. Those that were left there were pushed into the water, both to deny their use to the Japanese and to make the port facilities all the more difficult to use.

several of the nurses stopped to assist wounded civilians. The sights and sounds and smells were overwhelming. A thick grey-black cloud hung over the city as it had for several days, the smoke from the fuel installations at the naval base at Selatar which had been set alight when the base was abandoned. That cloud was joined by smoke from the hundreds of fires in the city and on the wharves, where godowns stacked with rubber had been set alight in earlier air raids, and from the oil storage depots on the small offshore islands in the harbour. There were people everywhere, some in formal groups, but mainly civilians in family groups with even smaller clusters of service personnel. At the main entrance to the docks, armed guards were checking names off lists and asking for identification when they thought the person may not have a right to be evacuated.

Hovering over everything was a pervasive smell that just wouldn't go away. It was partly the smell of the East – monsoon drains and rotting vegetables – but there was an evil underlay to it. The loss of the city's water supply and the destruction of the sewerage systems meant that raw sewage had seeped out into the streets and gutters, and that was offensive enough. Worse though was the smell of bombed buildings that seemed to come from everywhere. There were bodies in the ruined buildings and sheds, in the cars abandoned at the roadside and in the warehouses and offices in and around the docks. There were even decomposing bodies lying in the streets, where bullets and shells and bombs had struck them down. There was no-one left to clean up the carnage, just as there was no-one at the docks who would ever forget the smell.

Following directions they assembled on one of the docks and waited for the swarm of launches and lighters, plus an incongruous tugboat to arrive. A small group of nurses began to sing 'Now is the Hour', but their words petered out under the glare of the other nurses. As the girls waited patiently another air raid commenced, and their reactions were noted by one of the senior Royal Navy officers supervising the evacuation:

> The incident that stands out most in my mind of those last hours was the magnificent bravery and fortitude of a group of Australian nurses who were waiting their turn to be evacuated. The air raids were following one another in quick succession and causing heavy casualties among the evacuees. To the noise of the guns was added the screams and cries of the dying and wounded. Smouldering and dismembered bodies lay everywhere among the pathetic remains of scattered, burst-open suitcases. It was essential to calm and succour the survivors if a complete panic was not to set in. These brave nurses were always the first to answer calls for assistance and by their bearing and spirit were in stark contrast to some of the opposite sex.

Colonel White had accompanied the nurses to the docks, and moved around them as they waited for the boats that would ferry them out to their evacuation vessel. He asked Mavis Hannah if she knew which ship they would be travelling on. Mavis replied that she'd just heard they were to be evacuated aboard a ship called the *Vyner Brooke*. White appeared horrified and said: 'Oh no, you're not. You haven't got a hope in hell of getting away. Wait here.' With that he stormed off, apparently looking for whoever was in charge of the evacuation. When he returned a few minutes later, he looked quite distraught. 'I'm sorry, Mavis,' he said, 'They've overruled me. You're going.'

When all the nurses and civilians had boarded, the small armada headed off across the harbour towards a coastal steamer painted a dirty grey. Some saw it as a 'small, sinister-looking dark grey ship', but at least one of the nurses recognised the vessel. A lifetime before, in September 1941, Vivian Bullwinkel and Nancy Harris had been the nominated representatives of the Australian Army Nursing Service at a dinner party hosted by reserve officers of the Royal Navy. The venue was a ship that appeared to be a cross between a very large private yacht and a regular coastal steamer. During the evening, one of the officers explained to Vivian that her description was actually quite a close characterisation of the vessel: it had been commissioned for, and partly designed by, the current White Rajah of Sarawak and given a family name, the *Vyner Brooke*.

Later that evening, a group of officers and staff from the 2/13th and the 2/4th sat on the grass outside their mess at St Patrick's, sipping drinks and smoking as they looked across Keppel Harbour to the oil tanks and godowns still burning brightly across the waters. Tom Hamilton was one of those present: 'From the lawn that night, we watched their small ship, the *Vyner Brooke*, sail out of the harbour, etched against the sunset that came redly through the smoke from the fires in the stricken city.'

The last of the Australian nurses were thought to now be out of harm's way. They would certainly face perils at sea, but those were perils that experienced seamanship and good luck could overcome. The soldiers they left behind were directly in harm's way, however, and their future was predictable in one respect at least – the Allies could not hold Singapore any more than they could have held Malaya. They would be surrendered to a numerically inferior enemy and, disturbingly, an enemy whose abilities and very heritage they had consistently underestimated and denigrated. The major concern for the senior officers was what would happen should they surrender, and whether their reputations would suffer irreversible harm. For their troops, the major concern was what would happen to them once they surrendered to an enemy with a reputation for cruelty.

Although it would not be known for some time, a significant number of Australians who surrendered to the Japanese were murdered after that surrender. The largest massacre was at a place called Parit Sulong as the Australians fell back from the battle at Muar River, but the pattern was repeated on Singapore island. On Monday, 9 February, a group from the 2/9th Field Ambulance went forward towards Kranji on the north of the island and part of the sector assaulted by the Japanese. Their plan was to assist in establishing an advanced dressing station for the increasing number of Australian casualties. Led by Captain John Park, a silver medallist at the 1938 Empire Games in Sydney, and containing Harold Ball, one of the best young footballers in Victoria, the small group and their ambulance was not seen again. Retreating Australian infantry later reported sighting an Australian ambulance tipped on its side beside the main road, but it was another four months before the mystery was solved. In mid-1942, a working party of Australian prisoners was labouring in the area where the 2/9th Field Ambulance men disappeared. They uncovered a shallow grave and recovered John Park's identity discs. They also found four bodies, all with their hands tied behind their backs. All had been decapitated.

On the night of 10 February, around 20 Australian troops were taken prisoner in a surprise attack, also near Kranji in the north of the island. The Australians were tied up – hands behind their backs – and taken into a jungle clearing where they were attacked with bayonets and swords. Two of the Australians survived, albeit with horrendous injuries, and eventually made it back to the Australian lines where they told their story.

Incidents such as these were widely known to senior civilian and military figures in what remained of free Singapore. Also known were some of the circumstances of the Japanese atrocities in Hong Kong; specifically that many of the Japanese soldiers were drunk when the atrocities occurred. Determined to try to avoid a repeat in Singapore, governor of what little remained of the Straits Settlements, Sir Shenton Thomas, ordered all stores of alcohol to be cleared by 12 February and all clubs and hotels to destroy their supplies by the following day. Subsequent events could not therefore be blamed on alcohol.

During the afternoon of Saturday, 14 February, Japanese troops stormed the grounds of the Alexandra Military Hospital, later claiming that they had been fired upon from within the hospital grounds by retreating Indian Army troops. The Japanese were met by Lieutenant Weston, Royal Army Medical Corps, carrying a white flag and seeking to formally surrender the hospital. He was bayoneted to death. Japanese soldiers then swarmed through the hospital, shooting and bayoneting patients, doctors, medical orderlies and support staff in frenzied and random attacks. During the attacks 320 men and one woman were killed, including some 90 members of the Royal Army Medical Corps. Three days after the massacre, the Japanese commanding general, Yamashita, called in at the hospital and expressed his regrets at the actions of his troops.

By then the Malayan Campaign and the Battle of Singapore were over. Pushed back into an ever-decreasing perimeter and with all water supplies in Japanese hands, Lieutenant General Percival finally accepted General Yamashita's oft-repeated call to surrender. Ten weeks after they had stormed ashore at Kota Bahru, Yamashita's 35,000 troops had routed Allied forces who numbered in excess of 85,000. When news of the fall of Singapore reached Japan there were special handouts of saki and beer for every household, and biscuits and rubber balls for all Japanese children.

CHAPTER 6

The Last Voyage of the *Vyner Brooke*

Shortly after 1700 hours, the last of the Australian nurses boarded the *Vyner Brooke* through a steel door in the ship's side; it would be another hour before the last civilian evacuees were on board. Captain Borton then steered the ship out into the middle of Keppel Harbour to await darkness and the chance to escape. The move also meant those on board no longer had to listen to the pleas for assistance from individuals and small groups who were paddling canoes from ship to ship seeking a passage from the doomed city. The nurses were welcomed aboard by Second Officer Jimmy Miller, a New Zealander and an engineering officer, and his Malay naval assistants, who escorted them upstairs to the main saloon. There they were told by Olive Paschke to find somewhere to sit and stay until the ship set sail, when all passengers would be addressed by senior officers in the saloon.

Small groups of nurses disappeared as they searched for the best spots they could find. Pat Gunther, Kath Neuss, Pat Blake, Winnie May Davis and Jessie Doyle formed a team and soon found a quiet area for themselves, well forward on the port side and out in the open.* Betty Jeffrey, Wilma and Mona and a number of other girls all found comfortable little nests on life rafts, lifebelts and assorted ship's equipment, and settled down to wait for further instructions. Others sought accommodation indoors. Mavis Hannah was one of several girls offered cabins by ship's officers but, on Olive Paschke's directions, the nurses declined these offers, and the cabins were instead allocated to civilians. The older civilians – and there were quite a few – were in the main directed to the staterooms, allowing those women with young families to occupy the interior cabins.

The next order of business for the nurses was a meal, as most had eaten little if anything since their breakfast. For many, the meal would probably be nothing more than biscuits, bully beef and water, all of which they had brought aboard with them. Some had a treat hidden away but were keeping it for something special, their arrival in Batavia for instance. Little though they had, it was still more than the civilians had brought aboard. Following an approach to the crew, and then to Olive Paschke, the nurses were called together in the saloon, apprised of the ship's minimal food situation and then formed into food preparation and distribution teams. Betty Jeffrey recorded what followed:

> The ship's crew were tired out and we were asked to go to the galley and prepare a meal. Some did this and produced a stew of

---

* Kathleen Constance 'Pat' Blake was 29, and another Sydneysider who had trained at the Royal Prince Alfred Hospital. Jess Doyle, also 29, and 30-year-old Kath Neuss where both also from Sydney.

army tinned meat and tinned vegetables. A chain gang of nurses was formed and the plates of food were passed from the galley to everyone on board; civilian men, women and children, ship's crew and finally, us. Army biscuits and cheese were the second wave.

The situation revealed a major flaw in the evacuation plan – there were almost no food supplies – and the ship's captain, Tubby Borton, and Olive Paschke met briefly to discuss this. Borton was happy to hand responsibility for the passengers' well-being over to the senior Australian nurse as it meant one less thing for him to worry about. Olive then met with Irene Drummond and the two drew up a list of items to be organised, and following their discussion they called the nurses to a meeting in the saloon.

Olive called them to order and then outlined the food situation aboard the ship. The majority of the available food consisted of tins of bully beef, baked beans and biscuits, supplies brought aboard by the nurses, which could be supplemented by tins of fruit that some of the evacuees had brought with them and the few supplies that could be found in the *Vyner Brooke*'s galley. Because of the shortfall, Olive announced that she and Irene Drummond had decided that all aboard would go onto rations for the remainder of the trip, crew and nurses included. Two meals a day would be prepared and served by the nurses, one in the morning and one in the evening, while tea and biscuits would be served each day at midday. Water was also an issue, and there would be none made available for washing until the *Vyner Brooke* was out of harm's way. The plan was fully endorsed by Captain Borton and should cause only minor discomfort during the two- to three-day trip.

Olive Paschke then reminded the girls that they were to wear their Red Cross armbands at all times and that they would be required to attend a comprehensive briefing in the saloon the following morning. She closed the meeting by informing the nurses that Captain Borton had told her that the *Vyner Brooke* was to depart Singapore within the hour. Wishing the nurses a good night, Olive dismissed them.

The nurses returned to the areas they had selected for themselves earlier in the day, both above and below decks, and made themselves as comfortable as they could. Most had been able to arrange rugs or chairs or stretchers to make something comfortable to sleep on, while others simply slept on life jackets. About an hour after sunset, probably some time around 2015 hours and shortly after a few last-minute evacuees arrived, Borton ordered the anchor lifted and the *Vyner Brooke* steamed slowly across Keppel Harbour towards the open sea. It was at this point that the observers at St Patrick's School waved a silent goodbye. Aboard the ship, the nurses looked back at Singapore rather than across to Katong. A small group of them gathered on deck, held hands and sang 'Waltzing Matilda' as the ship moved quietly across the water, but it was too poignant with memories of the men left behind, and the song faded away after a chorus and a verse. Jenny Greer commenced an upbeat version of 'Wish Me Luck as You Wave Me Goodbye', but her heart wasn't in it, and her voice also faded into silence before the song was finished. The Singapore they were leaving was a city clearly in its death throes, and the spectacle made a deep impression on the girls.

For Betty Jeffrey: 'It was a never to be forgotten scene – huge fires were burning along the whole front of Singapore and the black smoke billowed higher and higher far behind the town.' Veronica Clancy would write: 'In the distance, Singapore appeared to be just ablaze, the flames almost reaching the sky. The planes of the enemy caught in the searchlights looked like silver moths around an enormous light. The smoke from the burning oil dumps seemed to hang in dark clouds overshadowing everything.' Even the normally phlegmatic Jean Ashton would always clearly recall the scene: 'As we sailed out of Singapore . . . large fires could be seen, burning oil tanks and ships. Huge black smoke clouds hung over the city – such destruction is war.' It was a far, far different scene from their arrival just 12 months previously.

Some of the girls set out to explore what they could of the ship they all hoped would carry them to safety. The Royal Navy Reserve officer who had described the provenance of the *Vyner Brooke* to Vivian Bullwinkel and Nancy Harris three months earlier had been accurate in what he said, but he had known only part of the story. The *Vyner Brooke*, of 1600 tonnes, had been built in 1928 for the Sarawak Steamship Company, part of a fleet that included the *Rajah Brooke* and the *Rajah of Sarawak*. It cost the princely sum of 300,000 pounds sterling, money that the company had to borrow. Although registered in Britain, the ship's working life had been spent primarily on the run between Kuching in Sarawak and Singapore. The ship, and the Sarawak Steamship Company, had been taken over by the Straits Steamship Company during the 1930s, although the third Rajah of Sarawak, Sir Charles Vyner Brooke, held an interest in the company and had, on occasion, used the ship as a private yacht for himself and his family. Sir Charles had no personal use for it in February 1942; he had evacuated himself and his family to Sydney well before Japanese forces landed in Sarawak on 25 December 1941.

The *Vyner Brooke* was around 80 metres long and 13 metres wide at its broadest point. As well as a forward cargo hold, the ship had 16 cabins for passengers – two, three or four berth cabins, of which five were classified as staterooms. These deluxe accommodations were towards the rear of the ship and were accessed directly from the promenade deck. The other passenger cabins were off a passage that led aft from the main saloon, a 13 by 9 metre room directly below the bridge. There were also toilets and bathrooms off this passage. The captain's cabin and officers' and crew cabins and quarters were forward of the bridge.

The *Vyner Brooke* had been requisitioned by the Royal Navy at the start of hostilities with Japan. At the Selatar Naval Base, the vessel was painted dark grey and fitted with a four-inch gun forward, two Lewis Guns aft and racks of depth charges. While the depth charges were of recent manufacture, the four-inch and Lewis guns both dated back to World War I. The ship was then handed back to its original master, Captain Richard E. 'Tubby' Borton, and a crew consisting of a mixture of reservists from the Straits Settlements Volunteer Naval Reserve and some survivors from the *Prince of Wales* and the *Repulse*. While the crew was a mix of Europeans and Malays, professional sailors and volunteers, they were very good at what they did.

'Tubby' Borton was a Yorkshireman and a professional sailor. He and his wife and their four children had lived in a distinctive home in Singapore's Orchard Road for most of the past decade, and he was regarded as one of the best sailors in and around Singapore. Earlier in the week he had farewelled his family, evacuated to India from where they would eventually make their way back to Leeds. Borton's senior crewmen were as experienced and professional as he was. His first officer was Lieutenant Bill Sedgeman, a 27-year-old originally from North Wales but more recently of the *Prince of Wales*. His second officer, and head of the engine room, was Jimmy Miller, a New Zealander who had been on attachment to the Royal Navy when he, too, was made redundant by the sinking of the capital ships on 8 December. Miller would be assisted by another engineering lieutenant, the elderly reservist from Singapore, David Reith. Another local, Lieutenant A.J. Mann was the ship's wireless officer. The ship's engine room and guns were manned by 20 Malay seamen, volunteer reservists.

The number of evacuees who boarded the *Vyner Brooke* during the afternoon of Thursday, 12 February 1942 has never been accurately determined. There were definitely 65 Australian nurses on board and probably about 150 civilian and military personnel; people of all ages and backgrounds. The crew numbered around 40, giving a total of around 250 persons, although it has been suggested the figure may have been a bit higher. By any reckoning it was a large number for a small ship, and to ease the overcrowding Borton asked that his officers give up their cabins to allow more comfort for the passengers. The officers would share the crew's quarters. Borton's sailing orders were more specific. Admiral Spooner, the Royal Navy officer directing the evacuation, instructed Borton that he was to form a convoy that evening with three other small freighters, the *Mata Hari*, *Giang Bee* and *Li Wo*. The ships were to sail to Batavia via the Durian, Bassee and Banka straits, laying up close to either the coast of Sumatra or the thousands of islands in the surrounding seas during the day. It was a voyage of some 800 kilometres, and was expected to take at least two days.

The voyage was almost over before it had really started. Five minutes after heading out across Keppel Harbour, Borton realised they were heading straight into one of the harbour's minefields. Normally, departing ships were escorted out of Keppel Harbour by HMS *Jarak*, a minesweeper, which had a special red light mounted on her stern for the other ships to follow. But the *Jarak* did not appear this evening. While the light from the hundreds of fires created enough light to read by, the smoke drifting across the harbour obscured many of the buoys that marked the passage through the minefields.

Borton had been in and out of the harbour many times, and had thought he was capable of navigating through them. Ordering the engines stopped and then reversed, he backed the *Vyner Brooke* out of danger. Not prepared to take the risk, he kept the engines slowly turning over until he spotted two other vessels making for the open sea in line astern. Borton followed them through the minefield before ordering an increase in speed and for the helmsman to steer for the Banka Strait and Java beyond.

The nurses settled and slept wherever they could, with some falling asleep as soon as their head hit their makeshift pillow, while others sat in pairs or small groups and talked long into the night. The two Pats – Gunther and Blake – with Kath Neuss, Jess Doyle and Winnie May Davis settled on deck and spoke quietly as the *Vyner Brooke* started its interrupted journey towards the open sea. The five had formed a friendship based on commonalities. They were of similar ages, with Winnie May Davis the youngest at 26 and Kath Neuss the oldest at 31. Kath, at least, was always conscious of her age and at times seemed a lot older than she actually was. Winnie May was the opposite – young in all ways, dark-haired and vivacious, and still excited by all the things that were new to her. The five were from the 2/10th and had learned how to work together under Olive Paschke's direction. They were also all from New South Wales.

The two Pats tended to provide the leadership and Kath Neuss the gravitas, while Jess Doyle provided the leavening that held them together. Outgoing and bubbly, Jess was always good for a story, many of which were directed against herself and her family who were prominent in sporting circles in Sydney. Jess's middle name was Gregory and she was forever explaining that the name was actually her mother's maiden name and not some wistful pining for a son on her parents' part. Her maternal uncle was Jack Gregory, the finest all-round cricketer that Australia had produced to that point. If asked, and sometimes without being asked, Jess could explain how, upon his retirement from first class cricket, her uncle Jack held the record for the fastest ever Test century, and how he then married a former Miss Australia.

Some slept fitfully, some deeply, and some not very much at all. In this latter group were the two matrons, who spoke long about how they would handle all the possible situations that might arise. They involved both Tubby Borton and Major William Tebbutt, the senior Australian officer aboard, in some of those discussions and by the time they found their own places to sleep it was closer to dawn than to dusk. They did, however, feel that they and their girls would be able to cope with most situations as their girls were very good and they now had some plans to follow.

The morning of Friday, 13 February 1942 was one of the most memorable that Vivian Bullwinkel had experienced: 'Friday was the most beautiful [morning] I can recall. We're just sailing among the islands, and it was difficult to think that there was a war raging not very far from us.' There was a clear blue sky and a deep blue sea, with a host of small islands visible in the middle distance. No other ships could be seen. Borton was worried because the delay caused by the unplanned excursion into the minefield the previous evening had caused a more significant delay of several hours to his sailing plans, and he had hoped to be safely anchored and concealed behind one of those islands by daylight. Shortly after dawn, fortunately, he found what he was looking for, Linggo Island, a small island with a hill behind which he could conceal the *Vyner Brooke* from prying eyes.

Jessie Simons, too, was struck by what she saw when she awoke that morning:

> It was like an unexpected holiday, unspoilt by anticipation, to stretch out in the warm sunshine without any responsibilities or the nagging reminder of duties demanding attention. Some of us dozed, drugged by the sun; a few admired the feathery beauty of palm-crowned islets, or idly watched the effortless sweep of snowy gulls; the gloomy and the anxious scanned the sky for planes, periodically stirring their neighbours to emphatic protests with false alarms; and the phlegmatic settled down to books which they had the foresight to stuff into bulging luggage.

Vivian and Jessie had both slept well, unaware that the night had not been without incident. For one thing, the convoy did not exist. The two ships Borton followed through the minefield may also have been part of it, but no-one was going to show lights in an area controlled by Japanese aircraft and ships, and the four little vessels all made their own way to their individual fates. Those crew and passengers who were awake in the small hours of the morning heard the distant thunder of naval guns and saw occasional flashes and searchlights playing across the sea. No-one was able to determine exactly what it was, but their ship apparently sailed past the fringes of one of many minor naval battles taking place in the area to the south of Singapore.

By mid-morning all the nurses had been up for several hours. Their first task had been to sort out their sleeping quarters and they then organised a breakfast of bully beef and fruit for themselves before doing the same for all the others aboard the *Vyner Brooke*. While they were undertaking these chores, Olive Paschke and Irene Drummond were meeting with their senior nurses, Nesta James, Kit Kinsella and Jean Ashton, to outline their series of plans and lists and tasks, as well as detailing just what would be said to the nurses when they all gathered in the saloon for their meeting at 1000 hours.

Olive Paschke opened that meeting by informing the nurses that Captain Borton had revealed that the *Vyner Brooke* was to sail to Batavia and, once there, a future determination would be made, with the ultimate objective of ensuring that all the ship's passengers reached Australia safely. To reach Batavia they would need to travel through the Banka Strait, a body of water between Banka Island and the southern end of Sumatra. Borton had also explained that Banka Strait was now generally referred to as 'Bomb Alley'. Paschke then introduced Major Tebbutt, who was a personal friend and adviser to General Bennett in both civilian and military roles. Bill Tebbutt had been involved in certain intelligence aspects of the campaign and was taking his knowledge back to Australia.* As the senior army officer on the ship, he gave the girls a brief pep talk designed to lift morale and focus their thinking on their duties.

Irene Drummond then explained the plans that she and Matron Paschke and the senior nurses had been working on. The senior staff had decided to organise the nurses into 'district nursing teams', each of which would be responsible for a clearly defined area aboard the ship. Each sister in each team

---

* Tebbutt survived all that followed and spent part of his time as a prisoner compiling a comprehensive report on his flight from Singapore and its aftermath. Although he was introduced as a Staff Officer from 8th Division Headquarters, the girls all believed that Tebbutt was actually a senior intelligence officer who was being evacuated from Singapore late in the day because he had knowledge too important to run the risk of him being captured and tortured by the Japanese.

THE LAST VOYAGE OF THE *VYNER BROOKE*

was to ensure that proper discipline, good morale and good hygiene were maintained within the team's district. Drummond explained further that the *Vyner Brooke* had only two toilets and one communal washbasin for those accommodated in the main part of the ship, the saloon and the cabins attached to it. All had seen the queues that formed to use those facilities. Drummond closed by reminding the girls that organisation and discipline would be the keys to all of them coping with what could become a trying situation.

One of the ship's officers, probably Second Officer Jimmy Miller, was then introduced to tell the nurses about the *Vyner Brooke*'s lifeboats and life jackets and rafts. He explained that while it was neither practical nor possible to conduct lifeboat drills in their present circumstances and, in fact, all unauthorised movement on deck was banned, he would walk them through the ship's evacuation procedures in the hope that what they heard would be something they could practise at a more appropriate moment. He went on to explain that the *Vyner Brooke* carried six lifeboats, three each on the promenade deck on both the port and starboard sides. If the order to abandon ship was given – long blasts on the ship's siren – crewmen would take charge of the lowering of the lifeboats to the water. Other blasts would be used to warn of any of the various emergencies that could arise. Two of the boats were designed for 30 passengers and the other four could comfortably hold 20 passengers, and each of the boats would be under the command of one of the ship's officers.

He then explained the obvious: that while the lifeboats would take up to 140 passengers without any overcrowding, they would probably hold up to 180 in a pinch. Unfortunately, that meant there would be anything up to 100 people unable to fit into them. He said that he had no doubt that the nurses had noticed the dozens of life rafts stacked up at a number of points on the ship's superstructure. Each of the life rafts was a bit more than one metre square and was made out of wooden slats, each slat about five centimetres wide, attached crosswise to each other and edged with other slats. The rafts were designed for one person, or two people sitting back to back. Looped ropes for swimmers to hang on to were fixed to the sides of the life rafts, and those ropes could also be used to tie individual rafts together to provide a larger surface area. Two paddles were attached to each raft, which would also have a canvas container of fresh water attached to it. Crew members would cut the stacks of life rafts loose if and when the order was given to abandon ship. They could then be thrown overboard, or else they would simply float to the surface.

Finally, the ship's officer explained the peculiarities of the life jackets they had been issued with when they boarded. They were, he said, vests rather than jackets and were made by sewing pockets onto the original vest then filling those pockets with squares of kapok and cork. The overall construction was then covered with canvas. The jackets had a number of tags or belts that needed to be tied together for the jacket to fulfil its purpose, and he advised them to forget their modesty as the most important of the belts was the one that passed between the wearer's legs. If this was not tied tightly enough, when they jumped into the water the jacket would shoot up over their head and possibly be lost. If they were particularly unlucky, it could catch them under the chin and break their neck. He also said that if they chose to jump into the water, they should remove their shoes, hold their jackets tightly with their chins tucked inside the jacket, and jump into the water feet first. He concluded by saying that the *Vyner Brooke* carried enough lifeboats, life rafts and jackets for 650 people, but they would probably never be needed.

Matron Paschke continued on the theme. She told the nurses that if the ship was sinking, they were to search the below decks accommodation to ensure that all the passengers had been evacuated, beginning with their own districts. The nurses would only evacuate the ship on the orders of either of their two matrons. As the ship's lifeboats were not capable of carrying all the passengers aboard the *Vyner Brooke*, civilians were to be given priority. The nurses were to ensure that they, and all the passengers from their district, were wearing life jackets, and they should be prepared to use the life rafts the crew would throw into the water. Olive asked them all to be honest with her and Irene, as they needed to know which of the nurses could swim. Those who could would be expected to swim to life rafts. Spots aboard the lifeboats would be sought for those who couldn't swim. She then closed the meeting by saying that she and Irene Drummond would conduct an inspection of the district teams' areas of responsibility at 1130 hours; the nurses had an hour to prepare for this.

The nurses returned to their duty areas to estimate how many people they were responsible for and just who those people were. Around 20 of the passengers were adult males, mostly in their late middle age plus some who were elderly. The majority of this group were retired colonial officials and rubber planters, men who had stayed on in Malaya or Singapore at the end of their working life rather than returning to the country they had grown up in and largely forgotten. All of them were accompanied by either their wife or, more rarely, by a daughter. There were a similar number of older women, some were married to the men, but others were widowed or the spouses of senior managers from commercial enterprises or the Colonial Service. The majority, however, were younger women and children, with around 40 of the passengers being children. Overwhelmingly, they were the wives and children of servicemen who had stayed behind in Singapore with their units.

Some of the nurses were concerned about the number of

children aboard the *Vyner Brooke*. Jessie Simons expressed the feelings of many when she wrote: 'I felt very sorry for the many children, but could only be coldly angry with their parents. For many weeks they had known of the approaching danger, and time and time again had put off the day of reckoning until now when it might be too late.' As well as unnecessarily placing them in danger, delaying their evacuation also meant that they were now occupying positions that could have gone to deserving adults. These feelings were strong but were kept within the group of nurses.

Among the civilian evacuees were several who quickly endeared themselves to the Australian nurses, or else drove them to distraction. The children were generally in the former group; a proportion of the adults in the latter. A sprightly little four-year-old boy named Misha was an instant hit with the nurses. From his parents they learned a little of his background. His full name was Misha Warman, he was an only child, and his parents were Polish Jews. Fleeing their homeland ahead of the German invasion, the Warmans had traversed the Soviet Union, before cutting down through Central China to Shanghai, where they formed part of a large European Jewish expatriate community. Fearful of Japanese forces, the Warmans sought further refuge, firstly in Singapore and now aboard the *Vyner Brooke*. Australia was about as far as they thought they could run.

There was another Jewish refugee aboard, a German named Dr Goldberg who would not give any personal details but who insisted on being given preferential treatment because of her profession and her status. This antagonised some, with the British passengers being annoyed that she was travelling on a British passport when there was nothing particularly British about her, her attitude and accent grating on many. There was some gossip that she had been interned by the British in Singapore, but had somehow managed to secure both a release and an evacuation permit. Both ways she, too, was a victim of circumstances, and so the nurses gave her a bit more leeway than they may otherwise have done.*

Another delightful child was the young June Bourhill, fleeing Singapore with her mother while her father, a member of the Singapore Municipal Council and reserve soldier, stayed behind. June was particularly impressed with the nurses' uniforms and the seemingly endless supply of *things* they were able to produce from the pockets; she delighted in following her district nurses as they moved around, trying to assist them in any way she could.

Along with Dr Goldberg, one of the dominant females among the passengers was the redoubtable Mrs Mary Brown, who was accompanied by her daughter Shelagh, then in her early twenties. Mary Brown was an enormous woman – estimates of her weight were generally around the 100-kilogram mark – and was married to one of the senior businessmen in the Straits Settlements and chief choirmaster of the St Andrew's Cathedral choir. In Singapore, Mary Brown was one of the arbiters of that society's rules and protocols and lived a life of privilege. She was not comfortable on the *Vyner Brooke* and let everyone know it. She claimed to be unable to help anyone with anything, 'Health issues, y'know', but expected all the others, including the nurses, to provide her with the special services she had assumed would be hers forever.

Her daughter Shelagh was somewhat shy, but was more than

---

* Dr Goldberg would also survive all the subsequent events, and became one of the better-known camp doctors. She was never really trusted because she used her nationality and her profession to ask for and receive preferential treatment. Many of the girls couldn't decide whether she was a German spy or a self-centred harridan concentrating exclusively on her own survival. By contrast, a young survivor named Ralph Armstrong recalled Dr Goldberg as 'charming and gracious'. He also referred to her as Dr Goldberg-Curth; if correct, she was probably a leading paediatrician in Singapore before the war.

happy to engage with the nurses. Her escape mechanism was partly her shyness and partly her writing. Every day, irrespective of the circumstances, she tried to write a few lines in the diary she kept. Jessie Simons regarded them as she would excess baggage: 'For many years a semi-invalid with a "heart", Mrs Brown was almost a living miracle in her own and her daughter's eyes. She was 60 years old and the 25 year old Shelagh constantly referred to her as Mummy.' Shelagh had just completed her entry for 12 February when the nurses returned from their briefing. That entry read:

> . . . Leave for unknown ship. *Vyner Brooke* (very small). As we boarded the *Vyner Brooke* we were issued with lifebelts by a kindly English sailor. No cabins. Take up a position on deck. When all on, find luggage and stack cases together beneath us. For three of us, four small suitcases. On deck with us, one stretcher. Told no rations aboard, Australian nurses share out theirs. Sail about dusk – 6.30 to 7 pm. Singapore is a sad sight – all fire and a pall of smoke hangs over her. Sleep on deck. No washing next morning.

But for every Mary Brown there was a Norah Chambers or an Olga Neubrunner. Norah Chambers was a singer, musician and a teacher and was prepared to give of herself to help make others' lives just a little bit easier. Norah and her husband, John, a civil engineer, had started their journey in northern Malaya, escaping down the peninsula just ahead of the advancing Japanese. Olga Neubrunner, married to a planter and army reservist, herself a Colonial Service nurse and now seven months pregnant, shared Norah's optimism and attitude. While concerned about her husband who was still fighting the Japanese, and her unborn child, Olga was more than prepared to help out. For optimism and good humour the nurses couldn't go past Maudie James, a young cockney girl, newly married to a soldier she had to leave behind in Singapore. And for companionship, several found a kindred spirit in Phyllis Tunbridge, a civilian who'd worked in the British Army's Headquarters Intelligence Section at Fort Canning.

Finally, a number of the older couples went out of their way to be pleasant towards the Australian nurses. The cabin offered to and declined by Mavis Hannah was the night cabin of the ship's radio officer, Lieutenant Mann. It was subsequently offered to and accepted by one of the older pairs of married evacuees from Singapore. Whenever they saw Mavis they would thank her for her generosity (Mavis never told them of Matron Paschke's orders), and would always address her as Nurse Hannah. Mavis never learned their names.

The remainder of the daylight hours of 13 February passed without significant incident. There were small happenings and alarms, but none developed into the kind of flight or fight confrontation everyone on board feared. Japanese planes were spotted some distance off at about 0900 hours and again at 1100 hours. Some aboard thought they could hear the sound of distant cannon fire at odd intervals. Other aircraft were seen in the far distance during the afternoon, but were too far away for identification, not that anyone had any doubts about who they were and what they were looking for. Matrons Paschke and Drummond completed their inspections of the nurses' districts, and then the nurses themselves moved through their areas serving the midday biscuits and cups of tea.

Captain Borton had no record of the numbers or names of his passengers, and asked Olive Paschke if her girls could collect and collate that information as part of their duties. Paschke agreed and further offered to use herself and her nurses to conduct training in what to do when abandoning ship. This would include details about who was assigned to which lifeboat, which of the nurses would accompany the six lifeboats, and which of the nurses would volunteer for swimming first. A surprising number, led by Veronica Clancy and Lainie Balfour-Ogilvy, volunteered to stay on board as long as possible before swimming to safety. The majority of the passengers slept for all or part of the afternoon, and had their evening meals of bully beef and tinned vegetables followed by a small serve of tinned fruit just on dusk. Some of the older children became bored and restless during the afternoon but perked up considerably when one of the adults gave them a game of Ludo. Most of the passengers and crew had been below decks all day, and many of them availed themselves of the opportunity to spend some time on deck after the sun had set. Everyone was anxious to move on and knew there would be only a short break before the *Vyner Brooke* was again heading south. Shelagh Brown's diary entry for the day read:

> Very little food. Just sit and lie all day. Ship stopped in amongst islands in daylight. Matron Paschke (just like Zaza Pitts)* organises boat drill, she was superb and took command of feeding arrangements, etc. Given half a tin of asparagus, sausage and potatoes at night. Best meal so far... Very exhausted after Singapore. Thankful for a quiet day in spite of water and food shortage.

Borton had not travelled as far from Singapore as he had hoped, and was determined to sail at or near his ship's top speed

---

* Zaza Pitts was a well-known silent movie actress and radio personality in Hollywood.

during the dark hours of that night. Around 2000 hours he ordered the anchor raised and steered his vessel into the open sea, setting the *Vyner Brooke* on a general southeasterly course. Half an hour later, with the ship proceeding at its cruising speed, a lookout spotted flashes on the horizon, followed immediately afterwards by the concussion and sounds of heavy naval guns. At first Borton thought his ship was sailing along the fringes of a major naval battle but when searchlights flicked on just a few kilometres away, he realised that it was a skirmish rather than a battle and guessed that it involved at least one vessel fleeing Singapore and much larger Japanese forces.

Rather than risk accidental discovery, Borton headed for a nearby island large enough to shield the *Vyner Brooke*, and anchored with that island between his ship and where the searchlights continued to play across the water. Within half an hour, all the lights were extinguished and there were no more flashes of light or rumbles of thunder on the horizon. Borton waited an additional half hour before again cautiously heading for the open sea, building up speed and then again bringing the ship around onto a course for Banka Strait. They were still short of the strait when the sun appeared above the horizon. Borton spotted an island ahead and circled it, looking for a suitable anchorage. The island – Tojou Island – was smaller than he would have liked and the anchorage was barely suitable, but it looked a long way to the next island and the Japanese scout planes would be warming up, so he made a virtue out of necessity and anchored in the lee of the island.

Those who were later able to clearly recall the circumstances remembered that Saturday, 14 February was very hot and still from early in the morning. The nurses were again up and about early, making and serving breakfast, eating their own, and then moving back to the saloon for morning orders with Matron

Paschke and the senior sisters. For Vi McElnea* and her friends it was a special day, her thirty-eighth birthday, and they had a small ceremony below decks to mark the occasion. Paschke and Drummond had met earlier with Borton, who had given them an updated briefing on their circumstances. They were well short of where he had hoped to be, he told them, and were probably around half a day behind schedule. He suspected the actions of the previous evening involved a Japanese force that could now be ahead of them. It had probably gone beyond the time for good seamanship; what was more important now was good luck.

Following their meeting, the two matrons met briefly with their senior nurses and planned what they and their nurses could do. Olive Paschke outlined those plans to the nurses gathered in the saloon, and she didn't beat around the bush. Wilma Oram would never forget her saying just how grim the situation was and warning them that it was virtually inevitable that they would be bombed. She then outlined what was expected of them in such circumstances, and if they were ordered to abandon ship. To begin with, if the siren sounded a warning of imminent attack, all were to return to their work stations and take cover after organising their passengers in the safest positions and locations. All the nurses had been given lifeboat stations to which they would proceed if the order was given to abandon ship. Once there, they were to assist the ship's crew in evacuating the ship. Two of the lifeboats had been specifically allocated to mothers with children and passengers who couldn't swim; nurses were then reallocated to those on the basis of their swimming ability. All who could swim were urged to give up their seats on lifeboats

---

* Violet McElnea was one of eight McElneas from Ingham in north Queensland who enlisted in the armed forces in World War II. Theirs was also one of the district's pioneering families. Vi was 38 years old and was a caring, compassionate nurse and mentor to many of the younger women.

to non-swimmers and take their chances in the water until a place was available in a lifeboat or on a life raft.

The nurses were again reminded of the necessity of wearing Red Cross armbands. While the *Vyner Brooke* was obviously not a hospital ship, any Japanese pilot flying close enough to see the armbands might realise the ship contained civilian evacuees and refugees rather than fleeing soldiers. All nurses were also to carry dressings, morphia and syringes pinned inside their uniform pockets and were also to prepare a small bag of 'vitals', things they would need to survive if they were forced to abandon ship. If the ship's siren sounded short blasts, it meant enemy aircraft were about to attack. All nurses would then proceed to their duty stations, put on their life jackets and helmets and await further orders. If the ship's siren sounded a continuous blast, the ship was to be abandoned and the nurses were to go to their lifeboat stations. And, added Paschke, there would be another inspection of the nursing districts at 1100 hours.

That inspection would never occur. At 1100 hours, the *Vyner Brooke*'s lookout spotted a Japanese scout aircraft at about the same time as the aircraft spotted the *Vyner Brooke*. It circled once and then swooped down in a low-level pass spraying the starboard side of the ship with machine-gun fire. The attack was over almost before anyone realised what had happened. There hadn't been time to sound the ship's siren or to man either the large gun forward or the Lewis guns on the bridge and aft. Damage to the vessel was slight; the lifeboats on the starboard side were all holed but could be repaired, and no-one was injured. Their battle plans had worked well. As the Japanese aircraft attacked, the Australian nurses went to their battle stations, where they remained until Borton gave the all clear. During the attack, Vivian Bullwinkel had shared a battle station with Nancy Harris, Lorna Fairweather, a 28-year-old South Australian who had specialised in paediatrics during her training,* and Jessie Simons. Jessie had remained supremely calm throughout, seemingly engrossed in a book she had started reading earlier that day. Years later, Vivian could still recall that book's title.

But they had been found, and Borton was well aware that the Japanese aircraft, as it flew away, would be signalling their position to Japanese bombers that were already in the air or that were about to take off. He held a brief conference with the senior military officers on board, and included Bill Tebbutt in the proceedings. Borton told them that he considered it 'suicide' to remain where they were; the ship could be easily detected from the air and would be a sitting duck for the bombers he knew were coming. His experience suggested that he might be able to avoid bombs in the open waters of Banka Strait, and he proposed to make a run for it.

Borton could also see what appeared to be a cluster of small islands on the horizon, near where the entrance to Banka Strait narrowed between Sumatra and Banka Island. He felt there was no choice but to act, so he ordered the anchor weighed and maximum engine revolutions for the dash across the open sea. It seemed to take forever, with lookouts scanning the skies for Japanese aircraft, but was probably only 90 minutes before the *Vyner Brooke* dropped anchor in the lee of another small island, one a lot smaller in fact than Borton had hoped it would be. With the ship at rest a vast silence settled over the island, the *Vyner Brooke*, and its passengers and crew. People seemed almost afraid to speak or even breathe, except for the children of course, but as the minutes passed and nothing happened, a kind of normality returned.

---

* Lorna Fairweather, 28, was one of the most highly qualified nurses in the AANS, and was relieving matron at the Crippled Children's Home at Somerton, South Australia, when she enlisted.

Those aboard realised it was now 1330 hours, well past lunchtime, and they still hadn't eaten their midday snack of tea and biscuits. The nurses set up their work parties to remedy this and prepared to serve refreshments. Two of them, however, opted out. Pat Blake and Betty Jeffrey wanted no part of that day's lunchtime process. They didn't want to prepare it and they didn't want to eat it. They were both very tired. Grabbing some life jackets and blankets, they made their way to a spot in the shade at the rear of the bridge, where they made a little nest that they then climbed into. Within a few minutes, both girls were asleep. Within a few more they were wide awake again, snapped out of sleep by the scream of the ship's siren blaring only metres from where they lay.

PART TWO

Banka

CHAPTER 7

Banka Strait

The siren that woke up Pat Blake and Betty Jeffrey from what was a pleasant nap was sounded on the orders of Captain Borton. The *Vyner Brooke*'s lookout had spotted another Japanese scout plane, which had circled both the ship and the island but had not attacked before it flew off towards the northwest. It was approaching 1400 hours, and Borton was determined not to present the bombers he suspected were approaching with a sitting target. There was a much larger island visible about 20 kilometres away and Borton reasoned that if the *Vyner Brooke* could make it there, it may find a more suitable hiding place and be completely overlooked by the searching Japanese. The anchor was weighed and Borton ordered the engineer to make all possible speed.

The siren blasts also initiated a flurry of activity both above and below decks. Above deck, Royal Navy reservists rushed to man the forward cannon and the two Lewis guns. The cannon would be next to useless against aircraft as it had been installed primarily for defence against surface attacks, but the Japanese would not know that and perhaps it would force them to keep a respectful distance. Equally, the machine guns could be effective against unarmoured targets within a few hundred metres but could not be expected to do too much damage against the type of opposition Borton was expecting.

Below decks there was not quite pandemonium, but neither were there scenes of calm and order. The nurses and civilian evacuees were all cleared from above deck to their attack stations, the nurses grabbing their helmets and life jackets before assembling in the saloon. Immediately astern and down the passageway, civilians had occupied the cabins, while further aft others had retreated to the staterooms. A number of nurses were positioned nearby in their district patrol positions. Sisters Mary Clarke, Lavinia Russell, Gladys Hughes* and Veronica Clancy and a number of civilians took cover in the main bathroom behind the saloon. Around half the nurses were in the saloon, with the others scattered both forward and aft of the saloon. Kath Neuss, Winnie May Davis and Pat Gunther were responsible for the most forward part of the ship, and made their way there and set themselves up as comfortably as they could in an officer's cabin on the port side of the ship.

Around ten minutes into the dash for the large island Borton had spotted, and with the *Vyner Brooke* travelling at its top speed of almost 15 knots, they were still a long way from their target. It was at that point that the lookout spotted nine specks in the distance, flying towards them in three V-formations, at a height

---

* Mary Clarke, 30, was from Rylstone in the New South Wales central tablelands; 32-year-old Lavinia Russell was from Hurstville in Sydney, and 33-year-old Gladys Hughes, born in New Zealand, was from West Brunswick in Victoria.

of about 2000 metres and closing fast. As Borton and his crew watched, one of the Vs broke away and formed into a single line astern for an attack. The first bomber, by now recognisable as a 'Nell', the twin-engined medium bomber that was the workhorse of the Japanese campaign, went into a shallow dive and from a height of only a few hundred metres released three bombs. As it did so, the *Vyner Brooke* commenced a violent turn, the start of the zigzag manoeuvres that Borton initiated. All three bombs missed by a wide margin. Borton had some previous and recent experience of commanding ships under attack by Japanese aircraft, and now used all that experience. Carefully watching the next aircraft's belly until he could see that the bombs had been released, Borton would then throw the *Vyner Brooke* into a violent turn to either port or starboard. It was a tactic that was working.*

The second and third aircraft in the first formation also dived in to release their bombs, and also missed. All three aircraft did, however, take the opportunity to strafe the *Vyner Brooke* with their machine guns as they pulled out of their bombing run. In return, the four-inch cannon and the two machine guns aboard the little ship also blazed away at the attacking aircraft without any obvious success, while it was Tubby Borton's tactics and timing that had thwarted these first attacks.

Below decks everything was by now relatively quiet and ordered. In the cabins, passengers lay on the floor, under their beds if possible or with bedclothes and other protection over them if not. In the saloon, passengers and nurses also lay flat in small groups and took it all in: the thump of the cannon, the chatter of the machine guns just above and behind them, the smell of

---

* In the days before the evacuation, the *Vyner Brooke* had been attacked on several occasions as it steamed around the islands off Singapore on Royal Navy duties. It was during those attacks that Borton perfected the tactics he used to evade the bombs.

gunpowder and cordite that was starting to spread throughout the ship and the swish of the water outside as Borton threw the ship from side to side to avoid the falling bombs. There were other noises too, and these were more sinister: the increasing scream of high-powered aircraft engines as the bombers went into their dives, the high-pitched whistle of the bombs as they plummeted down, and the deep *whump* – part sound, part concussion – of those bombs as they exploded nearby. Under their breath and just to themselves, most of those aboard the *Vyner Brooke* had started to count those explosions. One . . . Two . . . Three . . .

The failure of the tactics used by the first flight of bombers made absolutely no impression on the second flight. They, too, attacked individually in shallow bombing runs and they, too, strafed the *Vyner Brooke* at the end of those runs. Because Borton employed the same tactics with the second group as he had with the first, their bombs also missed his vessel. Ten . . . Eleven . . . Twelve . . .

Betty Jeffrey felt calm and fatalistic and uncomfortable all at the same time:

> I felt certain that the bombs would miss us . . . We were able to relax a little while the planes gathered themselves to try again, but it was nerve-wracking really. It was most uncomfortable on the floor . . . it did not leave much room for my long legs and I always seemed to have a small child's foot under my stomach. The poor little kid was wonderfully brave . . . She didn't utter a sound. Her mother had four small children with her and she calmly prayed aloud – the Lord's Prayer. Poor soul, if anyone needed help, she did.

The attacks were continuous over a five-minute period – nine bombers and 27 bombs, all of which missed their intended target.

Those below decks felt that it had lasted a lot longer than five minutes, but agreed on the bomb total. There was a temporary hiatus, a two-minute respite while the bombers climbed and reformed well off in the distance and at a height where they were mere specks against the blue backdrop. Those who watched included several nurses who had snuck to the doors of the saloon and were peering out anxiously. They were noticed by a ship's officer, who snapped at them and ordered them to return to their stations.

The Japanese pilots learned from their previous errors. This time they flew a little faster and lower and in line astern, so that if the *Vyner Brooke* turned away from one attack, she would be turning directly into another. As the leading aircraft released its bombs, Borton ordered the helmsman to turn the vessel hard. The nurses and passengers below counted . . . 28 . . . 29 . . . Before the count reached 30, the *Vyner Brooke* was rocked by explosions.

In quick succession, a number of bombs rained down around and upon the *Vyner Brooke*. One bomb, possibly the first to hit, went straight down the ship's funnel and exploded in the engine room, killing or badly injuring all the crew there. A second bomb struck the vessel between the bridge and the stern, and penetrated to the between decks area before exploding. It destroyed many of the staterooms, killing most of the elderly passengers who had sought shelter there. That explosion also destroyed many of the life rafts that were stacked towards the stern of the ship. A third bomb landed on the forward deck, destroying the gun there and killing or wounding the gun crew. This bomb also smashed the ship's radio shack and demolished the radio operator's night cabin, the cabin that was to have been Mavis Hannah's. The elderly couple who occupied it were both killed. All were serious hits to the *Vyner Brooke* and the combination of the three was fatal. The coup de grace, however, was not a direct hit but a near miss that opened up the starboard side of the ship.

The *Vyner Brooke* was dead in the water, all forward motion lost, as the last bombers released their loads and flew over and up to observe their handiwork. Their target was already starting to list to starboard, smoke was rising from the funnel and from several holes in the main deck and from the sides of the vessel. Tubby Borton had survived the attack and was still on the bridge. A quick look around at the damage and the engine room's failure to respond to any calls reinforced his conviction that his ship was doomed. He ordered the ship's whistle to be sounded.

The situation below decks was becoming increasingly grim. When the first bomb hit, little Misha Warman's father just snapped, ran out onto the deck and jumped overboard. He disappeared below the waves and was not seen again. The bomb that had landed aft had done most of the damage to the civilians aboard. Several in the staterooms and the rear cabins were killed outright, while those sheltering in the passageway behind the saloon also suffered some severe injuries. Throughout the main accommodation space, people had suffered horrendous injuries from bomb splinters and shrapnel from demolished walls and decks. One of the elderly Englishmen had his abdomen sliced open by shrapnel and had been partially disembowelled. Wilma Oram was the nurse nearest him and, as she moved to treat and comfort him, she noted with clinical calmness that the wound would be fatal. As she squatted alongside him, the Englishman softly sang 'Rule Brittania' and died. The cries and yells that rent the air suggested that many more people had been hurt.

Betty, still lying flat in the saloon, was quite dispassionate as she lived through the terrible moments of the successive bombing runs:

Back came the planes . . . and this time we were just about lifted out of the water. The little ship shuddered and rattled. There was a terrific bang and after that she was still. No more zigzagging. A bomb hit the bridge. Another went straight down the funnel. For a minute the place was blacked out. We were told by an officer to stay put so, moving the child's leg to another part of my tummy, I chatted with Sister Ennis about near-misses. Down the planes came again and what a crash! It felt as if the bomb had landed right in the room with us. Then shattered glass, tons of it, smoke and the sound of crashing walls.

A number of the nurses were injured in the bomb blasts, primarily by the one that caused all the damage to the aft of the vessel. The worst of the injuries appeared to be those suffered by sisters Rosetta Wight, who was one of the older nurses, and Clare Halligan. The two nurses had been in the rear of the saloon near the passageway to the cabins when the bomb landed behind them. Both had been facing towards the front of the boat and suffered deep shrapnel wounds to the back of their thighs and buttocks, wounds that penetrated to the bone.

Partially in shock and bleeding profusely, both women were unable to move, and their wounds were treated where they lay by fellow nurses, who then half carried them to the upper deck. In another part of the saloon, Flo Casson, the 33-year-old former matron of the Pinnaroo Soldiers Memorial Hospital in rural South Australia, was also in trouble. The blast that knocked over Rosetta and Clare had also caused severe damage to both her legs, one of which was possibly fractured. She, too, was eventually assisted to the main deck. Sylvia Muir* was quite close to

---

* Sylvia Muir was a young Queenslander from the outback centre of Longreach, while Rosetta Wight was also a country girl, from Fish Creek in Victoria's South Gippsland region. Clare Halligan was from Ballarat.

the blast, and reeled away after the explosion, noting that the older Englishman who had been lying next to her appeared to be in trouble. Although there were no obvious injuries, he sat and stared without seeing and appeared incapable of either thought or action. She staggered forward, seeking assistance to get to the main deck.

Wilma Oram was also bleeding, but she was unaware of it until she stood to move away from the dead man. She and Mona had been further forward, lying along the side of the ship that was blown open by the near miss, and both had been hit by shrapnel. Wilma's legs had been gashed by flying glass. Fearing that they might require amputation, Wilma examined them carefully, touching the edges and gauging their depth; all were only skin surface and Wilma was relieved to find that she was unlikely to require hospitalisation let alone amputation. Mona, alongside her, had also been flattened by the same blast and had suffered cuts to the backs of her legs.

Kath Neuss received a nasty shrapnel wound from the bomb that hit aft. Struck in the left hip, she struggled to walk and had to be helped up onto the deck by Wilma and Mona. Sylvia Muir had suffered shrapnel wounds to her arm, and tore up her petticoat to bandage them. Jessie Simons had been struck in the forearm by a bomb splinter, but it was not a serious wound and the splinter would remain in her arm for the rest of her life. Most disturbingly, however, a number of nurses had not been seen since the first bomb hit. The nurses were lucky in that they at least were able to assess the wounds they had suffered and respond appropriately to the seriousness of those wounds. The civilians were less able to make realistic assessments, and many were on the verge of panic. The nurses went directly to their districts, and took charge of what was left of them.

When the ship's siren sounded the abandon ship signal, the

nurses who were able to walk moved to their evacuation stations. The plans explained to them just a few hours earlier were put into effect and were found to work quite well under the circumstances. Olive Paschke had insisted that all civilians had to be evacuated before the nurses could leave the vessel, and that the nurses must be prepared for anything they might confront in putting those plans into effect. As nurses, their first responsibility was to the physical wellbeing of those in their charge so, en route to their designated evacuation points, the nurses who were able to collected extra emergency dressings and morphia to treat the wounded and to prepare them for evacuation. Some also grabbed the extra dressings they had made on board the *Vyner Brooke* in their spare time over the last two days.

Around five minutes after the first bomb hit, a formation of three Japanese bombers commenced another bombing run, although it was plain that the ship was in its death throes. The first aircraft's bombs fell well ahead of the *Vyner Brooke* and caused no further damage. As the aircraft pulled out of its shallow dive, its gunner sprayed the port side of the vessel, holing the lifeboats there and severing some of the ropes that held them in the davits. The second of the bombers was well into its run as the nurses began leading small groups of people out onto the main deck.

While some of the nurses treated the injured where they lay, others had gathered civilian evacuees around them from the various meeting points on the ship. As most of them had been in or near the saloon during the attack, it was from there that the first passengers emerged to make their way towards the lifeboats. Leading this group of a dozen or so were Betty Jeffrey and

Caroline Ennis, each of them carrying a small child.* They had been the last into the saloon, and were now the first to leave. Depositing the children with an Englishwoman and leaving the remainder of the group sheltering behind the lifeboats on the starboard side, Caroline went aft while Betty returned to the saloon, stopping near the burning bridge on the way to put a field dressing on the badly gashed leg of a Malay soldier, using an emergency field dressing she had originally been issued in Melbourne. As she re-entered the saloon, another Japanese bomber flashed past, machine guns chattering, as its bombs exploded off the port side of the *Vyner Brooke*.

By now, one of the ship's officers, resplendent in the whitest uniform some of the girls could remember seeing, had entered the saloon and was directing passengers towards the exits in a calm and clear voice, something which helped take the edge off the panic that might have developed. The situation was not without its lighter moments. As people were scrambling towards the exits, a woman's high-pitched voice cut through the hubbub: 'Everybody stand still!' It was a voice that brooked no dispute, and it had an immediate effect, with passengers, crew and nurses stopping in their tracks. The same voice then said, in a slightly lower tone: 'My husband has dropped his glasses.' Those who heard it laughed and then resumed their passage towards the lifeboats.

The final check of the rear of the saloon and the passageway behind was heartbreaking. A number of the passengers there had been injured beyond any reasonable hope of recovery, and their injuries were simply too extreme or painful for them to be moved. The nurses checking there, led by Veronica Clancy,

---

* Caroline Ennis was born in Swan Hill and was nursing in northeastern Victoria when she joined the AANS.

made the decision to give those too badly injured to survive an extra injection of morphia, hoping that it would both ease the pain and perhaps end their suffering before the ship sank and they drowned. There were also a number of bodies and one of the nurses recognised one as being Mrs Warman; in 15 short minutes little Misha had been orphaned.

Although the bombs missed, shrapnel from the explosions further damaged the lifeboats on the port side. The shrapnel also inflicted injuries. As Betty Jeffrey was returning to the saloon, Jessie Simons was leaving it at the head of a group of passengers, with the intention of leading them to the port side lifeboats. The bombs exploded as Jessie emerged onto the deck and a piece of shrapnel sliced open a neat cut on the arm of one of the passengers she was leading. As the bombs exploded, Jessie thought, 'This is it!' But she survived the blast and didn't realise for some further time that she had been injured in the earlier attack.

A small group of nurses was neither treating the wounded nor leading passengers to the lifeboats. The plan put together by Paschke and Drummond stressed that all the civilians aboard be accounted for and evacuated before the nurses could leave, and several of the nurses had been charged with verifying that the civilians had been evacuated. Beth Cuthbertson, Vivian Bullwinkel, Iole Harper and Louvinia Bates* all had different areas of the ship to check, while Jessie Simons was also responsible for ensuring that the saloon had been cleared. She returned below decks after leaving her passengers at the lifeboats to do just that. As the nurses moved through the stricken ship, the things they saw were horrendous; flames and bursting bombs can do things to the human body that make even experienced nurses pause. In a few short minutes, however, the nurses checked all the public

---

* Louvinia Bates was a 30-year-old nurse from Fremantle in Western Australia.

areas, the passageways, bathrooms and cabins, and were certain there were no passengers still alive in the below decks area. Bill Tebbutt did his part as well, double-checking the wrecked staterooms at the rear of the vessel before returning to the boat deck to assist with the starboard lifeboats.

By then, the last Japanese aircraft had dropped its bombs, all of which missed the stationary vessel by a considerable margin. Strafing the *Vyner Brooke* as it completed its bombing run, however, succeeded in cutting some of the ropes attaching the lifeboats on the port side to the davits. One dropped straight down into the water, where it immediately sank. A second also dropped to the water, but hit at an angle, turned upside down, and immediately started to drift away from the ship. The third, containing two of the Malay sailors, also dropped to the water, but remained upright. Badly holed, it began to take water straightaway as it, too, drifted away from the *Vyner Brooke*. Betty Jeffrey, who witnessed it all, could not help but laugh at the expression on the faces of the sailors as they dropped but then quickly returned to assisting passengers to the lifeboats on the other side of the ship.

By now, just a little over 10 minutes from the time the first bomb struck, the ship was struggling to stay afloat. She was starting to tilt increasingly towards her starboard side, increasing the pressure on the crew and the nurses to complete the evacuation of the ship. With no lifeboats now available on the port side, efforts on the starboard side were redoubled. The three lifeboats there had all been holed by machine-gun fire and shrapnel, but all appeared reasonably seaworthy and could be lowered by the crewmen standing alongside them awaiting orders to do just that. Olive Paschke took charge of the evacuation process and issued instructions in a clear and calm voice.

* * *

Matron Irene Drummond entered the first lifeboat and she and Olive Paschke supervised the loading of the wounded into it, while the lifeboat itself was under the command of Bill Sedgeman, the *Vyner Brooke*'s first officer, who directed the two sailors aboard and those manning the davits. Seriously injured passengers were the first priority, and the nurses helped several of these aboard. Two more of the *Vyner Brooke*'s sailors joined Sedgeman, and additional supplies were passed up to them to stow aboard the lifeboat. When it was full – it could only hold around 20 because of the wounded – the lifeboat was lowered slowly into the water. As it was descending, nurses on the deck threw some greatcoats and blankets down to the waiting sailors. The lifeboat was successfully launched but immediately started drifting away, caught in a strong current. Those aboard the *Vyner Brooke* watched as the sailors in the lifeboat began to bail furiously.

As the first lifeboat was being filled and lowered, a second was also being filled, a process temporarily interrupted when another Japanese aircraft made a final strafing run over the ship. No-one was struck and no more damage was inflicted on the stricken vessel. Paschke directed that this lifeboat be filled with the frail elderly and with mothers who had accompanying children, with priority in both cases being given to those who couldn't swim. The more seriously wounded nurses were among the first to be assisted aboard – Rosetta Wight and Clare Halligan – joined shortly afterwards by Kath Neuss who had been practically carried all the way by Wilma and Mona, and assisted by her best friend, Pat Gunther. There was a moment of farce when one of the older women complained loudly that one of the sailors helping people climb into the lifeboat was also trying to look up the female passengers' dresses. Again, two sailors climbed into the lifeboat which was filled with 30 or so people before it, too, was lowered towards the water. It may have been that some aboard the lifeboat moved suddenly or that there was greater damage to the lifeboat than was apparent for, as soon as it entered the water, the lifeboat overturned, throwing most of its passengers out.

Unfortunately, the situation with the third lifeboat on the starboard side was becoming problematic. As the *Vyner Brooke* continued to list to starboard, this lifeboat started to swing away from the ship, making it increasingly difficult to get people aboard and also making it unlikely that the boat could be lowered even if it could be filled. The list also meant that loose items aboard the ship were sliding across the decks and into the water, creating additional hazards for those still on board as well as for those in the water. Jean Ashton, Wilma Oram and Mona Wilton were helping passengers across the growing gap and handing them to the two sailors already in the lifeboat. One of those sailors recognised the danger not only of the falling debris but also of the ship rolling over on them, and ordered the nurses away from the lifeboat and into the water. All three jumped in, but while Wilma and Mona swam away from the *Vyner Brooke*, Jean Ashton swam parallel to it, eventually kicking away from the ship's stern.

Wilma and Mona hoped to swim to the second lifeboat and hang on to one of the ropes that trailed from it. Although it was still upside down, a number of people had already swum to it and were either hanging on to the ropes or making futile attempts to turn the heavy wooden boat over. Swimming in the bulky life jackets was not easy, and the two nurses had made little progress when the *Vyner Brooke* gave a lurch and debris rained down into the water from the ship's upper deck. Among this debris were several life rafts that had been cut loose when the order to abandon ship had been given. Wilma did not see the life raft that struck her a glancing blow to the side of her head. Although glancing, the blow was heavy enough to render her unconscious and open up a gash on her scalp deep enough to expose her skull.

Mona Wilton was less fortunate. The life raft that struck her crushed her skull and killed her instantly.

All over the ship, passengers, crew and nurses took to the water. There were several individual instances of hysteria but no widespread panic. Bill Tebbutt, who had been assisting at the starboard lifeboat station, made a quick circuit of the main deck to ascertain if there were any problems elsewhere. At the rear of the ship he found two female civilians in their lifebelts, seemingly uncertain about what to do next. Judging that it was too high to jump from the listing boat, he led them down one level and suggested they drop the short distance to the water from there. Both women hesitated. Judging that it was time for direct action, Tebbutt simply pushed both into the water and then jumped in himself.

There were now signs of fear at the lifeboat station. Veronica Clancy was there and noted: 'Many of the civilian women were hysterical. One would do nothing but abuse her husband – "He shouldn't have left me! He shouldn't have left me!" I pointed out to her that unless she got over the side in a few minutes she would never live to tell him so.' Through a mixture of cajoling and threats, the nurses eventually made sure that all civilians had left the *Vyner Brooke*, which by now was only minutes away from sinking, and all knew it.

Olive Paschke again took control of the nurses around her on the main deck and led them away from where the lifeboats had been launched, on the damaged area below the bridge, and towards the stern of the ship. She called out to some girls already in the water that she would soon see them again on dry land where they would get 'teed up' and start afresh. Olive spoke calmly to the girls around her, instructing them to look for anything that would float and to throw it into the water, taking care to avoid the passengers already swimming away. She then ordered them to remove their shoes and lower themselves into the water using the ropes that had been deployed for that purpose by the *Vyner Brooke*'s crew. Then, in a very dignified way, she led her nurses down those ropes and into the water.

Once in the water, Olive directed the swimmers towards the planks and other flotation devices they had just thrown in. The non-swimmers, herself included, began to make their way towards a cluster of lifeboats and life rafts about 50 metres off the *Vyner Brooke*'s starboard side. Included in the non-swimmers' group was one nurse who had just disobeyed a direct order from her commanding officer. The anonymous nurse, well aware of her complete inability to swim, believed she was going to drown and that it didn't really matter if she drowned barefoot or not. She didn't drown and was still wearing her shoes six months later.

Elsewhere, other passengers, crew and nurses made their own way off the sinking ship. Jessie Simons had removed her shoes as instructed but she, Iole Harper and Louvinia Bates decided against going over the side of the ship. Instead, the three climbed down to the deck below them where they believed they could simply step off into the water. When they saw broken glass in a companionway they planned to take, Jessie went back and collected shoes for all of them. When she returned to the companionway there was no sign of Bates or Harper, so she went back to the boat deck, grabbed a rope and slid into the water, taking most of the skin off the palms of her hands as she did. Like the others, Jessie pushed off from the side of the ship when she entered the water and headed towards the cluster of boats and rafts a short distance away. A few other nurses also lost skin in the process of abandoning ship, but through it all the girls showed a discipline and a compassion that saved many lives.

The evacuation of the *Vyner Brooke* was not without its difficulties. Like some nurses, a number of passengers failed to heed the advice about descending the ropes hand over hand rather than sliding and lost all the skin from the palms of their hands in the process. Others, all civilians, either didn't heed the advice about securing their life jackets or jumped from too high on the ship. A number of bodies floating in the water had obviously died from broken necks. The nurses' sense of care and duty was also apparently not shared by all the civilians or, indeed, the crew. Some of those who claimed a place in the first lifeboat because of wounds did not appear to be quite as badly wounded as they claimed, while others who were perfectly capable of swimming refused to give up their places to non-swimmers. Fortunately, there were very few in either category.

Among the last to leave the *Vyner Brooke* was a small group of nurses that included Vivian Bullwinkel. A non-swimmer, Vivian removed her shoes and very carefully adjusted her life jacket before entering the water. By the time they left the ship it had heeled over so far that there was just a short drop from the deck to the water. Once in, the nurses swam to a partially submerged lifeboat where 12 nurses, three of them wounded, two civilian women, an elderly man and a ship's officer, Jimmy Miller, had already gathered. Nearby were Jenny Greer and four other nurses sitting on a plank they had somehow thrown off the ship. To everyone's amazement, Jenny led the group in a rousing rendition of 'We're Off to See the Wizard'. Winnie May Davis and Pat Gunther had seen where Vivian and her group had left the *Vyner Brooke*, and they entered the water from the same place less than a minute later. By then, they were able to literally step into the water.

The last person to leave the *Vyner Brooke* was probably Jessie Blanch. As the ship continued to roll over onto its starboard side, it also began to sink bow first. This meant that the stern started to rise out of the water, and the stern was where Jessie found herself. With the other nurses in the water calling for her to jump, Jessie took off her shoes and her life jacket, which she threw ahead of her, and jumped. She closed her eyes as she hit the water and went so deep that she thought she would never see the surface again. But she eventually bobbed back up, found a life jacket and put it on. Hearing the others cry out, she turned to watch the *Vyner Brooke*.

With a mixture of what seemed to be both majesty and regret, the *Vyner Brooke* completed its roll onto its starboard side and slipped gracefully beneath the waves, bow first, with hardly any accompanying fanfare of convulsions or explosions. Jessie Blanch noted that her watch had stopped at 1425 hours, and that she had been in the water about three minutes when the *Vyner Brooke* sank. First spotted by the Japanese scout plane at 1400 hours, the *Vyner Brooke* had been hit by the first bomb around ten minutes later. It was hard to believe that had been just 15 minutes ago.

The *Vyner Brooke* was one of about 70 ships sunk in and around the entrance to Banka Strait in a 48-hour period commencing at daylight on Friday, 13 February 1942.* She was sunk

---

* Many hundreds of people also escaped in small boats, launches, junks, yachts and the like. Most who left this way sailed across the Malacca Strait to Sumatra and then headed overland to that island's Indian Ocean coast. From ports like Bencoolen (Bengkulu) and Padang, they sailed in merchant vessels for Ceylon (Sri Lanka) and India. Casualties among those ships were probably a little lower than among those who headed for Java, but were significant nevertheless. Japanese aircraft and submarines patrolled the waters they were sailing through. Among those who perished was Brigadier General Archie Paris, who had commanded the 11th Indian Division during the Malayan Campaign. Paris was notable on several counts. When the Japanese attacked, he reported to his headquarters with two Irish setters and a shooting stick. Paris was also one of the officers ordered to flee rather than surrender, as he was considered an expert in jungle warfare. Gordon Bennett fled via a small boat to Sumatra and trekked to its west coast. There he was collected by flying boat and returned to Australia to tell his story.

approximately 15 nautical miles north of Banka Island and almost at the northern entry point into the strait. It is impossible to know how many people died during the sinking, because any passenger lists for the evacuees' vessels did not survive the war, even if those lists had been accurate, itself an issue. Based on what we know of the subsequent histories of the survivors of the *Vyner Brooke*, it seems likely that the death toll at the sinking was somewhere between 40 and 50. Crew members were killed in the engine room by the bomb that dropped down the funnel, the elderly reservist Lieutenant Reith and at least three Malay volunteer sailors among them, and up to 15 were probably killed in the staterooms and the furthest cabins from the saloon. Two other Malay sailors were never accounted for, and are presumed to have perished in the sinking. About half a dozen passengers were killed while jumping into the water wearing ill-fitting life jackets. Little Misha Warman's parents died and it seems that June Bourhill's mother drowned, most likely when the second lifeboat capsized. Mona Wilton was killed instantly when struck by a falling life raft and several other passengers disappeared after the bombing or after they entered the water.

Some of the Australian nurses were either killed during the bombing, were unable to evacuate the ship with the others as they were badly wounded or trapped, or were killed once in the water. Louvinia Bates made a safe escape from the ship and a short time later was seen alone on a life raft. She soon drifted away from the main groupings of survivors, however, and was never seen alive again. Badly concussed, Wilma regained consciousness and believed she had a conversation with Kit Kinsella, who drifted past wearing a life jacket. That may or may not have been so as Kit, also, was never seen again after the sinking of the *Vyner Brooke*.

Others simply disappeared. After the *Vyner Brooke* was

attacked they were not seen in a lifeboat, on a life raft, or in the water. Most of the names of those who perished aboard the *Vyner Brooke* may never be known, but there are some we can identify: Ellenor Calnan, 2/10th AGH, from Culcairn near Albury in southern New South Wales; Marjorie Schuman, 2/10th AGH, friend and confidante of Buddy Elmes and general character from northern New South Wales; and Lavinia Russell, 2/10th AGH, from the southern suburbs of Sydney, all members of the Australian Army Nursing Service who had served with distinction in Malaya and Singapore.

CHAPTER 8

Adrift

Most of the nurses and many of the civilians would later recall just how cool and welcoming the water felt when they first entered it, and also that it was a great relief to be away from the sounds and scenes of a ship under attack by enemy bombers. As well as the coolness of the sea water, they welcomed the relative silence that now engulfed them. Those who watched the *Vyner Brooke* slip beneath the surface did so without any real sense of loss; they had survived the last two months in Malaya and Singapore and they had survived the last two days under a constant threat of destruction. They would survive this.

A first priority for many was to find something to sit on or, at the very least, to hold on to, then to find friends who may have drifted away. Most of them continued to swim or drift from where the *Vyner Brooke* disappeared. Planks, boards and anything that would float rose to the surface, followed almost immediately by a huge bubble of oil that covered everyone and everything within a radius of 200 metres. People still in the water within that radius were immersed in it, with eyes and ears stinging from contact with the dark, greasy substance, which also covered the shapes the girls knew were the bodies of those who had not survived. In some ways, those first few minutes were surreal, and the individual experiences reflect the state of semi-shock that most were in.

For Mavis Hannah, the overwhelming sense was one of the untidiness and disorder that surrounded her; thousands of dead fish, some of unimaginable colour, several dead bodies, oil drums, life rafts, general debris among a scene of chaos. Others were more matter of fact. Joyce Tweddell, 'Tweedie', realised that something was wrong as soon as she entered the water, but it took her several minutes to work out what that could be. She then realised she was still wearing her tin helmet. Not too far away, Christian Sarah 'Chris' Oxley, who was a practising and devout Catholic, was praying quite loudly, 'Holy Mary, Mother of God . . .' Mavis Hannah, who had caught hold of one of the life rafts and was struggling to control it, said: 'Shut up, Chris. Grab an oar and get this raft away from here. Then you can pray.' A little stunned by the outburst, Oxley did as she was told.*

Individuals formed small groups when they could, and then those small groups looked for others they had seen, especially their leaders, Olive Paschke and Irene Drummond, who they thought would be able to organise them to make it relatively easy to reach the big island they had seen from the *Vyner Brooke*, a large land mass with what appeared to be a very high mountain

---

* Joyce Tweddell lied about her age to join the AANS, the young Brisbane woman adding an extra year to the 24 she could legitimately claim. Christian 'Chris' Oxley (Christian was her given name) was also from Queensland. Born in Charters Towers, the convent-educated Oxley was probably the most deeply religious of all the nurses.

in its hinterland.* Catching up with their friends and leaders was proving to be a lot harder than they imagined, however. The nurses and the other survivors found there were exceptionally strong currents in the water and that those currents seemed to change direction rapidly. In a few short minutes, the first lifeboat launched with Irene Drummond and the wounded nurses aboard had drifted a long way from the clusters of survivors clinging to rafts in the general vicinity of the *Vyner Brooke*. As it drifted to the limits of their eyesight, they could see several people aboard bailing as though their life depended on doing so.

It was now that luck, and the fluky currents of the Banka Strait, began to determine the fate of the individual nurses. Mavis Hannah had abandoned ship prepared for anything, carrying a pair of scissors, her pay book, a little bag which had safety pins attached, morphia, a syringe, two Straits dollars and a powder compact. Shortly after she entered the water, Mavis heard her name called, and looked across about 50 metres of water to where she spotted her friend, Lainie Balfour-Ogilvy, hanging on to a rope that trailed from Irene Drummond's lifeboat. Lainie called to Mavis to swim across and grab a rope, just as Peggy Farmaner and Peggy Wilmot had done.† Although she wanted to, Mavis was a non-swimmer, and could only watch as the lifeboat and its passengers were swept away. After bobbing in the water for several minutes, she was able to grab and hold on to a life raft as it drifted by.

The 'Wizard of Oz' group on the plank comprised Jenny Greer, Joyce Tweddell, Beryl Woodbridge, Flo Trotter and Jessie

---

* The high point spotted from the *Vyner Brooke* was probably Mt Menoembing which, at 455 metres, is the highest point on that part of Banka Island.

† The two Peggys were both from Western Australia and were both 28 years old. They were part of Tom Hamilton's 2/4th CCS. Hamilton was especially fond of Farmaner, who he would later refer to as, 'a pretty little Western Australian who was full of fun'. (Hamilton, p. 63.)

Blanch.* Still singing, they drifted away from the main group of survivors quite rapidly. They drifted past Wilma Oram, who was slowly regaining consciousness in the water. When she was fully awake – a process that occupied several minutes – Wilma conducted a self-examination of her head wound. It stretched across the side of her head, from a point just behind her temple and towards the rear of her skull. It was very deep and, as she drifted, Wilma calculated how many stitches would be required to close it; she thought about 20 would do the job. Fortunately, the sea water had cleaned out the wound and it was no longer bleeding. Temporarily satisfied with her position in life, Wilma was able to grab a life raft and climb onto it. Shortly after she did so, a voice called out, and a woman swam a short distance to the raft and asked if she could climb up. Wilma welcomed her aboard and the woman introduced herself as Mrs Dorothy Gibson, a civilian evacuee. The two then untied the oars and decided to try to row to the nearest land, which they believed to be Banka Island.

The injured Pat Gunther had been thrown into the water when the second lifeboat overturned, and had drifted alone for a short while before she was joined by Winnie May Davis. Together, they grabbed an upturned canvas stretcher which they held on to until they were close enough to touch a life raft, on and around which were gathered a number of other survivors. They both recognised Jessie Simons in the group. Realising that Pat was injured and couldn't swim, Jessie helped her up onto the raft.

Sylvia Muir also had some good fortune. While floating in the water, she had been grabbed by a panicking Chinese man, and she was only able to break his grip when Joyce Tweddell came

---

* Always called 'Woodie', Beryl Woodbridge was, at 37, one of the older nurses. A Melburnian, she was both pretty and petite. Florence Trotter, another devout Christian, was a Queenslander and part of a group of nurses from the Brisbane General Hospital who enlisted together in 1940.

to her assistance. These two soon drifted apart, however, with Tweedie catching Jenny Greer's plank and Sylvia trying to swim to a partially submerged lifeboat where she could see her friend Pearl Mittelheuser. Sylvia was almost at the end of her tether when Mitz was able to reach out and pull her into the lifeboat, probably one of those that had dropped into the water from the port side of the *Vyner Brooke*.

Betty Jeffrey, who was a strong swimmer, spent her first few minutes in the water swimming from group to group looking for Olive Paschke; that morning, Olive had requested Betty's assistance if the worst came to fruition and they were all in the water. None of the nurses she spoke to had seen Olive, and so Betty continued to swim towards any grey uniform she could see. She spotted Winnie May Davis and Pat Gunther and their canvas stretcher, and stopped to rest with them for a while, then swam on through a large oil patch to a raft packed with people, several of whom were wearing grey uniforms.

Among the dark heads in the water alongside the raft she found Olive Paschke, who seemed 'terribly pleased' with herself for having kept afloat for what was now more than an hour. Betty told her she had every right to be pleased as punch. The raft, or rafts, as several had been tied together, contained two Malay sailors, one suffering from burns, both of whom were ineffectively trying to paddle. Also sitting out of the water was Caroline Ennis, who was holding two small children, a Chinese boy who looked about four years old and a little English girl who was probably a year younger. Around the raft and in the water were four or five civilian women, plus Iole Harper, Merle Trenerry and Gladys McDonald* from

---

* Gladys McDonald, a Queenslander, was one of the group who joined from the Brisbane General Hospital. Merle Trenerry, from South Australia's Yorke Peninsula and a member of a pioneering Cornish tin-mining family, was a nurse with wide experience in both city and country hospitals.

the 2/13th, Jess Dorsch from the 2/4th CCS, with the 2/10th representatives being Mary Clarke and now Betty herself.

Not too far away, another group had coalesced around an upturned lifeboat, the second one launched from the starboard side of the *Vyner Brooke*. Vivian Bullwinkel was part of this group. She had made it through the water to the lifeboat and grasped the rope that ran around the boat's gunwales. Also clinging to the rope were several other nurses, including two who had hurt themselves in the evacuation, an elderly civilian couple and Jimmy Miller, the *Vyner Brooke*'s second officer. All were covered in oil. Introductions were hardly necessary as just about everyone clustered around the lifeboat knew everyone else, but they were exchanged anyway. In the general chatter that followed the introductions, a number of the nurses expressed a fear of sharks. Jimmy Miller admitted to some expertise on the subject, and reassured the nurses by explaining that the concussion from the bombs dropped on and around the *Vyner Brooke* would have driven all the sharks well away from the area.

Others were on their own for all or most of their various journeys. Nesta James found a life raft, climbed aboard and was carried away from the others by a current. She would not see anyone else for the next 12 hours. Cecilia Delforce[*] had a similar experience, and hers lasted several hours longer. Lavinia Bates was also sighted alone and aboard a life raft, caught in a current and drifting away. Unlike the others, however, Lavinia was never seen alive again.

About 90 minutes after the sinking, a Japanese scout plane swept low across the area where the survivors floated in groups

---

[*] Del was 30 years old and hailed from outback Queensland, where she had also spent all her nursing career. The other nurses believed she was one of the best swearers they had ever heard, with a gift for combining traditional vernacular with modern idiom.

or individually. They all watched it but no-one waved as they wondered if it was the same plane and pilot who had brought about their present situation. They also feared that he may turn his machine guns on them but, after one pass, he flew off. Had some of the survivors had the inclination to wave a greeting, it would have caused them considerable pain to do so. The canvas life jackets had rubbed the skin under their chins and around their armpits almost raw, and the salt water was adding to their misery. Had the Japanese pilot looked down as he flew above them, he would have seen a few individuals sitting on life rafts or clinging to debris. He would also have seen three or four large groups sitting in or on, or clustered around a couple of battered lifeboats and groups of life rafts roped together. As the plane flew off to the northwest to an airfield recently captured in Malaya, the survivors continued to drift towards Banka Island, now growing dark ahead of them.

One of the little groups the scout plane passed over contained Mavis Hannah. After watching her friend Lainie Balfour-Ogilvy drift away with Irene Drummond's lifeboat, Mavis held on tightly to her life raft. During the next half hour she had been joined by several other survivors, including sisters Violet McElnea and Val Smith. The group around the life raft continued to grow and by nightfall there were 16 survivors sitting on or clinging to the several rafts that they had been able to tie together. Although a non-swimmer, Mavis considered herself to be the senior nurse in the group and therefore had to set an example. She remained in the water, allowing a couple of children and some elderly survivors to crowd together on the life rafts.

The raft that Jessie Simons, Winnie May Davis and Pat Gunther attached themselves to also contained badly injured crew members from the *Vyner Brooke*. There were three of them, two British and one Eurasian. One of the British sailors, who the girls only knew as Stan, spent a lot of time contemplating the fact that the *Vyner Brooke* sinking was his fourth of the war to date. He had been on the *Prince of Wales,* and had been sunk twice before then in European waters. The Eurasian had been one of the *Vyner Brooke*'s radiomen, while the other British sailor had been one of the gun crew of the forward four-inch cannon. He had extensive flash wounds from the bomb that destroyed the gun and was in a very bad way.

After climbing aboard the life raft, made larger by lashing a second one to it, Winnie May Davis gave the burned gunner an injection of morphia from her emergency kit, and this seemed to ease his pain. The raft and its passengers continued to drift on what was becoming an increasingly empty sea. Just as the sun was setting, three civilian women grouped together drifted close to their raft. One of the women was unconscious, and drifted straight past Simons; she was not identified and was never seen again. As the other two were being helped onto the raft, Jessie recognised them – it was the redoubtable Mrs Mary Brown and her daughter, Shelagh.

A little further away from Olive Paschke's group, Sylvia Muir was joined at Mitz Mittelheuser's overturned lifeboat by several other nurses: Veronica Clancy, Gladys Hughes, Mina Raymont, Shirley Gardam and Jean Ashton, plus a civilian evacuee who introduced herself as Mrs Bull and who was accompanied by a four-year-old daughter named Hazel, a Malay sailor named Billy, two civilian men and a few women of various ages. Mrs Bull was worried because her two other children had drifted away from her, but she was reassured by the nurses who said if they were wearing life jackets, they would certainly be rescued by other nurses, good swimmers whose role was to perform such rescues. Hazel was also concerned. When she tried to hold onto a rope she had let go of her teddy, which was now drifting away. Jean

Ashton swam after it, recovered the sodden bear and returned it to Hazel, thereby making a friend for life.

Working together as a team, the survivors decided they would try to right the lifeboat and, after several attempts, succeeded in doing so. Some of the nurses gave up various parts of their clothing to plug the machine-gun and shrapnel holes in the boat while the men bailed furiously. The lifeboat was able to take aboard all those who had been in the water but there were no oars. Although two nurses gave up their dresses to be used as sails, it was to no avail.

As the sun continued to dip towards the horizon those aboard the lifeboat made a major decision. Their lifeboat was going nowhere except deeper into the water. Conjoined rafts occupied by several civilians drifted close by, and their occupants agreed to share them with those aboard the sinking lifeboat. The nurses retrieved their dresses and anything else they had used to plug the lifeboat's holes and, as their craft sank beneath them, became part of a group of 23 survivors clustered on and around the life rafts.

It was agreed that, to ease the strain on everyone, some form of arrangement should be introduced whereby everyone took turns both in the water and on the rafts. One exception was made: an elderly civilian named Mrs Maddern was in a bad state emotionally. Her husband of many years had been injured in the sinking of the *Vyner Brooke*, and the couple had been together in the water for several hours with Mrs Maddern supporting her fading partner, who had died in her arms shortly before she was collected by those on the raft. It was agreed that she could remain on the raft. It was also agreed that Olga Neubrunner should remain aboard. Seven months pregnant and pining for her husband still fighting the Japanese somewhere behind them, Olga's nursing experience made her more than aware of the dangers to herself and her unborn child.

Also aboard was Dr Goldberg, whose sense of self-importance had survived the sinking. Goldberg steadfastly refused to share the burden and take a turn in the water and said, in her heavily accented English: 'I'm a mother of three and more important than any of you.' Veronica Clancy was more incensed by the comment than by the attitude. She clambered half aboard the raft and started to punch Dr Goldberg as hard as she could in the middle of the back. Goldberg screamed at each blow but still refused to budge. As the struggle continued, Blanche Hempsted climbed onto the raft, put Goldberg in a headlock and dragged her backwards into the water, where she subsequently directed sullen looks at anyone who spoke to her. In the midst of this uneasy peace, the sun set as the rafts drifted closer to the island ahead.

As darkness increased on that first night adrift, a number of groups and individuals afloat in Banka Strait saw a bonfire spring to life on a beach in the distance. It seemed to be a beacon, and those who could see it set about trying to reach it. Others believed they could hear distant shouts and cries. While probably just an illusion, for some it added to the fears that were already starting to build.

Vivian Bullwinkel, Jimmy Miller and the others clinging to the upturned lifeboat felt the strength of the current taking them towards land all afternoon, and when they saw the fire on the beach some distance ahead after dark, discussed what it might be and decided it was a beacon deliberately lit to guide shipwreck victims like themselves. Their circumstances meant they were not able to steer their boat, but the current continued to take them in the general direction of the island and at around 2200 hours on the Saturday evening they felt sand beneath their feet. Those who were able to staggered ashore and took a few moments to catch their breath. Then, taking off their life jackets, they waded back into the water and helped Clare Halligan and Rosetta Wight up onto the beach and made them comfortable on the sand. They had all been in the water for almost eight hours, and it took a while for them to recover all their faculties, both physical and mental. There was general agreement that they needed to ascertain what the beacon, if that was what it was, had been lit to signify, and to find out who had lit it. The bonfire appeared to be at least a couple of kilometres away from where they sat on the beach. After a few minutes, Jimmy Miller and Vivian said they would go to investigate. Two other nurses agreed to accompany them. The four set off down the dark beach towards the light in the distance.

As the sun went down, those aboard Jessie Simons' raft also took stock. As well as the badly burned British sailor, other occupants were starting to suffer from their injuries. Jessie's rope-burnt hands were an agony to her and Pat Gunther, although also wounded in the sinking, searched through her little carry bag and found a tube of lipstick. Working on the theory that it could not do any more harm, Pat rubbed this into Jessie's palms as a kind of salve. The lipstick made it look as though she had two slabs of raw meat at the end of her arms, but it did provide some relief.

Just on dusk, Jessie and the others thought they saw a number of black-hulled ships in the distance, but they were too far away and the light was too dim for them to be able to recognise anything other than the shape of the vessels. At one point after dark they thought they could see a fire on a beach in the distance, and although they tried to paddle their raft towards it, the current was too strong and the fire soon disappeared. At another point, their raft drifted past an old man in the water, lying back in his life jacket, an unlit pipe clamped firmly in his teeth. He had drifted away before Jessie realised that he was not an apparition, and he didn't respond to her calls as the distance between them widened. At some stage during the night the badly burned sailor slipped off the raft and into the water. He simply disappeared without saying a word or uttering a sound.

No-one was able to estimate the exact hour, but during the first few hours of Sunday, 15 February, Jessie Simons' raft drifted into the middle of what seemed like dozens of small landing craft packed with troops or equipment being lowered from a large transport ship and despatched towards a shoreline they could just begin to make out, and which they assumed was some part of southern Sumatra. As the life raft continued to drift, several of the landing craft changed direction and one pulled up alongside. Using gestures, the Japanese soldiers aboard indicated that the nurses should climb onto the vessel. Although apprehensive, they did so and were treated with courtesy and dignity by the soldiers. A line was thrown to the others on the life raft and it was towed to the beach behind the landing craft. There, the *Vyner Brooke* survivors were left under guard until mid-morning, squatting in the shade at the edge of the beach and being offered water and cigarettes by the Japanese.

At one point shortly after they arrived on the beach, a curious incident occurred, something they would be able to look back upon and laugh about later, but at the time was a potentially serious occurrence. Jessie Simons had very short hair, which had been plastered down against her skull by a combination of fuel oil and sea water. She no longer had a dress as her uniform had disappeared during the night along with the body of the British sailor. She was now wearing only a petticoat and underwear. One of the Japanese guards wandered over to Jessie, pulled out the front of her petticoat, and peered in at her breasts. Although he was checking to see that she wasn't a soldier trying to disguise himself, for a moment it appeared to be something more sinister. As the Japanese soldier walked away, the Eurasian radio operator gave Jessie his shirt to wear.

Around mid-morning, the group was led down and around the water's edge to a road that took them to a small town, and there they were taken to an old cinema on the main street. The cinema contained at least 200 people, mostly European and mostly in various stages of dishevelment and shock. One man walked across to address the group of newcomers: 'Congratulations on making it this far alive,' he said to them. 'You are in the town of Muntok on Banka Island. Good luck to you all.'

The large group of nurses that included Sylvia Muir, Veronica Clancy, Gladys Hughes, Blanche Hempsted and Jean Ashton had continued their vain efforts to direct their life raft with its mothers and children, and Dr Goldberg, and had continued those efforts until well after dark. At any one time there were in excess of a dozen people in the water swimming, pushing and pulling, but despite their best efforts the raft still travelled wherever the currents took it. Some became concerned about Mina Raymont and Shirley Gardam, who seemed to be doing more than their fair share of the work. On several occasions they had almost drifted away from the raft, so the other nurses started to take turns just watching them while they were in the water. At one point during the night those around the raft could clearly see a fire some distance away to their left, but the life raft refused to go against the current and the flames soon disappeared into the gloom behind them.

Towards morning, everyone could clearly hear shouting from a shoreline that now appeared to be a lot closer that it had been at any time since they had abandoned the *Vyner Brooke*. Shortly afterwards, those on the raft spotted a Malay native swimming towards them and in a few minutes he had reached the raft. He was quite exhausted when he arrived and had to be hauled aboard to recuperate. When he had done so, he used a combination of gestures and common Malay words to let them know that they were between one and two kilometres from the shore.

After a brief discussion, Veronica, Gladys and Blanche volunteered to swim to shore to see if they could find any assistance. All three claimed to be good swimmers and said that, if any one of them should find herself in trouble, the other two would be there to help out. The three swimmers set off and had gone around 500 metres when they heard a boat engine, and shortly afterwards an old motor launch pulled up alongside them. Stranger still was the sight of two RAAF airmen who were aboard. After pulling the three swimmers into the boat, the launch continued on to the life raft, and eventually the Australian airmen were able to fit all the survivors onto their motorised launch.

The girls must have given the airmen a shock in more than one way. Veronica recalled that when they were hauled aboard the launch: '. . . we were practically naked, our uniforms had been taken for sails, our brassieres and singlets, straps broken, were down around our hips somewhere from swimming for so many hours. The boys gave us their coats . . .'

The airmen spoke to the survivors, telling them to lie down in the boat and to remain as quiet as possible as they were in enemy waters. The launch then headed off, travelling parallel to the coastline, until it came to a long jetty that extended some distance into the sea. The airmen tied the launch to a landing stage near the end of the jetty, and helped all the passengers disembark. The ongoing trauma proved too much for Olga Neubrunner who, calling for assistance, collapsed in agony on the end of the jetty. In labour and in pain, Olga delivered a stillborn baby surrounded by the nurses who could only hug her and clean her up.

At the landward end of the jetty, some 400 metres away and through the early morning mist and smoke, a fairly large township could be seen, with figures moving around its streets. One of the airmen told the survivors to stay where they were and asked his mate to keep an eye on their boat, saying that he was going into town to see if he could get some help.

The airman hadn't quite reached the end of the jetty when he stopped, peered intently ahead, then turned and started running back towards them. As he drew closer, he yelled to his mate to get into the launch, untie the ropes and start the engine. Those tasks were completed just as he arrived at the landing stage. The airman ran straight past the puzzled group of survivors and leapt into the launch which pulled away as fast as its old engine could manage. Looking back down the jetty, the survivors saw a group of Japanese soldiers running towards them. When they reached the end of the jetty, the soldiers unslung their rifles, crouched and fired several shots at the rapidly disappearing launch, without any apparent effect. They then turned to look at the bedraggled group of women and children who had watched the preceding scenes with amazement. After an animated conversation among themselves, the soldiers indicated that the survivors should form into a group. With one soldier leading and the others providing an escort, the survivors marched down the long jetty and into the town beyond. Two nurses supported Olga Neubrunner, and another two helped Mrs Maddern. Dr Goldberg walked by herself. Veronica Clancy noted the headless body of a Chinese off to one side of their path. A half hour later, they were settling in at the Muntok cinema.

* * *

Jenny Greer's group – Woodie, Flo, Tweedie and Jessie Blanch – finished their version of 'We're Off to See the Wizard' and launched into a series of popular songs. As the afternoon dragged on and they realised that they had little, if any, control over their destinies, they talked of childhood, adolescence and adulthood, of the things they had done and the things they hoped to do before their lives were over. As the sun set and their world contracted to their plank there were periods of silence, but they were very much a group of positive young women and, sooner or later, one of them would come up with a topic that would start them talking again.

At some stage during the night the nurses quite clearly saw a lighthouse and a short time later spotted a large fire on a beach. The current carried them fairly close inshore, close enough for a couple of the girls to say they could see women in AANS uniforms in the light of the bonfire. But then the current swept them past, and the fire and those around it were lost from view.

Early on Sunday morning, a flukish cross-current carried the plank and the nurses directly onto a gently sloping beach. They staggered up to the palm trees that fringed the land side of the beach, took off their life jackets and simply sat down for a few minutes – time that slowly stretched into the first few hours of daylight. In the light, they saw smoke rising from a small village hidden in the jungle behind the beach. Hungry and thirsty, and deciding they really had nothing to lose, the nurses walked into the village and conversed with a villager who could understand their questions. He was able to indicate to them that the local area had been occupied by the Japanese that very morning, and that they were based in a town a short distance away. He pointed in a direction, and the nurses set off to find the town. After a short distance, they came to a road and had only been walking along it for a few minutes when a Japanese soldier appeared around a bend. The soldier stopped and waited for the nurses to reach him. When they did, he turned around and the little group walked for perhaps 20 minutes before they entered a small town. They were taken to an old cinema in the town's main street and led inside.

Although there were times when all she really wanted to do was let go and drift away, Mavis Hannah was just not prepared to give up so easily. To let go was to die, and Mavis thought that she was not quite ready for such a final step. Nothing really significant had happened during the first afternoon, evening or night, and nothing much happened the next day, which they all knew was Sunday. Nothing much happened during the day on Sunday and nothing much happened on Sunday night either, although by then Mavis and the others were starting to relinquish a little of the grip they had on reality. Mavis was quite convinced there had been 16 people sitting on or clinging to the life raft, but she couldn't remember where that figure had come from. During that second night, she thought that their raft had almost touched a lighthouse, and she believed that she could feel seaweed beneath her feet, but there was nothing to grasp on to, and then the lighthouse was behind them. And, it seemed, just a little while later, the world was lit up by the sun and it was a new day.

In a dream, Mavis heard someone calling to her in a language she didn't understand. When she looked up it was not a dream; a Malay fisherman in a canoe was calling and gesturing to the group still holding on tightly to their raft. He threw a rope to them, which one of the girls grabbed and looped around a corner of the raft. Soon they were on a beach and sitting down and listening to the fisherman who spoke softly and pointed to a town they could see on the other side of a little half moon–shaped bay. Some time later – it could only have been a few minutes but seemed much longer – Mavis found a banknote, two Straits dollars, in her pocket and gave it to the fisherman who went away and returned with food and water. The nurses ate and drank with the other survivors and then slept for many hours. When they awoke, it was another morning, and they sat around discussing their options. They didn't really have any, so they stood and stretched and began to walk to the town on the other side of the bay. The fisherman had called it Muntok. The nurses decided that they would surrender to whoever was in charge of the town.

Among those who joined the band that grew around Olive Paschke's raft were her 'bodyguard', Betty Jeffrey, and Iole Harper. For a long time afterwards, Betty could recall that first afternoon in the water, the soporific effect of the sun, the cool, welcoming water and the sensation of floating, weightless, on a sea of glass. She suspected that some of those who survived the sinking simply drifted away and fell asleep and drowned. While Betty had swum to join the group, Iole had arrived by way of another life raft. As she floated in the water after abandoning the *Vyner Brooke*, she had grabbed a young Chinese boy as he floated past in a life jacket. She was able to lift the child onto an empty life raft and pull it across to Olive Paschke's raft, where she passed the child up into the waiting arms of Caroline Ennis.

Iole then grabbed one of the trailing ropes alongside Betty, and the two AANS nurses, who had never seen each other to this point in their lives, formally introduced themselves. Iole explained to Betty, who hadn't even asked, that she was not really worried about sharks because, with all the ships that must have been sunk in recent days, they would already have eaten their fill. Not, thought Betty, if we have drifted from one hunting ground to another, but she kept that thought to herself. The girls'

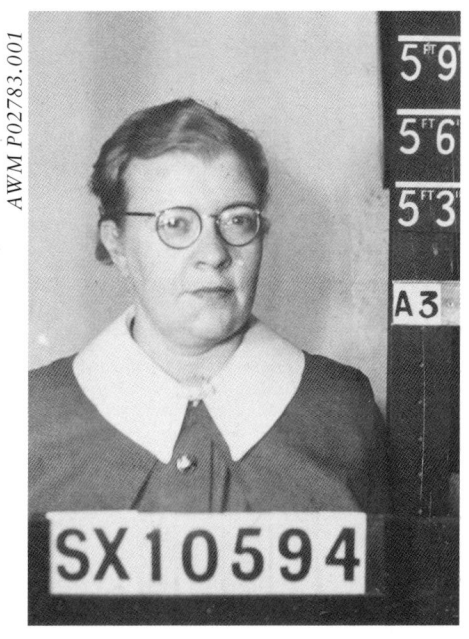

Top left: 'Dashing Dot'. Matron Olive Dorothy Paschke RRC.

Top right: 'Like a mother hen…' Matron Irene Melville Drummond.

Left: 'Kit'. Sister Kathleen Kinsella.

Right: 'Bully'. Staff Nurse Vivian Bullwinkel.

Bottom right: 'A nightingale sang...' Sister Elaine Balfour-Ogilvy.

Bottom left: 'Buddy'. Sister Dorothy Gwendoline Elmes.

AWM P03960.001

P01180.001

AWM P01021.001

Mary Cuthbertson, Clare Halligan, Ada 'Mickey' Syer and Ruby Wilson en route to Singapore.

The 2/10th AGH waiting to entrain at Selatar Naval Base, February 1941.

The 2/13th AGH waiting to disembark, Singapore, August 1941.

Sisters of the 2/13th AGH at a concert party at St Patrick's School. Second and third from left, front row, are Louvinia Bates and Jean Ashton, and third from the right is Veronica Clancy.

The 'White Elephant' at Malacca, with a flat roof for marching and the mess building at left.

An operating theatre at the 'White Elephant', Malacca, mid-1941. The nurse at the far right is 'Buddy' Elmes.

AWM P01295.001

A nurses' swimming party heading out from the 'White Elephant'. Kath Neuss is sitting at left.

AWM P01701.005

The 2/4th CCS at Tampoi, November 1941. From left: 'Kit' Kinsella, Peggy Farmaner, Major Adrian Farmer, Peggy Wilmott, Mavis Hannah, Elaine Balfour-Ogilvy.

'Doing the rounds': Matron Irene Drummond pours tea for her nurses at Tampoi, November 1941. Vivian Bullwinkel is at left.

The 2/4th CCS shortly after arrival, probably at Port Dickson. Back row from left: Jess Dorsch, Peggy Wilmott, 'Mina' Raymont, Elaine Balfour-Ogilvy, Peggy Farmaner. Front row: Shirley Gardam, Irene Drummond, Mavis Hannah. Only Hannah would survive what was to come.

'Going native': 2/4th CCS nurses trying on saris. From left: Jess Dorsch, Peggy Wilmott, Mavis Hannah and Elaine Balfour-Ogilvy, with two members of the local Indian community.

St Patrick's, Katong, February 1942. Nurses and wounded after a bomb strike.

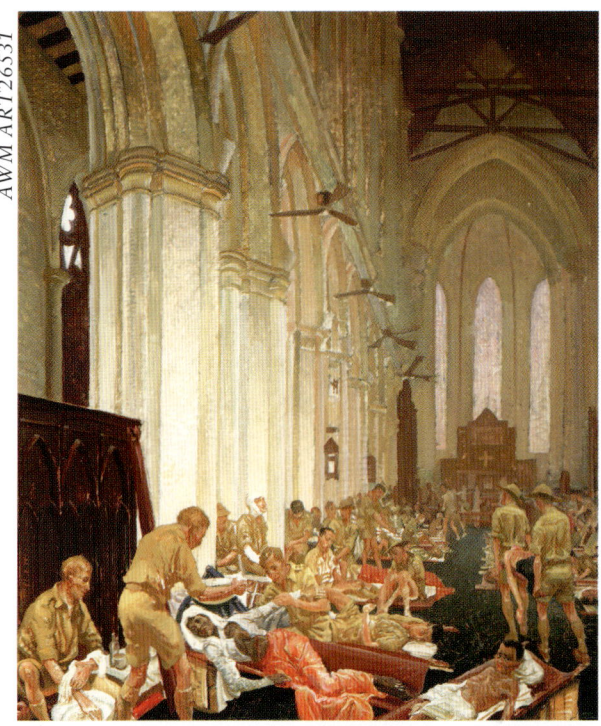

Murray Griffin's painting of St Andrew's Cathedral, Singapore, in the days before the surrender. This was the meeting point for the nurses prior to their evacuation.

'Alive.' Survivors of the ordeal arrive in Singapore in September 1945, most wearing their original uniforms.

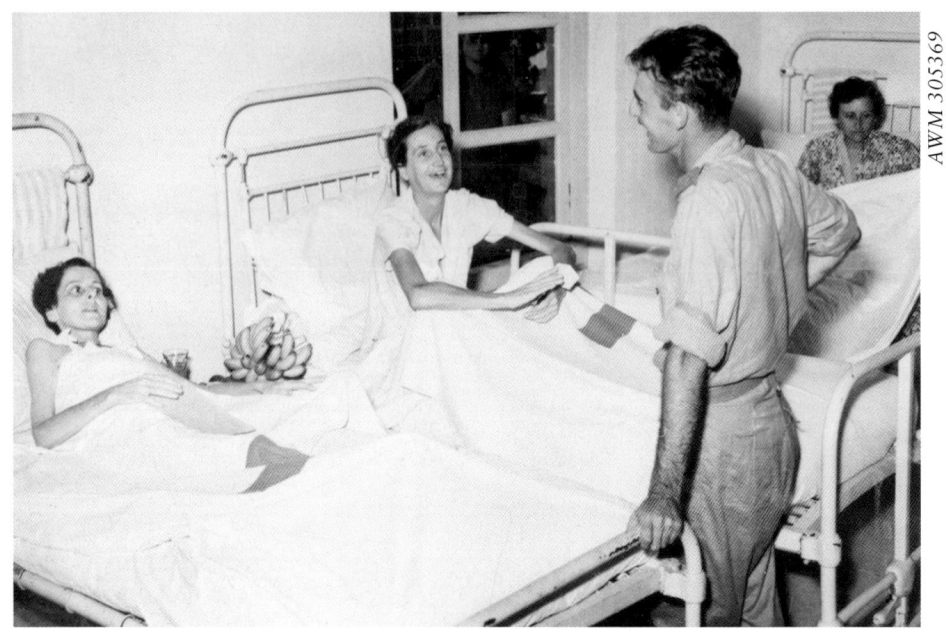

Jenny Greer (left) and Betty Jeffrey recovering at St Patrick's.

Enjoying a Gracie Fields concert, September 1945. Front, left to right: Beryl Woodbridge, Jessie Simons, Veronica Clancy.

AWM P01701.003

The official welcome back to Australia, aboard the *Manunda*, Fremantle, October 1945. In this group photo, the nurse in dress uniform in the centre of the picture is Colonel Annie Sage, Matron in Chief, Australian Army Nursing Service.

Vivian Bullwinkel (centre) and Wilma Oram (right) at a welcome home reception in Melbourne, October 1945.

Jean Ashton (left) and Mavis Hannah are welcomed home in Adelaide, October 1945.

Left and below: St Andrew's Cathedral today.

Raffles Hotel, Singapore.

'The Spotted Dog': the Royal Selangor Club today.

The Australian section of the Commonwealth War Cemetery, Jakarta.

One of the many: Pearl 'Mitz' Mittelheuser's grave in the War Cemetery, Jakarta.

A memorial plaque for the lost nurses in St Andrew's Cathedral, Singapore.

conversation ranged over a number of subjects, and they discovered that they both had brothers serving in the Royal Australian Navy. In fact, their brothers had actually served together on the same ship in the Mediterranean.

Olive Paschke, ever the organiser, motivator and leader, arranged for the two Malay sailors on the raft to be relieved from their paddling duties by Australian nurses. When they weren't paddling, the nurses were either sitting on the raft and helping with the children, or taking their turn in the water. Not that the paddling seemed to make much difference. The oars that had been attached to the raft were long gone, and they had to make do with two slats taken from a packing case. Iole Harper assumed responsibility for the swimmers and for general work divisions. She put people into shifts, making certain she did more than anyone else, and would occasionally drop into the water to check on those already there. She even found time to give lessons in the proper and effective use of the feet when attempting to propel the raft.

During their first night adrift, the Paschke raft passed other small groups of nurses and civilians being pushed somewhere else by the currents. Also, at dusk those on the raft had seen at least five large ships on the horizon, and during the night those in the water had felt the thump or concussion in the water of large engines close by. In the distance they could all see searchlights playing across the water, and although several of them called out at regular intervals there was never a reply.

At one time, their raft was pushed towards the shoreline and came tantalisingly close, maybe only a hundred metres or so, to a large bonfire that had been lit on a beach. They could see figures moving around the bonfire and thought they could also hear voices, but they were unable to break the iron grip of the current and were once again swept out to sea. At another time, a ship's officer clinging to a piece of debris was carried to within hailing distance of the raft. He, too, drifted by and was not seen again. In the early hours of Sunday morning, a number of nurses thought they spotted a very long pier jutting into the sea. It was too far off to reach, but they were encouraged nevertheless as it meant they were probably drifting closer to populated areas where the chance of rescue was higher.

Aboard the raft, Caroline Ennis had assumed responsibility for the children, and had developed a particular affinity with the little English girl, who was soon calling her Auntie Caroline. During that first night, the other nurses heard the little girl ask Ennis if she could 'go upstairs'. Uncertain about what she meant, Caroline asked the girl what she wanted to do, to which she received a whispered reply about going to the toilet. Auntie Caroline informed her that it would be all right for her to go where she was, but the child would not go until her sodden underpants were removed. Like all aboard the raft she was soaked, and also insisted on washing her hands in the salt water afterwards.* A little squall also threatened to overturn the raft at one point, and everyone aboard was given a fresh soaking.

As the hours passed, the currents continued to play tricks with the life raft, at one time sweeping it towards a lighthouse before suddenly whisking it back out to sea. The paddlers paddled furiously and the swimmers gave a mighty heave, but they could not break the grip of the current. Before dawn on Sunday morning, the raft drifted through a convoy of small Japanese transport vessels carrying soldiers and equipment. Although the raft actually bumped into some of these craft, there was total silence as they passed through them. When dawn finally broke,

---

* Because of the shortage of both food and water, going to the toilet ceased to be an issue for most of the survivors by the second day adrift.

the survivors could see that they were as far from land as they had been when the *Vyner Brooke* went down, although they had drifted a good way down Banka Strait. In the distance they could see a Japanese warship lobbing shells over a small coastal town. They could no longer see beaches; the nearest shoreline presented a solid vista of large trees and mangroves.

The nurses had been taking turns to row or sit on the raft, or to lower themselves into the water to hang on to the ropes and drift with the raft. During the night, however, the rotation system had broken down and there appeared to be too many people on the raft. The new best friends, Betty and Iole, volunteered to lighten the raft, and entered the water. Both were good swimmers and they joined the two Malay sailors who were already in the water. To begin with, the four in the water swam alongside the raft, joking that they should slow down as they were outpacing it. Although almost within touching distance, in an instant everything changed; the swimmers were suddenly five metres and then ten metres from their friends on and around the raft, which had been caught in a strong cross-current.

As the raft was swept away from the swimmers and from the nearest land, Betty and Iole called out, but there was nothing either group could do about their situation. Betty and Iole watched the raft grow smaller, with Mary Clarke and Gladys McDonald sitting either side of Olive Paschke, and Jess Dorsch and Merle Trenerry in the water alongside hanging on to the trailing ropes. And there, back to back with her matron, sat Caroline Ennis, cradling two small children on her lap. The raft and its occupants were never seen again.

Many of the survivors of the sinking of the *Vyner Brooke* reached land some time during that first night or during the morning of

Sunday, 15 February. Like many of the larger groups of survivors, the pair of Wilma Oram and Dorothy Gibson, sitting quietly on their life raft, was almost run down by the Japanese invasion fleet supporting the occupation of southern Sumatra and Banka Island. They, too, had seen the bonfire on the beach, but it was too far away and the current was too strong for them to have any possibility of reaching it. As daylight appeared, so did the realisation that they appeared to be right in the middle of a significant Japanese landing. The current eased a bit, and Wilma and Dorothy were able to paddle ashore amid the Japanese landing craft. Once ashore, they were promptly taken prisoner by the Japanese who were already there. They were equally promptly marched under guard to one of the larger buildings in the town the Japanese had just occupied; it was an old customs house just down the road from what appeared to be an old cinema.

Nesta James and her life raft drifted with the current for 12 hours or more, bumping into debris on occasion but not really seeing or hearing anyone else. In the early hours of Sunday morning, Nesta washed up on a beach not far from a large lighthouse, the historic Tanjung Kelian fortified lighthouse that many of the other survivors had almost reached. She approached the lighthouse and knocked on the door of what appeared to be the residence. There were two Malays inside and from them Nesta learned that the Dutch lighthouse keeper had fled the previous day, leaving them in charge. Shortly after this information was gathered, some Japanese soldiers arrived to secure the lighthouse and prevent its destruction. Held at bayonet point, Nesta was relieved of her 100 Straits dollars and pay book by the Japanese, who left immediately afterwards. Uncertain of what to do, Nesta returned to the beach where she met another *Vyner Brooke* survivor, Phyllis Tunbridge, the British Army intelligence clerk, who had also been confronted by the Japanese group.

They had relieved her of significantly more than $100 – she was attempting to take several thousand dollars in several denominations away – and had her face slapped before the Japanese left. Both Nesta and Phyllis had short, dark hair; the Japanese tested the sex of each woman by the simple expedient of feeling their groins.

The two returned to the lighthouse residence, but the next morning the Malay caretakers made it plain that they did not want the Australian women to remain. They decided to seek shelter in the nearby jungle, where they were soon joined by a number of other survivors from their ship. They, too, came to the conclusion that there was nothing they could realistically do beyond walking to the town the Malays had indicated was an hour or so down the road and surrender to the Japanese. This they did, and within the hour they were in the old customs house at Muntok.

Probably just one beach away and in the opposite direction to Muntok, Cecilia Delforce was also washed ashore. She set off towards the jungle at the back of the beach and, as she followed a track that led through it to the rear of some sand dunes, she heard a rifle shot. In front of her, a Japanese soldier had just shot a prisoner, probably a local volunteer with the Netherland East Indies Volunteer Forces. Several others, with their hands tied behind their backs, stood nearby. The soldier seemed surprised to see Cecilia, and indicated a small hut nearby. When she opened the door, Cecilia saw there were several women inside, including some nurses wearing uniforms that she did not recognise. There was no further shooting and within an hour another group of Japanese soldiers arrived and marched the women the relatively short distance to Muntok.

* * *

Out at sea, Iole Harper and Betty Jeffrey were now by themselves; the two Malay sailors must have struck out for the nearest land without telling the Australian nurses. Taking time to swim, then float, then talk for a while before swimming again, Iole and Betty were washed into a mangrove swamp on Banka Island. Mangroves have spikes on their roots and soon both women had puncture marks all over their arms and legs. Any of their skin not covered by water was attacked by mosquitoes, and there seemed to be no way out of the swamp. As they entered their second night in the water, they swam into and then out of several muddy creeks. There were no settlements, no people and no roads, paths or tracks.

They snatched some sleep while holding on to mangrove roots, and when the sun rose on Monday, 16 February, they repeated their efforts of the previous afternoon, swimming into and out of muddy creeks, but feeling weaker and weaker as the day wore on; they were soon spending less of their time swimming and more of it hanging on to trees. Another night came upon them and then another morning. Talking was becoming an increasing effort, but they discussed their position dispassionately and knew they would not survive another day. As they headed upstream in one of the tidal creeks, they began to hallucinate. Some time, probably during the early afternoon, they imagined that they could hear voices. Then they were being helped into a canoe and into a hut. They were given water and, a little bit later, scraps of food. They slept on reed mats that night and in the morning they were fed again. Their rescuers, Malay fishermen, explained that the Japanese had occupied the entire island and that the nurses should give themselves up. Later, they helped Betty and Iole out to the main road behind the village they had brought them to and pointed down that road to Muntok, a few kilometres away. As they walked towards captivity, Betty and Iole did the calculations – they had spent 72 hours in the water.

The town of Muntok was the second largest settlement on Banka Island, and had grown to the size it was partly as a service centre for the tin mines found some distance inland. The town really began to grow after the state-run Banka Tinwinning Company started operations there in the late 1920s. In 1940, the mines it operated had produced 24,000 tonnes of tin, or 55 per cent of the entire output of the Netherlands East Indies. Most of the mines – open-cut mining was the norm – were located well away from Muntok in the eastern and northern parts of the island, but Muntok was the location of one of the island's main tin smelters. The smelter and the mines were worked primarily by labourers brought in from elsewhere in the archipelago, who lived in camps specially built for them and known locally as the 'coolie lines'. At Muntok, the coolie lines – also sometimes called the Chinese camp – were located on the western fringes of the settlement. Elsewhere in that part of Banka Island, fishing provided the main source of food and income. Most of the small local villages were built slightly inland from the beaches and waterways, where food gardens could also be established and tended. The area behind the sandy northwestern beaches was crisscrossed with tracks and paths, while many of the beaches had small huts and shelters for the fishermen who worked the area.

As Muntok grew in size, it also became a centre for the local village trade as well as the tin industry, and the Dutch colonial authorities built a coastal road linking the nearest villages with Muntok. The town became an administrative centre as well as the focal point for local trade; a customs house near the base of the Muntok jetty, a police station and other government facilities were built and, to cater for the developing tastes of those who lived and worked there, a cinema was erected in the main street in the late 1920s. By mid-February 1942, that cinema contained many more people than it had ever attracted for a film showing. A single-storey, timber and corrugated-iron structure, the cinema comprised a large hall capable of holding over 200 people in comfort, an entrance hall and a projection booth. By 16 February 1942, around 1000 people had been crowded into it.

In Singapore's last week as one of the Straits Settlements and part of the British Empire – General Percival surrendered it to General Yamashita at 2030 hours on Sunday, 15 February – a flotilla of up to 300 vessels of all shapes and sizes attempted to escape the closing trap. While a proportion tried to make their way to India or Ceylon, most headed through the waters and islands to the south of Singapore, down towards Banka Strait and Bomb Alley and, hopefully, on to Java, the Indian Ocean and Australia beyond. About 90 per cent of those that tried did not make it to the eastern end of Banka Strait. Forty of the 44 ships that departed Singapore on the same day as the *Vyner Brooke* were sunk within two days; 20 of the 25 that left the next day suffered the same fate. Three-quarters of the people who fled were either killed or captured by the Japanese. By the end of the month, Japanese naval authorities would consider closing the strait to shipping because of the hazards to navigation many of the wrecks were beginning to pose. The currents that swept the survivors of these sinkings away were very capricious; of the *Vyner Brooke* survivors, some made landfall within eight hours of the sinking, while others like Betty Jeffrey and Iole Harper spent three days in the water. Some, like those on

Olive Paschke's raft, were swept out to sea and may not ever have made it to land.

Those who made landfall on the northwestern side of Banka Island would, sooner or later, finish up at Muntok. All the roads in that part of the island led there, and it was the only town that could provide the facilities and support the survivors would need. Muntok was occupied by Japanese forces in the early hours of Sunday, 15 February. The destroyer that escorted the occupation troops fired several rounds over and beyond the town as the troops swarmed ashore to discourage any possible resistance, and the experienced soldiers of the Sumatran invasion fleet swept into Muntok, occupying a few key points without loss or any real distress. Around mid-morning several aircraft from the Dutch Army Air Force bombed the vessels grouped in Muntok Bay, causing slight casualties and stiffening the resolve of the troops ashore, including the senior officer, Captain Orita Masaru. Any possible opposition would be severely dealt with.

There were already both shipwreck survivors and refugees in Muntok when the Japanese arrived, and Orita Masaru ordered his junior officers and men to simply direct all the Europeans they saw to the customs house, where they would be kept under guard. By nightfall on 15 February, the customs house was badly overcrowded and the prisoners of war and internees, for that is what they now were, were escorted under guard to the cinema, the largest building in Muntok. By nightfall on 16 February, there were up to 1000 people confined in the cinema. The Japanese guards became increasingly frustrated and there were several minor acts of intimidation and abuse. The culmination of the frustration that all were by now feeling came when Vivian Bowden, a senior Australian diplomat who was fleeing Singapore after earlier fleeing China, made loud and strident objections to the two Japanese soldiers who wanted him to hand over his watch. They took the watch and then took Bowden outside and marched him a short distance into the jungle. There they made him dig his own grave and then shot him.

In many ways, the Muntok cinema and incidents like the murder of Bowden summed up the sea change that the Japanese attacks throughout Asia had begun, with their casual brutality reflecting their desire to show that Asia was now going to be run by Asians, and that the days of colonial authority were over. It was a lesson that would take some of those who had occupied privileged positions a long time to comprehend. Squashed in the cinema, an English Colonial Service officer spoke to Veronica Clancy: 'You know, Sister, the real tragedy of all this is the levelling of classes and nationalities.' After all she had been through, Veronica was flabbergasted by the statement, and it took her a minute to recover. When she did, all she could think to say was: 'It is fools like you in responsible positions that cause war', before moving as far away from him as she could in the circumstances.

Wilma Oram and Dorothy Gibson were taken to the customs house during the morning of 15 February, and within an hour had been joined by Jean Ashton, Jenny Greer, Blanche Hempsted, Eileen Short* and Veronica Clancy. A group of eight men arrived next, and explained how they had narrowly avoided execution after surrendering to a Japanese patrol. Throughout the day, the small groups and individual swimmers who had made it ashore on Banka Island were brought firstly to the customs house and later to the cinema. More and more arrived over the next few days and, naturally, the Australian nurses sought each

---

* Eileen Short was from regional Queensland and joined the AANS while serving as Matron of Isisford Hospital, a small town in the middle of nowhere.

other out to swap news about the sinking, their time adrift, and what they thought might have become of the missing. The cinema was becoming increasingly unsuitable to hold the numbers crowded into it, and on 17 February the Japanese marched their prisoners through the town and into the coolie lines on the outskirts. While the coolie lines had originally been constructed for the native labourers who worked the mines and the smelter, the war had left them pretty much vacant. The lines consisted of a number of huts built around an open central area, with the complex enclosed within a high stone wall. Within the lines was just one well which produced brackish water, while the entire area was overlain by the smell that emanated from the open drain that ran through the middle of the complex. There were neither baths nor showers, just the ubiquitous 'tong', a concrete, open-topped trough from which water was ladled over the body for washing. The coolie lines also contained a small hospital which, within a few days, had a full complement of medical staff and patients. Unfortunately, it did not have any medicines.

It was to the coolie lines that Iole Harper and Betty Jeffrey were brought late on the afternoon of Wednesday, 18 February. They told the nurses who clustered around them of their ordeal in the water and how they had last seen Matron Paschke's raft, with its cargo of nurses and children, being swept away from Banka Island some three days previously. They spoke of their decision to surrender and how, after an initial fear that the Japanese wished them ill, they had actually been treated quite well. They were fed, given water and taken into a room attached to the police station where a number of wounded Japanese were lying on the floor clad only in G-strings. They were asked to treat the wounded, but could only provide advice as their hands were still recovering from rope burns and mangrove punctures. They were unable to say anything about the fate of the two *Vyner Brooke* lifeboats that had been launched, however, or about Matron Drummond and the nurses still missing with her group. But they confirmed that they also had seen the bonfire on the beach and suspected that it might represent part of the mystery.

It was to the coolie lines ten days later that the Japanese brought Sister Vivian Bullwinkel, who was able to tell the nurses about the bonfire on what the locals called Radji Beach, and what had taken place there on the morning of Monday, 16 February 1942.

CHAPTER 9

On Radji Beach

The only two lifeboats successfully launched from the port side of the *Vyner Brooke* drifted away on currents, separated from the life rafts and spars and stretchers and barrels to which most of the survivors clung. Some fluke of nature oversaw this separation and gave the lifeboats and their passengers destinies of their own. Matron Irene Drummond's lifeboat was the first launched and it contained a number of wounded, four sailors from the *Vyner Brooke*, several nurses, medical supplies and a number of blankets and overcoats that had been dropped into the boat as it was being lowered into the water. The lifeboat and its human cargo were all under the command of Bill Sedgeman, Royal Navy, first officer of the *Vyner Brooke*. The lifeboat had quickly begun to drift away from the sinking ship, and within a few minutes had been caught by a current that took it further and faster than the other survivors could either swim or paddle.

It had many holes from machine-gun fire and bomb splinters, but none were fatal and it could, and did, float. The last sight many of the survivors had of the lifeboat was of Sedgeman standing in the bow looking back, Irene Drummond in the stern looking forward, and in between them, two sailors bailing furiously.

This lifeboat was also the first of the survivors' craft to reach land. After a little over three hours in the water, the lifeboat and its 20 passengers washed up on a long crescent-shaped beach just as the sun was starting to drop into the sea. Although those aboard did not know it, the beach had a name – Radji Beach – and it was located just a few kilometres to the west of Muntok, the largest settlement in this part of the island they had found, Banka Island. It was starting to grow dark as Sedgeman and Drummond finished sorting through all the things they needed to do to make safe and comfortable those under their control. The wounded were their first priority. The blankets and greatcoats were arranged in sleeping positions towards the rear of the beach by one squad of nurses under the direction of Irene Drummond, while Bill Sedgeman took another group of sailors and nurses to explore the beach and its immediate environs. This group also collected driftwood from along the high tide mark. Returning to the wounded, they used the firewood to build a bonfire in the middle of the beach, with enough firewood stacked alongside it to keep the bonfire burning throughout the night. It was dark when the bonfire was lit and, as Sedgeman and Drummond had hoped, it became an instant beacon to dozens of people in the surrounding waters, many of whom were from the *Vyner Brooke*.

Throughout that night of 14 February, individuals and small groups of shipwreck survivors attempted to reach the beacon on Radji Beach. For many, it was never anything more than a bright light in the distance, and for others it seemed to offer a tantalising chance of survival, almost in their grasp, before it was snatched away by the ever-changing currents. A few were so close to the beacon that they could recognise the clothes being worn by some of the women on the beach as being AANS uniforms; others could clearly hear the voices of those nurses and recognised them as being Australian. But that was as close as they got. Those already on the beach could not hear their calls above the breaking of the waves, or see their white hands waving in the darkness, well beyond the light cast by the bonfire.

A few did make it to the beach, generally in ones or twos. Among them were several crewmen from the *Vyner Brooke*, including at least one officer, a number of civilians – mainly women and children – and several nurses. Around 2230 hours, the tall figures of Vivian Bullwinkel and Jimmy Miller walked into the firelight and greeted Bill Sedgeman, Irene Drummond and the others gathered around the fire. As recounted, Bullwinkel and Miller had attached themselves to the second lifeboat launched, and had travelled with it until it ran ashore some distance away. Included in the number they had drifted with were the badly wounded nurses Clare Halligan, Flo Casson and Rosetta Wight. Miller and Bullwinkel outlined the circumstances that brought them there, and how they would need assistance to bring all their survivors back to the larger group.

Bullwinkel was particularly concerned about the condition of the wounded. Some of the servicemen had wounds that would require professional treatment in hospital, while others, not so seriously injured, would need sterile bandages and sutures – as well as medications – if their relatively minor wounds were not to turn septic. The nurses were naturally a special concern. All three were Victorians and had been nursing with the 2/13th at the time of their evacuation. Clare Halligan, the oldest, a 38-year-old from Ballarat, was the least severely wounded. Her thigh had been cut deeply by a bomb splinter but she was able to walk and simply needed some stitching and some medication to be guaranteed a full recovery. The other two, Flo Casson and Rosetta Wight, were much more seriously injured. The two 33-year-olds were both from country Victoria – Warracknabeal and Fish Creek – and Flo had been the matron at a Riverland hospital before joining the AANS. They were both strong and brave women, but their wounds were severe. Again, shell splinters had caused the damage, with both women suffering deep wounds to the buttocks and upper thighs. They were unable to walk, and had to be fed and helped with their toilet functions. The wounds appeared to have caused nerve damage, perhaps fractures, and they needed more specialised treatment than any that could be provided on the beach.

Some of the elderly appeared to be suffering from shock as well as physical injuries, and Vivian asked what medical supplies and expertise were available within the group on the beach. Among the survivors around the bonfire was a Chinese doctor who had boarded Drummond's lifeboat to assist with the wounded before it was launched. Twice he was asked and twice he refused to accompany Miller back to the second lifeboat, saying that he could not afford to leave the wounded already on the beach. Miller eventually put together a rescue party and set off. The journey to the second lifeboat and back with its survivors took over two hours, and the wounded nurses were in agony on the return journey, having to be half-dragged, half-carried for most of the distance. Their pain was obvious and it, in turn, increased the distress of the other survivors.

Shortly after the rescue group under Jimmy Miller set off, the main group around the fire thought they heard thunder and saw flashes of light on the horizon. The nurses and the civilians thought it was a tropical thunderstorm; the sailors judged it was a naval battle. It was still some hours to dawn when the rescue party returned from the second lifeboat. Their wounded were made as comfortable as possible and the able-bodied joined the others around the fire, talking over their recent experiences. The officers discussed bringing all the survivors together into one big group and then seeking food and assistance from any local villagers they could find, and then going further afield to establish contact with local authorities, whoever they may be. Most of the others simply stared into the flames or sought out a comfortable spot where they could sleep.

In the hour before dawn, another lifeboat grounded itself on Radji Beach. The sailors had been correct earlier, and what they had seen had been a naval battle, although a very lopsided one. A Japanese cruiser caught and sank another evacuation vessel from Singapore in Banka Strait. The lifeboat contained the biggest single group of survivors from that clash. Among its complement of men, women and children were several wounded servicemen. A Royal Navy officer, Lieutenant Commander J.C.S. White, was also in the group; originally on another vessel, he had been picked up as he drifted on a life raft. All survivors were made as comfortable as possible and settled down for what remained of the night. An hour later, the sun rose. It was Sunday, 15 February 1942.

Shortly after dawn, the senior officers on the beach – Bill Sedgeman, Jimmy Miller and Irene Drummond – held a meeting to plan what to do. A headcount revealed that there were now more than 70 people gathered together on the beach; 22 of these were Australian nurses, three of whom were so severely wounded that they were patients themselves. There were the two senior officers and several sailors from the *Vyner Brooke*, around a dozen soldiers from the night's battle, and about the same number of Royal Navy sailors. The remaining survivors at the site were all civilians, most of whom had come from the *Vyner Brooke*. Included in the number were several children. The wounded were made as comfortable as possible on the landward side of the beach, placed in the shade and brought water at regular intervals. A kind of roster was arranged among the nurses to check regularly and report on their condition. Small parties moved off in different directions, seeking to learn more about where they were and what was on the beach and in the jungle around them. They also kept a weather eye out for Japanese aircraft and soldiers.

The officers made their decisions and called the other survivors together in the shade on the edge of the beach to fill them in and seek both comment and commitment. Sedgeman explained to the group that they were in a certain amount of trouble. Daylight had revealed they were on a sandy beach that stretched into the distance to the north and was about 20 metres wide at high tide. To the south there was a rocky outcrop that extended into the water and separated their beach from another, smaller but equally sandy beach. At the back of the beach to the north was jungle, although there were coconut palms scattered at the littoral between beach and jungle. The second lifeboat was not visible, but its occupants were able to identify where they had trekked from the previous night.

Their first priority, Sedgeman said, was the welfare of the wounded, and the Chinese doctor, Matron Drummond and a group of her nurses would assume responsibility for this. Before the meeting, the nurses had already started this duty. With the help of half a dozen naval ratings, Drummond and several of her nurses had assisted the doctor in his assessment of the wounded, and then carried or supported them to the shade at the rear of the beach before the sun became too hot and tormented them further. A number of nurses remained with them when the meeting started just a few metres away.

Sedgeman went on to explain that their provisions were the next concern. While they had enough water in bottles and canteens to last a couple of days with rationing, food must be regarded as a priority, as they could barely scrape enough together for one meal. There were also sanitary arrangements, and it was suggested that two areas – one for males, the other for females – be identified an appropriate distance apart in the jungle. A number of able-bodied survivors were briefed to go beachcombing, seeking anything that would be of use to the survivors, while the able-bodied women and children were asked to assist the men by looking for driftwood and other timber suitable for the bonfire, just in case they were to stay another night on the beach.

There was a track leading from the beach into the jungle, Sedgeman said, and he proposed taking a party along it to see where it went. It was his hope that it would take them to a village. If it did, he hoped to be able to bring back food for the survivors. He then selected five sailors, all of whom had survived the sinkings of the *Prince of Wales* and the *Vyner Brooke*, and all of whom he knew well. He also asked for five volunteer nurses as he felt that a mixed group of that size would be less threatening to any locals they might meet than a similarly sized group of servicemen alone. Vivian Bullwinkel was one of the nurses who volunteered. Sedgeman finally nominated four sailors to explore the beach beyond the southern headland, and delegated Jimmy Miller to assist Irene Drummond in organising the survivors on the beach in his absence. He then set off with his own little group to the track behind the beach.

The track led them into thick jungle, and they walked slowly and cautiously for perhaps half an hour – a distance of over a kilometre – before they came to a kampong, a small native village, set in a clearing in the jungle. Sedgeman halted the group and went forward alone to three old men who were sitting under a crude shelter in the centre of the kampong. Using a combination of gestures and the few Malay words he knew, Sedgeman tried to explain about the shipwreck survivors on the beach, the wounded and the nurses, and their need for food and water. One of the old men replied in kind. He indicated that they could not assist and that he should lead his survivors to a much larger settlement nearby. The old man continued to gesticulate, and again Sedgeman believed he was being told that the survivors would be able to surrender to the Japanese at this larger settlement, and that the Japanese would then supply them with both food and water. Thanking the old man, Sedgeman returned to the group and led them back to the beach, explaining the conversation as they walked.

While Sedgeman had been talking to one of the old men, another of the three had called to a woman, possibly his wife, who in turn had approached the group of survivors while Sedgeman and the old man continued their pantomime talk. There, she repeated some of the words and gestures of the old man to the female members of the party. Vivian attempted to explain to her the circumstances of the survivors and what had brought them to this place. She felt that this woman appeared to be sympathetic; a call resulted in another woman appearing with water for the group to drink. However, another of the old men began to rebuff the first woman, as yet another woman was bringing food and clothing. Using what appeared to the Europeans to be very forceful gestures, he seemed to tell the women that as the island was now controlled by the Japanese that the villagers were free of any obligation to assist white people, while they should also be aware that, if the white people stayed in the area for too long, they could also expect possible retribution from the

Japanese. The villagers moved away from the group of survivors as Sedgeman returned, but this interchange, as well as Sedgeman's discussions with the old man, gave them plenty of food for thought as they returned to the beach.

Back at Radji Beach, Sedgeman, Miller and Drummond sat in the shade to discuss what had occurred during the morning. Sedgeman spoke first, outlining what had happened at the kampong and his belief that they were unlikely to receive any support or succour from the villagers. Jimmy Miller had slightly better news. The exploration parties sent out had found a freshwater spring bubbling out of the rocks behind the headland. This spring formed a small stream that flowed inland into the jungle, disappearing into a swampy area back from the beach. The water at the spring was both fresh and sweet, and there was more than enough to supply the needs of all the survivors. Nearby, among some palm trees that fringed the beach, they had also found a fisherman's hut, a lean-to really, and Irene Drummond had supervised the transfer of a couple of the more seriously wounded to that place. The sailors had made crude stretchers to assist with the move. The hut was also down towards the headland, less than 50 metres from the bonfire whose embers still smoked on the beach. It was a help but, coming on top of Sedgeman's gloomy assessment, it was still not enough.

After their brief discussion, Sedgeman called all the survivors to a meeting. He reiterated to them everything that had happened that morning and then proceeded to outline the alternatives, as he saw them, from which the survivors needed to choose. The first alternative was to repair the lifeboats, provision them as best they could, and attempt to sail them to some place not yet occupied by Japanese forces. The second alternative was for the party to move inland and attempt to live off the land with the help of friendly natives until they could make contact with

Allied forces. The final alternative was to surrender to the Japanese in the town the villagers had spoken about. Sedgeman told the survivors that he thought the number and condition of the wounded and the elderly made the first two alternatives impractical, and that he didn't believe there was a fourth alternative of waiting where they were until something happened. As it was early afternoon, he said that surrendering that day was impractical and they would all meet again the following morning to make a final decision. He then suggested they all conserve their energy for what lay ahead.

Nothing much happened during the rest of that day. The nurses had been organised into work groups early in the morning, and while some collected and sorted all the medicines and medical supplies, others collected water containers and filled them at the freshwater spring. Still others washed the bandages and gauze pads they had used on the wounds they continued to treat, while others performed the numerous duties nurses undertook, albeit under the unusual and quite trying conditions.

When the Australian girls weren't nursing or scrounging, they were talking. At the professional level, they discussed how several of their patients had suffered additional injuries from being in the water when explosions occurred nearby. Many of these injuries were ruptures or hernias of internal organs. Interestingly, the nurses observed, women wearing elasticised corsets appeared to suffer fewer injuries of this type than those who didn't. They also talked about their own situation, and what each thought the most likely and most attractive outcomes would be. The consensus among them was that the condition of the wounded meant that surrender to the Japanese was the only viable alternative.

As darkness fell, the bonfire was relit and everyone on the beach settled back to grab whatever rest they could before facing the challenges they knew the next day would bring. It was an interrupted rest. The nurses were back on shift work, helping the wounded, changing dressings and taking water to their patients at regular intervals. Some time late at night when most on the beach were drifting into their troubled sleep, the sea in the distance was lit up. Those awake watched as, out in the middle of Banka Strait, a ship was caught in Japanese searchlights and sunk by gunfire. Shortly before morning, another lifeboat and several life rafts washed up on the beach. An additional 30 British soldiers and sailors joined their group, many of them injured. One of the latter was an English infantryman named Pat Kingsley, a private soldier from East Yorkshire whose unit had been part of the 18th Division, reinforcements who had arrived in Singapore just in time to surrender. The shells that had sunk his ship had also removed most of his bicep and part of one shoulder.

The nurses moved among the newly arrived wounded, following the Chinese doctor and adding their own assessments to his. They could offer only limited treatment, but even this was more than those they were treating could have expected in the circumstances. Most of the nurses were still working when the sun once again crept above the horizon. It was Monday, 16 February 1942.

The headcount that preceded the survivors' meeting that morning revealed that there were now well over 100 people on Radji Beach. The demographic balance had changed with the overnight arrivals; half of those present were servicemen, with soldiers outnumbering sailors. Also around half of those who had arrived overnight had been wounded. In the harsh light of day it was obvious that most of the seriously injured would survive no more than 24 to 48 hours. This was the first point Bill Sedgeman made when he opened the morning meeting of the fit survivors. Some of the servicemen present, soldiers and sailors alike, expressed concerns about reports that the Japanese army appeared to have a policy of not taking prisoners. Others countered this by pointing out that the large number of women and children in their group meant that, if they all stayed together, all of them would be safe.

Sedgeman called the meeting to order and reiterated the points he had made 24 hours earlier. They could not attempt an escape by land or sea without abandoning the wounded and elderly, something neither he nor the nurses were prepared to consider. Many of the nurses had been very upset after they had been ordered to leave their wounded behind in Singapore; they were determined it would not happen again. The only realistic alternative available to the survivors was to send a party to the nearest town and surrender the entire group to the Japanese. It was this alternative that Sedgeman asked them to consider and to then cast a vote. When they did so by a show of hands, the vote was unanimous – they would surrender to the Japanese that day.

After the vote was taken, Sedgeman explained that he would not order his sailors to do anything that he was not prepared to do, and so he would lead the surrender party. He asked two of the sailors from the *Prince of Wales* to accompany him. Before departing, he told Irene Drummond that he would ask the Japanese if they had any stretchers and, if they did, if these could be brought back for the severely wounded. Then he led the two sailors down the jungle track. It was 0900 hours.

As soon as they left, Drummond put her nurses to work. She approached Miller, who had been left in charge of the British servicemen, and suggested they start to put together stretchers for the badly wounded in case the Japanese did not bring enough. Miller agreed, and detailed some of his sailors to do just that. Others joined nurses who were working to construct a large Red Cross on the beach. As Irene was overseeing this, she was approached by several of the civilian women. They were, they said, concerned primarily about the welfare of their children. All had been without a proper meal for almost two days and were becoming increasingly restive. If no-one objected, the women proposed to follow in the footsteps of Sedgeman and march to the town they believed was close enough for them to be able to reach it without too much distress. Once there they, too, would surrender to the Japanese. Doing so would relieve some of the pressures on those who remained at Radji, and would mean that their children would be that much closer to their next meal. Irene and Jimmy Miller agreed with the proposal, and the civilian women and children set off soon afterwards, led by a middle-aged man who appeared to have assumed command of the group, and accompanied by a couple of the walking wounded. Both were sailors and both had survived the sinkings of the *Prince of Wales* and the *Vyner Brooke*. After walking for 20 minutes, a number of the children were footsore and tired, so the group sat down to rest a few minutes in a jungle clearing. As they were resting, Bill Sedgeman led a party of armed Japanese soldiers, accompanied by an officer, past them. Although both groups looked at each other, no words were exchanged.

Back at the beach, the nurses were trying to figure out how much time they had left to complete their various tasks. None of the nurses had a working watch, but they guessed it was around 0930 hours.

With the departure of the civilian women and children there were now considerably fewer than 100 people left on Radji Beach. Apart from the 22 Australian nurses there were about

25 uninjured men – mainly soldiers and sailors – but also a number of civilians including the Chinese doctor. The military group that Sedgeman handed over to Jimmy Miller included an engineering officer who had been aboard the *Vyner Brooke* and a number of NCOs from both the Royal Navy and the British Army. The numbers of uninjured men were matched by the numbers of wounded, most of whom were incapable of walking and who would have to be carried out on stretchers. There was also one elderly European woman who had politely declined the offer to leave with the other civilian women and children. Her husband was among the seriously injured. They had not been separated in almost 50 years of married life and they would not be separated now.

Irene Drummond called her nurses together and explained to them what she wanted them to do. There should be a final check of the Red Cross: was it large enough to be visible from the air? Large enough so that there could be no mistaking, even by Japanese, of what it was supposed to signify? She also insisted that the stretchers under construction be checked and improved where possible. They did not know how far they would be expected to carry the wounded and she suspected it would not be the Japanese who would be doing the carrying. The nurses, soldiers and sailors continued to work together and worked quickly. Using spars and planks, belts and driftwood, they constructed about a dozen sturdy stretchers to replace the makeshift beds the wounded were now lying on, and moved some of the lightly wounded across to the new stretchers. Any stretchers the Japanese brought would probably be a lot better than those they had built, and would be used for the more seriously wounded. As they were moving the last patients onto these stretchers, all chatter on the beach ceased. Sedgeman had returned, and he was accompanied by a small and dapper Japanese officer and a heavily armed patrol of what seemed to be around 20 soldiers. It was just after 1000 hours.*

Bill led the party of Japanese soldiers onto Radji Beach and, gesturing with his arm, indicated the various groups of people – servicemen and civilians and nurses, injured and whole – and pointed to the stretchers, the almost-completed Red Cross on the beach and indicated that these were the people who wanted to surrender. Vivian Bullwinkel observed the exchange. The Japanese officer seemed to look straight through Sedgeman to the survivors on the beach and, for a brief moment, she thought that he was doing some sort of calculation, thinking through a new problem that had been unforeseen. But it was only briefly, however, and Captain Orita Masaru snapped out his orders to a sergeant major, who in turn had his men load and cock their rifles.

Speaking quietly and with no discernible expression on his face, the officer explained to the sergeant exactly what he wanted done. Relaying the orders to a small group of the soldiers, the sergeant showed signs of anger, perhaps, or frustration at something Vivian could only imagine. Using gestures that were reinforced by jabbing their bayonets at those who were slow to move, the unwounded survivors were quickly divided into three groups: the nurses, a group that included the elderly European

---

* There have been several variations on the make-up and numbers of Japanese in the patrol in the many books, articles and interviews given on the incident, with numbers ranging from six to in excess of 30 soldiers. Some reports have the soldiers carrying automatic weapons and setting up machine guns on the beach. The structure of the Imperial Japanese Army, the occupation of Banka Island and the weapons extant in the IJA all make the likely number to be something around 18 soldiers, led by a sergeant major and accompanied by a captain, Orita Masaru. Six would not have been able to do what they did, and more than 20 would have taken too many away from their occupation duties. One officer and 20 men was the make-up Vivian Bullwinkel included in her postwar affidavit for the International War Crimes Tribunal.

woman; and two groups of servicemen and civilians, the smaller of which included the remaining officers and NCOs Bill Sedgeman, Jimmy Miller and four others. With a nod of his head and a hand gesture, the officer continued his directions. The sergeant and about a dozen Japanese soldiers marched the group with the officers and NCOs down the beach towards the rocky headland. As they were being led away, one of the officers called out to the servicemen remaining behind on the beach that they were only required to give the Japanese their name, rank and serial number.

Perhaps some, and maybe all, of the officers and NCOs glanced back at Radji Beach as they were led around the rocks at the end and onto the small beach beyond. Once they were well out of sight, they were stopped and several of the Japanese soldiers produced lengths of material which they used to blindfold their prisoners. Then Lieutenant Bill Sedgeman, Lieutenant Jimmy Miller and several other British servicemen whose names will never be known were bayoneted to death. It was over in two minutes, and their bodies were thrown into the jungle at the edge of the beach.

As the Japanese soldiers strode quite smartly back from beyond the headland there was growing disquiet among those who had been forced to sit silently on the sand in their two groups. Some of the nurses had become concerned when the Japanese had appeared without any stretchers, but Irene Drummond had warned them that they couldn't rely on Japanese goodwill and that she had expected all along that it would be their responsibility, and theirs alone, when it came to transporting the wounded into whatever town they were to be taken to. So they sat on the sand under the guard of the Japanese officer and several of his men as their friends and fellow survivors were marched out of sight and did not return with the soldiers.

Once back with their officer, the Japanese soldiers advanced to the two groups left on the beach and indicated to the remaining servicemen and male civilians that they were to get to their feet. They then directed the men down the beach in the same direction and in the same manner as the officers before them. This was a larger group though, and more Japanese soldiers went with them, including one who was carrying a light machine gun. This group was also halted on the far side of the headland and, again, some of the Japanese soldiers produced blindfolds and indicated that the prisoners should put them on. With this larger group there were not enough blindfolds to go around, and the Japanese sergeant indicated to some of the prisoners that they were to tear strips off their shirts and use these for blindfolds.

By now one or two of the prisoners were becoming agitated and when one Englishman, near the sergeant, spoke back at a Japanese soldier, the sergeant major drew his sword and struck the man in the face with it, opening up a terrible wound that stretched from temple to chin. Bleeding profusely, the man slumped to the ground, while the sergeant barked a new set of orders. The prisoners were jostled into a ragged line facing the beach, and the machine gunner set up his gun on a tripod and lay down in a firing position behind them. Most of the prisoners had a fair idea of what was about to happen, but stood silently, almost as if waiting for orders after the shock of seeing their comrade struck down. As the guards attempted one last time to blindfold the prisoners at one end of the line, several from the other end tried to escape.

Three men, including a Royal Navy stoker named Ernest Lloyd, grasped what was about to happen, and the man standing next to Lloyd whispered out of the side of his mouth: 'Here's where we get it in the back.' Lloyd, who'd survived the sinking of both the *Prince of Wales* and the *Vyner Brooke,* was not going easily, and said in reply: 'Well, I'm going to give it a go!' The two, and a third further down the line, broke away from the main group, sprinted to the edge of the water and dived headlong into the waves. Surprised, the Japanese guards were slow to respond and the prisoners were in water deep enough to start swimming before they did. But the guards recovered and unleashed a fusillade of rifle fire at the three escapees. Two were killed instantly. A bullet creased Lloyd's scalp, opening up a long wound, while a second bullet passed through his leg and lodged in his shoulder. Unconscious, he drifted away from the beach and eventually washed up on a sand spit at the other end of the beach. Satisfied that the three men were dead, the Japanese turned to the prisoners still lined up on the beach. Within a few minutes, all had been blindfolded and bayoneted. This time, the Japanese did not bother to hide the bodies.

The nurses had continued to sit on the beach under the gaze of the remaining Japanese soldiers and their officer, as the second group of male prisoners had been led beyond the headland. They had heard a volley of rifle fire in the distance and, five minutes later, watched as the Japanese soldiers returned, walking in single file, with several appearing to be cleaning their bayonets with small cloths. As soon as the second group of prisoners had been led away, most of the nurses became aware of what was to come; they had been told that the Japanese did not take prisoners and their worst fears were realised as they watched the returning Japanese. Jenny Kerr, a no-nonsense girl from near Young in New South Wales was sitting alongside Vivian, and turned to her and said: 'Bully, they have murdered them all!' while Nancy Harris said to no-one in particular: 'It's true, then. They don't take prisoners.'

Only Lainie Balfour-Ogilvy spoke up with an alternative, suggesting that if they all ran in different directions at least some of them would probably get away. For instance, the good swimmers could run into the water, and those who could run fast could take off down the beach or into the jungle . . . Her thoughts and words faded away. Irene Drummond spoke softly, reminding them that there were wounded lying behind them who were relying on the sisters of the AANS for both support and succour. Yes, the Japanese had probably murdered the men, but everything in their training and everything they stood for and believed in meant that they could not abandon their patients, even if the consequences of fulfilling the oath they all took were too horrible to contemplate. While there is life there is hope, she said, and the little group fell silent.

Others in similar situations have reported experiencing a number of emotions, everything from rage to acceptance of the inevitability of death, but for Vivian at least, the overwhelming emotion at that point was one of disbelief. She, like her fellow sisters and friends around her, had come a long way in the past few months. They had seen and heard and experienced things that most had never dreamed of and, through it all, they had maintained the highest standards of their profession. They were committed to the saving and not the taking of life, and Vivian was not aware of any of them ever knowingly causing physical harm to another human being. Individually and collectively, they had done nothing to deserve the kind of ending that seemed to be their destiny. It was wrong, it couldn't, wouldn't and shouldn't happen.

The Japanese squad stopped in front of the nurses and squatted down to clean and reload their rifles, glancing across at the officer and at the girls themselves. After an eternity that lasted no more than two minutes, Captain Orita Masaru called out a command and the soldiers stood up and – again using both gestures and bayonet tips – forced the nurses into a line facing the sea about 10 metres away. At the far right of the line stood Irene Drummond, quietly encouraging and bustling over the wounded girls like the mother hen that she was. To her left were Clare Halligan, Rosetta Wight and Flo Casson, each too weak and in too much pain to stand alone so they were supported on either side by sisters and friends. A line of 23 was formed, the 22 nurses joined by the elderly civilian who had refused to leave her husband and who now stood weeping in the middle of the line. On the far left, the line ended with Alma Beard, a 28-year-old from Toodyay in Western Australia, Vivian Bullwinkel and Jenny Kerr. There was no shouting and no tears, no panic and no hysteria, even when two of the nurses had to be prodded into line by Japanese bayonets.

At the end of the line, Alma Beard leaned across and said to Vivian: 'Bully, there are two things I've always hated in my life, the Japanese and the sea, and today I've ended up with both.' Vivian was unable to reply as she was in another place. She was looking out to sea, thinking: 'How can something as dirty and evil as this be happening in a place that is so beautiful?' The thoughts swirled around and around and flashed into and out of her consciousness. The one that gave her both comfort and solace was that, in a very short while, she would be reunited with her dead father and that, some time in the future, her mother and brother John would join them, and it would all be like it had been when she was young and free and happy. There was no direct order given, but the line began to shuffle forward. As they began to move, they all heard Irene Drummond call out: 'Chins up, girls. I'm proud of you and I love you all.' There was a moment of almost supernatural silence as they set off. Several of the girls looked across and made eye contact with friends, but most just looked straight ahead, seeing something that no-one else would or could ever see. And then the killing began.

The machine gunner was good, but that was his business.

He fired in short bursts, concentrating on two or three prisoners at a time and not rushing up and down the line. He aimed for the middle of the back, where the vital organs are, and he made sure that what he aimed at, he hit. Irene Drummond was still a couple of metres short of the water's edge when the machine gunner opened fire. She was hit immediately and knocked head first into the sand. The impact of landing hard knocked her glasses off and, as she groped for them in the sand, a second bullet struck her, killing her instantly. Flo and Rosetta and Clare and the sisters supporting them fell under the gun, grouped together in death as they had been in life. The other girls didn't falter but kept walking, now in water that reached their ankles and then reached their knees. Several now prayed aloud, the Lord's Prayer mixing with the Hail Marys as one by one the nurses were hit and knocked headlong into the water by the force of the bullets.

Second last in line, Vivian glanced quickly to her right and saw some of her friends die, most of them silently and some saying the names of their loved ones. She wondered whether she should be saying something but that thought was never fully formed because something like a sledgehammer smashed into her back and she felt herself falling forward as everything around her turned to black.

At another shouted order, the firing ceased. Issuing staccato instructions, Captain Orita split his men into three sections. One section approached the bodies of the nurses on the beach and in the shallows; any who showed the least sign of life was bayoneted through the heart. A second section worked its way through the wounded on the makeshift stretchers in the shade of the trees, bayoneting them all, while the third section went to the fishermen's hut where the severely wounded had been treated. They, too, were bayoneted to death and left where they lay. Re-forming on the beach, the soldiers cleaned their bayonets before forming up into a single file and following their captain off the beach and onto the track that would take them back to Muntok. Just before the track joined the main road to Muntok, the patrol walked past the struggling group of mothers and children. The Japanese officer stopped and looked very carefully at them before, with a tilt of his head, he led his men away.

Behind them, Radji Beach was at peace again, silent and still but for the lapping of the waves where the sea met the shore. Among the crumpled forms lying individually or in little groups on the sand or in the shallows were the earthly remains of Irene Drummond and the girls whose lives she had shared with Olive Paschke. They were their girls, their sisters, and they had loved them all. Lainie Balfour-Ogilvy, Alma Beard, Ada Bridge, Flo Casson, Mary Cuthbertson, Buddy Elmes, Lorna Fairweather, Peggy Farmaner, Clare Halligan, Nancy Harris, Minnie Hodgson, Nell Keats, Jenny Kerr, Mary McGlade, Kathleen Neuss, Florence Salmon, Jean Stewart, Mona Tait, Rosetta Wight and Peggy Wilmot. The great letter writers and the beautiful singers, the raconteurs, the social butterflies and the serious thinkers were all gone. The city girls and the country girls, and the girls from in between had their lives ended long before they should have. They were gone and would not be coming back to families and friends. All had seen and experienced more than their fair share of pain and suffering. But now, all too soon, their own pain and suffering was over and they, too, were at peace.*

* * *

---

* Ada Bridge was a Sydney nurse who was originally from the Hunter Valley; Minnie Hodgson was a 32-year-old from Western Australia's wheat belt. Flo Salmon, a native Sydneysider, was just 26 when she died, while Jean Stewart, also from Sydney, was 37. Mona Tait was a Queenslander who trained in Canberra and nursed in Sydney.

As efficient as they had been with their guns and bayonets, the Japanese had failed to kill all their prisoners at Radji Beach. On the small beach beyond the rocky headland that marked Radji's southern extremity, an American civilian named Eric German started to move when he was certain that the Japanese had gone and would not be returning. He had been bayoneted once from behind and, looking down below the blindfold he was wearing, had actually seen the tip of the Japanese bayonet emerging from his chest. Unbelievably, the blade had missed all his vital organs and German had lain flat and still, convincing the Japanese that he was dead. When he was certain that he was alone, German tested his body; he was alive and he also found that he was mobile, so he moved into the jungle at the back of the beach and spent the rest of Monday and Tuesday recuperating and regaining his physical and mental strength. Eric German would eventually follow a series of paths and tracks out of the jungle and onto the road to Muntok where he surrendered to the Japanese, telling them that he was a shipwreck survivor who had suffered a number of wounds when his ship was sunk by Japanese bombers. Interned in a succession of Japanese camps, he would survive the war, but would not mention his Radji Beach experiences to anyone until it was over.

Some 80 metres from where Eric German lay feigning death, Stoker Ernest Lloyd had washed up on the spit of sand that, at low tide, extended seawards from the rocky headland. The salt water had washed out the bullet wounds to his scalp and leg, but he had been unconscious for perhaps 30 minutes. The nurses had been shot around 1030 hours and it was probably past 1100 hours when Lloyd regained consciousness, realised where he was, and made his first tentative movements in an effort to stand up. When he made it to his feet, Lloyd found that he was able to walk, slowly and with a limp, but he was mobile enough to make it back to the headland, down Radji Beach and as far away from the murder scenes as possible. He did not want to be in the area in case the Japanese returned. When he felt his strength giving out, he moved a few metres into the jungle until he found a place to hide.

As he traversed the beach, Lloyd saw the bodies of several nurses. Although he did not stop to make any sort of formal examination, he noted that all had been shot, while several of the bodies also exhibited bayonet wounds. The dresses of some were above their waists, exposing their underwear, but it appeared to Lloyd that the bullets and bayonets and the waves had conspired to leave several of the bodies in the unnatural positions in which they lay. After several days of sheltering in the jungle, and seeking water and food from a Chinese man who befriended him, Lloyd realised he could not last much longer. He was barely surviving and he was putting both himself and the Chinese man in danger. Lloyd walked into Muntok and surrendered to the Japanese. Keeping his own counsel, Ernest Lloyd would also wait until the war was over to tell his story.

Neither German nor Lloyd saw the tall, slender figure of Vivian Bullwinkel wash up onto Radji Beach. The bullet that hit her like a sledgehammer had entered on her left side, just above the hip but below her ribs, and had passed through her body, exiting just to the left of her navel and without hitting any major organs or blood vessels. The impact of the bullet had knocked her face forward into the water and she had lost consciousness, only regaining it partially, but enough to turn her head to the side in the low and sloppy waves. As she drifted on those waves, she also drifted in and out of consciousness; at one point, she imagined she could hear Japanese soldiers laughing and running down the beach, while at another time she felt she vomited up several litres of sea water. Eventually, Vivian drifted back onto

Radji Beach, probably around 20 minutes after she had been shot.

It was like a bad dream for Vivian. Despite being a nurse, and one who had seen all the horrors of war in Malaya and Singapore, she still believed that when you were shot, you died. She had been shot but she was still alive. When she glanced back at the beach, she saw bodies floating in the shallows, while a look to one side revealed more cast haphazardly across the sand. She knew she was alive, though, and that to stay alive she had to move. She also felt cold: 'So cold that my only thought was to find some warm spot to die.' It was shock setting in, and Vivian had both the training and the discipline to recognise it for what it was and to react accordingly. She rose and made her way across the beach and to the jungle track that she had walked down the day before. She only made it 20 metres back into the jungle before an overwhelming fatigue washed over her and she knew she was about to collapse. Leaving the track, Vivian went another dozen or so metres into the jungle to where two shrubs had created a den, a small dark cave where she knew she would be safe. She crawled in, curled up, and went to sleep.

She awoke later in the day, just as the sun was setting. Her first action was to examine where she had been shot. The entry and exit wounds appeared to be clean and there had been relatively little bleeding, so she assumed the wound wasn't life threatening and would respond to whatever basic treatment she had available. She also mused over her fate: 21 of her friends had been killed while she had survived. This may have been part of some larger cosmic design but there was also a more practical aspect to Vivian's survival; she was the tallest of the Australian nurses, several centimetres taller than those on either side of her in the line. Had she been their height, the bullet that struck her below the ribs would probably have passed directly through her heart.

Vivian again drifted into a deep sleep and awoke to bright sunlight and the sound of voices. Peeking through the leaves and branches that provided her cover, she caught glimpses of a small group of Japanese soldiers on Radji Beach. Although they appeared unaware of the possibility of anyone surviving the killings on the beach, she waited at least half an hour after they had disappeared up the jungle track before she was prepared to move. She knew that she did have to move, though, as several days had passed since her last proper meal, and she was very hungry and had a raging thirst. She took the path to the beach and turned towards the fishermen's hut and the freshwater spring nearby. She was not prepared to walk on the beach proper though, and moved slowly through the palms and shrubs that fringed it. As she approached the hut, Vivian heard a hoarse whisper: 'Sister, sister . . .'

The nurse had found another patient, one who, too, had survived Radji and who needed assistance. He was, he said, an English soldier, a private, and his name was Pat Kingsley. He was in a very bad way, but revived a little after Vivian brought him water from the spring. He told her that he, too, had been fleeing Singapore when his ship was caught up in a Japanese invasion fleet on the night of Sunday, 15 February. Illuminated by searchlights, it had been quickly sunk by Japanese shellfire. Shrapnel from one of those shells had sliced through the upper part of Kingsley's right arm, removing most of the muscle and other tissue, and smashing and exposing the major part of the shoulder socket. He could recall being dragged out of the water and into a lifeboat, and later the lifeboat washing up on a beach with a bonfire, but not a lot else. He thought he had heard gunfire and knew he had been bayoneted through the chest, but that had been two days ago. When he realised he could move, he had crawled into the jungle and had been lying there, waiting to die, when he had seen Vivian's light grey uniform going past.

Vivian examined Kingsley and quickly determined that he was lucky to be alive. The splinter wound to his upper arm appeared particularly severe – a large bone mass was visible – but it was a clean wound, and Vivian believed that it would not be life threatening and would probably respond to simple medical procedures. Kingsley also had two bayonet wounds in his chest and although one of them had clearly missed all the vital spots, the second had pierced a lung. While the entry wound would heal, Vivian was concerned about internal damage and bleeding. It was not necessarily a mortal wound, but one that would require X-rays and hospital treatment.

Kingsley was too weak to be able to move any distance, so Vivian explored further into the jungle and found another den that was large enough for both of them. She was surprised to learn that she had slept through an entire day, and finding Kingsley had, she admitted, given her another reason to try to go on. After making certain that he was comfortable and that their den was well hidden, she returned to Radji Beach. She was unable to look closely at the cluster of bodies near the water's edge, but did see that one or two other bodies had washed up further down the beach. An examination of the lifeboats revealed that most of the medical supplies had disappeared, but she was able to retrieve some water bottles on that first trip. These she filled and took back to Kingsley in the den.

On her second trip later in the day, Vivian collected some life jackets. She thought that she and Kingsley might be able to pick them apart and use the canvas to floor their den. On later trips she collected more life jackets plus any little odds and ends she thought may prove useful. On one trip, she removed a shirt from one of the dead sailors. It was only slightly torn and bloodstained, and was in much better condition than the one Kingsley was wearing. He seemed to appreciate her thoughtfulness. During each of these trips to the beach, Vivian's eyes were inevitably drawn to the bodies of her friends. She knew they should be buried, but neither she nor Kingsley had the strength or the implements to undertake such a task. In time, they became just another part of the background. Exhausted by their exertions, Vivian and Kingsley slept well that night.

During the next day, which Vivian calculated was Thursday, 19 February, Vivian and Kingsley discussed the future they now dared to believe they had. During one of her trips to the beach Vivian found a tin of condensed milk, which she brought back to share with Kingsley. Using part of a spar and a jagged piece of steel, Vivian punched a hole in the tin. Although they shared the contents, Vivian made sure that Kingsley got the lion's share. It was food, of course, that formed the basis for many of their conversations about the future. What it was, where it could be found, and how they would eat it. It was obvious to both that if they stayed where they were and relied on windfalls and flotsam for food, they would soon starve to death. They had a plentiful supply of fresh water, enough for both drinking and washing themselves, but there was no way that they could supply themselves with enough food to live. Their two alternatives were to surrender to the Japanese or to beg food from the villagers in the kampong that Vivian had visited with Bill Sedgeman just a few days earlier.

Neither believed that surrendering to the Japanese was an alternative they would survive. While they could claim that they had only recently been shipwrecked and washed ashore, their bullet and bayonet wounds would suggest a different story. As the only survivors of a massacre that had claimed the lives of up to 100 unarmed prisoners they could expect to be summarily executed, if only to cover up the larger crime that had been committed.* In the end there was really only one alternative – Vivian would walk to the native kampong to beg for food.

Around 0900 hours the next morning, Friday, 20 February, Vivian walked the kilometre or so to the kampong. While no-one in the village seemed too surprised to see her, she was ignored by the old men who had spoken to Bill Sedgeman, and had to again tell her story to a group of slightly younger women. This she did using a combination of gestures and the smattering of Malay words she knew, although it is likely that her gaunt appearance said more than any of her words. Vivian left the kampong with several little packages of food wrapped in banana leaves – vegetables, rice, with some kind of meat mixed in. She estimated that she and Kingsley could make these food supplies last for two days, which they did.

The food and shelter worked well for Kingsley, and over the next couple of days Vivian thought he was beginning to recover from his shocking injuries. The wound on his arm had not become infected and new skin appeared to be growing around the gaping edges of the wound. The bayonet wounds in his chest also appeared to be healing nicely, but they were both concerned that he may have internal injuries. Kingsley's breathing rattled and wheezed, while coughing hurt him and brought up dark phlegm. But he said that he did feel better, and when Vivian set off to walk to the kampong on the Sunday he said he might accompany her on the next visit. The women at the kampong again gave Vivian little packets of food but the atmosphere was a little strained, and Vivian quickly thanked the women before returning to the beach.

---

* At the subsequent Tokyo War Crimes Tribunal hearings, it was accepted that 50 men, 22 women and 10 stretcher cases were murdered on Radji Beach.

Because they had so little to do in and around their den, Vivian and Kingsley often talked together as they sat on their life jackets at the edge of the beach. Some of their talk was about the future, as both believed they would survive for the short term at least, and some was about the past. Kingsley told Vivian about his native Yorkshire where he had grown up and where he had left behind a wife, Elsie, and a young family. Vivian spoke of growing up in Broken Hill, of her father's work in the mines there, and of living on the edges of the vast and empty interior of Australia. She also continued her daily visits to Radji Beach, noting how the tides would sometimes wash bodies up on shore while a subsequent tide would wash them back out again. One morning she was surprised to find a beach empty of all bodies: a particularly high tide appeared to have scoured the beach clean of all traces of the killings, including the bodies of the Australian nurses.*

That was probably around Wednesday, 25 February, the day Vivian made another visit to the kampong. Although Kingsley was by now walking without too much difficulty, Vivian was not comfortable with the older men of the village and did not know how they would react to the presence of a European male. She convinced Kingsley to remain behind for this visit. Her concerns were not without foundation. Upon her arrival at the kampong the old men shouted what seemed to be abuse at her and made threatening gestures. Two of the women approached her with

---

* In the evidence she presented to the tribunal, Vivian stated that in the days following the massacre, nurses' bodies were washed up onto the beach then washed away on a regular basis. She said that she was unable to identify any of them and did not think to go to collect their identity discs. In later recollections, she noted the usual flotsam and jetsam from the sea was washed up on Radji Beach and one morning she found the body of a young Asian woman. It, too, was reclaimed by the sea at the next high tide. Another *Vyner Brooke* survivor, the teenaged Ralph Armstrong, wrote years later that he believed a party of prisoners were taken to Radji Beach to construct a large funeral pyre. All the bodies were placed on this and were reduced to ashes. There is no evidence that anything like this ever occurred.

food parcels though, and after handing them over they explained to Vivian that this was the last food they would be giving her. They suggested that the village elders were both angry and afraid because they had been told that any native who assisted Europeans would be executed by the Japanese. The women also told Vivian that there were others like her already in Muntok, European ladies wearing uniforms with Red Cross armbands. Then they turned their backs on Vivian and walked away.

Back at Radji Beach, Vivian discussed these events with Kingsley. They were not quite back to where they started as both had put on some condition since the morning they met, but they were faced with the same dilemma they had faced on that morning. If they remained at Radji Beach they would starve to death and if they surrendered to the Japanese they might be killed. Both considered that this latter outcome was a little less likely as it was well over a week since the massacre, and no physical evidence remained to suggest that it had ever occurred. They believed that they could concoct a credible story about being shipwrecked a long way away and struggling along jungle trails to Muntok. In the end, it came down to a choice between the certainty of death by starvation and neglect versus the possibility of death by shooting. There was really no choice at all; they would surrender to the Japanese at Muntok and take their chances.

The decision being made, Kingsley had a favour to ask of Vivian. His birthday was on 27 February, he told her, and he would be turning 39 that day. Because of the uncertainty about what would happen after they surrendered he wanted to spend his birthday as a free man, and so asked Vivian if they could delay their surrender until 28 February. Vivian liked the idea and agreed.

PART THREE

Setting Sun

CHAPTER 10

Sumatra

Quite early on the morning of Saturday, 28 February 1942, Vivian Bullwinkel and Pat Kingsley finished the last of the food given to them by the women of the kampong. Vivian filled water bottles with fresh water from the nearby spring, and together they walked away from Radji Beach. They followed the jungle track to the kampong area, which they skirted, and continued on the other side of the village. Within ten minutes they came to a surfaced road and turned in the direction the village women had indicated would take them to Muntok. They walked along this road for barely five minutes when a motor car appeared around a bend ahead of them, slowed down and came to a stop alongside them. The back door opened and out stepped a Japanese officer, complete with sword.

The officer did not appear surprised to see Vivian and Kingsley walking along the road and, using polite gestures, he invited them to join him in the back of the car. Once they were settled he spoke to the driver, who turned the car around and headed back the way it had come. In the back, neither side spoke the other side's language, so there was no real conversation. The officer had some bananas which he shared, and Vivian and Kingsley had barely finished eating before the car pulled up in front of a police station in what appeared to be the main street of Muntok. The officer hopped out first and opened the back door for his passengers before escorting them into the police station, where he saluted another Japanese officer inside and then departed without saying a word.

Chairs were provided for the prisoners, and they were asked a few simple questions by an English-speaking sergeant. They answered along the lines of their agreed story, that their ship had been sunk a long way away over a week ago, and after their life raft had been washed ashore they had started walking, using native trails and living off fruit they had found or stolen from kampongs and drinking water from the many streams they had to cross. The sergeant seemed disinterested in their story, but Vivian kept her water bottle in front of the bullet hole in her dress just in case. After a few minutes the sergeant stopped writing and called out to soldiers in the yard outside. Indicating that this was an escort, he led Vivian and Kingsley outside and pointed towards structures that seemed to be part of a camp a fair way off in the distance.

The structures were part of the coolie lines, and some time later, two of their escorts led Kingsley through the gate into the men's quarters, while another two took Vivian another 50 metres to the women's quarters. They unlocked and opened the gate, led Vivian inside, then returned the way they had come. A number of women in the yard stopped to look at her when she was brought in. One of them, wearing the uniform of an AANS nurse, waited until the Japanese soldiers had left and then took a step forward, opened her arms and said: 'Welcome, Bully.' Vivian could not hold back any longer; she simply burst into tears.

Wilma Oram was among the first nurses to reach Vivian and hugged her tight as she cried. The small group then moved into one of the coolie huts that had been taken over by the Australians, and waited until all the other Australians had arrived. In the absence of matrons Paschke and Drummond, Nesta James was the senior nurse among the survivors from the 2/10th, and the senior nurse among them all. Jean Ashton was the senior survivor from the 2/13th and Mavis Hannah her equivalent from the 2/4th CCS. When these three were present, Vivian told the girls what had happened at Radji Beach, and of how she alone had lived when all their friends had died. She told the story sparely and without emotion, and in a way that all present would remember and several would record, almost verbatim, in the diaries and notebooks they had begun writing.

As Vivian told her story there were gasps and caught breaths among the listeners, but they let her continue uninterrupted and, when she had finished, most of the nurses had tears streaming down their faces. There was a brief silence and then Nesta James spoke up. Vivian's story, she said, must never be shared with anyone outside the small remaining group of Australian nurses. If the news of her survival became known to the Japanese, it would be a death sentence for her and probably for anyone else who knew the story as well. All those present were asked to pledge their silence about the events on Radji Beach, and to always support Vivian's fictitious story of shipwreck and survival, which had apparently been accepted by the Japanese as truthful. Vivian was led to a sleeping space and encouraged to rest while close friends looked after her. The other nurses returned to their various tasks and to their main recreation – attempting to piece together the puzzle of what had happened to their friends. Vivian had supplied the largest piece of that puzzle to date.

Although they did not know it at the time, the coolie lines at Muntok brought together all the surviving nurses who had sailed from Singapore aboard the *Vyner Brooke*. Before Vivian's arrival, most of the discussions about the fate of the missing nurses had been speculative. Several of the girls had seen Olive Paschke's life raft on its voyage down Banka Strait, and Betty Jeffrey and Iole Harper had confirmed that it was swept a lot further than any of the others had known. Many more of the girls had seen either the bonfire on the beach in the distance or else had been close enough to see people around it, and now Vivian had been able to explain the circumstances of that bonfire and what had happened to the people there with it. The fate of Olive Paschke and her raft, with Jess Dorsch, Merle Trenerry, Gladys McDonald, Mary Clarke and Caroline Ennis with her little children, would forever remain a mystery.

All the girls felt the loss of Matron Paschke, even those who had not been under her direct command. Jessie Blanch recorded: 'Matron didn't arrive, and we were terribly upset about that. She was such a wonderful person. We thought everything would be all right if Matron was there.' Other losses were felt equally as keenly. It was at the coolie lines that Wilma was first informed about Mona's death, after her friends felt that she had recovered sufficiently from her wounds. The news came as a shock to Wilma, and it left a hole in her life that could never be filled. But it also started something else, a desire to help those who seemed helpless and, at that moment, Vivian seemed the most helpless of all. Wilma determined that she would not let Vivian go the way Mona had gone, at least not while she still had breath in her body. She moved Vivian next to her in their sleeping quarters and began sharing her food and her mosquito net with her.

As Vivian grew stronger, seemingly taking strength from the solidarity of the Australian nurses, her friends brought her up to date on what had happened to them in the two weeks since they had been shipwrecked. Many of them spoke about coming ashore or being picked up covered in oil, so heavily saturated with it that the clothes they were wearing had to be discarded and their hair so matted that it had to be cut as close to their skulls as possible. Others spoke of being brought to Muntok in the hours after the Japanese had occupied the area, how they were first held in an abandoned pigsty before being crowded into the customs house, and of how they were then moved just 100 metres to the Muntok cinema to join hundreds of others from about 28 different ships, and where the Japanese violence had been both casual and random. How the sick and badly injured were removed and taken to the police barracks which had been converted into an emergency hospital.

Many spoke of the fortitude and sheer will to live displayed by Betty Jeffrey and Iole Harper. Vivian learned of the 72 hours they had spent in the water, the first day as part of the group around Matron Paschke's life raft and the rest alone, the two of them swept along by the fluky currents and struggling through impenetrable mangrove swamps. Both were in the camp hospital being treated for an assortment of injuries including mangrove spike wounds that had become infected and, in Betty's case, badly rope-burned hands. On their arrival at the camp both were in such a bad way that they were given morphia shots and had basically slept for the next three days. Their prognosis was now positive. Vivian also heard the sad news about Olga Neubrunner's stillbirth and how little Misha Warman had been orphaned.

The coolie lines were also described to Vivian as she was

taken on a guided tour. The lines themselves were basically an earth quadrangle with dormitories on either side. The Australian nurses occupied part of one of those dormitories and were expected to sleep on platforms within. The main problem was the platforms were made of concrete, angling down slightly, and while each of the girls was given about her own body width to sleep on, they felt like sardines in a rather large tin. At the foot of each dormitory was a deep concrete drain which they used as the toilet, and which continued to flow through and out of the camp. Their drinking water came from one tap, which had a very limited flow and was always attended by a long queue. There was also a fairly constant trickle from another tap into the tong, a concrete basin with ladles for splashing water on dirty bodies, which, in its turn, usually had a queue lined up for the sluicing down which constituted a wash.

When Vivian arrived there were around 600 people held in the lines, and they represented a wide cross-section of people. There were nuns as well as servicemen from various services and countries, civilian men, women and children who had been captured and interned, or who had surrendered voluntarily. An informal survey conducted by one of the nurses suggested there were shipwreck survivors from at least 70 different vessels. Among those taken to the coolie lines were a number of wounded, and senior nurses and officers decided that an area should be set aside for them. Part of one of the dormitories was used for this purpose and there were three doctors, all women. One was an Englishwoman, a Dr Smith, and the second was Dr Jean McDowell, a Scotswoman who would become a favourite of the Australians. The third was Dr Goldberg, still not trusted by most of the Australians. A hospital was organised and staffed as well as could be expected in the circumstances. Only half of the surviving Australian nurses were considered fit enough to work in that hospital, and those who did work could only do so in short shifts because of their weakness from injury and exposure. Their hospital also had no soap and only one towel.

The food situation was only marginally better. All prisoners were given two meals a day by the volunteer kitchen crews, and both meals consisted of rice, but rice that was hard to cook and harder to eat. To receive their rations, men and women prisoners had to line up in separate queues, using whatever they had in the way of crockery and cutlery. Fortunately, some of the Australian nurses had gone scrounging within the lines, and were especially successful in some of the recently abandoned storage areas, returning with a set of quite exquisite little Chinese bowls. These served all of them. Mosquitoes were a problem at night, as were the Japanese guards, who seemed to delight in walking through the dormitories and shining torches on the faces of anyone they suspected was asleep. Occasionally, some variety was added by pricking people on the soles of their feet with bayonets, or turning all the camp lights on, waiting until babies and children were awake and screaming, and then turning them off again.

A second Australian scrounging expedition was also fruitful, with a double mattress being discovered and brought back to the girls' dormitory. It was less successful when put to use though, as Winnie May Davis, Pat Gunther, Jessie Doyle, Pat Blake and Betty Jeffrey, who had found the prize, also found that sleeping on it gave them less space than sleeping on the concrete.

Vivian was also brought up to date on her new circumstances. For instance, there were no opportunities to beg, borrow or steal clothes that may have been lost or damaged in the sinking of the *Vyner Brooke* or in the subsequent time spent adrift. Fortunately for them, there had been a supply of sailors' trousers in one of the huts at the coolie lines; one pair of trousers easily converted into two pairs of shorts and a suntop for the nurses, and that was what many of them would be wearing for the foreseeable future. Those who didn't have shorts and tops were generally dressed in sarongs, with their uniforms repaired and put away for the time being.

Vivian was forced to revisit painful memories at the end of her first week in the coolie lines. A message was sent to her from a civilian doctor at the camp hospital saying that one of the patients there was dying. The patient was an English soldier named Pat Kingsley, and he had asked if he could see Sister Vivian Bullwinkel, AANS, before he died. When Vivian arrived, the doctor explained that his patient had a perforated lung and that the internal wound had become infected. In a modern hospital with modern medicine, Kingsley would be treated and would recover without any complications. But this was not a modern hospital and the doctor simply did not have any medicine capable of stopping the infection that would shortly end Kingsley's life.

Pat Kingsley was in a deep coma when Vivian arrived at his bedside, and he never regained consciousness. He died a short time later with Vivian holding his hand. She held it for a while longer before folding Kingsley's arms across his chest and turning to leave. As she did so, she nodded to the patient in the next bed, a man with crude bandages around his head, shoulder and leg. His name was Ernest Lloyd, and he was a stoker in the Royal Navy.

The next morning, the Australian nurses were given one hour's notice of movement. They were to pack their belongings and fall in at the camp's makeshift parade ground. They were leaving the coolie lines at Muntok and were transferring to a new camp, across Banka Strait, in the city of Palembang in Sumatra. It was 2 March 1942.

* * *

The move occurred in a disjointed and haphazard way that the girls would come to associate with most aspects of Japanese wartime administration. Having been awakened very early and given one hour to prepare, they set off just before dawn and on empty stomachs. They marched in a ragged line with the civilian internees through Muntok to the jetty, where they waited a while before boarding a small and dirty coastal freighter for the short trip across the strait and the considerably longer trip up the Musi River to Palembang, the largest city in southern Sumatra. Short it may have been but sweet it definitely wasn't. The sanitary arrangements aboard ship were challenging. The single toilet available to the prisoners was a 60-centimetre square cubicle made of rough timber and attached to the side of the freighter. While an effort for some to use, for Mary Brown it was an almost insurmountable challenge. She was too large to fit easily into the cubicle, and several of the Australian nurses were required to help her squeeze in backwards; an even greater effort was required to extricate her.

And then there was the weather. Crossing Banka Strait was simple and the breeze refreshing but the Musi River leg was undertaken in increasingly hot and oppressive conditions. There was no protection from the sun and most of the girls were hatless. At one point it rained and they were all drenched through. As the rain was easing off, the Japanese guards reappeared from wherever they had been sheltering and produced some old tarpaulins for shelter. The rain finished, the sun came out, and those underneath the tarpaulins broiled.

The boat reached Palembang around 1830 hours and there they disembarked via a small and rickety plank and sat on a wharf with their little bundles of possessions for two hours. They were then taken by trucks through darkened streets and jeering crowds – a few of the Australians took the opportunity to jeer back – to an abandoned school, the Mullah School at Bukit

Besar, which was to be their home for who knew how long. They were met at the school by British and Dutch servicemen who had a surprise for them, a hot meal of stew containing things most of the girls didn't recognise, followed by a nice hot cup of tea. The group was divided into groups of 40, each of which was assigned one of the schoolrooms. The lights were left on all night and the windows were left open, with thousands of mosquitoes responding to this obvious invitation.

The next day the senior serviceman present at the school, Air Commodore Modin, approached the Japanese with a request that the Australian nurses be treated as military personnel rather than civilians, and therefore accorded the status of prisoners of war rather than internees. The Japanese refused the request in less time than it took to translate it.* They also informed Modin that all the women and children would be relocated to a separate camp later that day. Before they did so, however, Vivian and two of the senior Australian nurses, Nesta and Jean Ashton, approached Modin and, in strict secrecy, told him the story of what had happened at Radji Beach. Vivian spared no details, and gave the air commodore the names of all those who had been killed. The Australians did so, they said, because they did not know what their fate might be and they wanted at least one senior officer to know the story.

From the school, the women marched that afternoon to a suburban enclave based around a street called Irenelaan, where the female internees were given houses to occupy. The whole enclosed area comprised 14 medium-sized brick houses arranged in an L-shape, and internees were assigned to each. The houses

---

* Appeals to the Japanese for Red Cross support for the nurses were dismissed at the same time. The Japanese, throughout the war, strongly resisted granting the International Red Cross access to their camps or to the nominal rolls which were kept only perfunctorily.

were typical Dutch colonial homes, freestanding, built above the ground with space underneath, with a front veranda and steps leading up to the front door. In occupying these residences, the women formed 'kongsis', the Chinese word for groups. Most of the kongsis at Irenelaan were based on personal friendship or, sometimes, family relationships or social status, especially among the Dutch internees. The largest kongsi was the single one formed by the Australian nurses, who were given two houses to themselves. The 2/13th girls occupied one and the 2/10th and 2/4th CCS the other. Although the barriers between the units were starting to break down, the girls still preferred to be with those they had known the longest.

Irenelaan was, at first glance, an attractive site for an internment camp. Situated on the top of one of Palembang's small hills, it was light and airy with a view across country to the oil installations around Pleidju, themselves a sight as they were surrounded by barrage balloons. One of the downsides of the location was the water supply which, because of gravity and increased demand, would often slow to a trickle by mid-morning. A second was that the Japanese used the hillside behind the camp for training, and on many occasions the girls would be startled by blood-curdling yells as soldiers practised bayonet drills. At other times they were startled by small groups of soldiers, covered in leaves and twigs, who darted from house to house across the camp in pursuit of invisible enemies.

Unfortunately, the houses were separated by two other houses occupied by Dutch internees, but were close enough for both formal and informal visits. There was also little in the way of furnishings left behind by the houses' previous occupants. One double bedstead and a few chairs seemed to be all that could be found, but, joy of joys, one of the houses contained a working electric stove. It also contained a child's cot; at barely

150 centimetres tall, Nesta James was the only one who could fit comfortably in it and, even for her, it was a bit of a tight squeeze. Mitz – Pearl Mittelheuser – was elected captain of one of the houses, with Jean Ashton captain of the other.

One of the most immediate effects of the Japanese refusal to recognise the nurses as prisoners of war rather than internees was that they were not eligible for any payments like the male prisoners were. Although these payments were barely more than tokens, as officers, the girls would have been able to afford to purchase foodstuffs and clothing that were now denied to them. Fortunately, on two or three occasions in the first two months they were there, some Dutch internees turned up unannounced bringing hot soup and a few small luxuries like soap and toothbrushes. It was not a lot, but it was a lot more than they had been able to bring to the camp.

Relations between the various groups started off pretty well, and there were never any real conflicts, partly because the Japanese allowed an internal administration to be formed. There were some differences between the various cultures, though. Veronica Clancy was always intrigued by the Dutch nuns and their quarters just down the road from the Australians: 'A weird assortment of clothes could be seen hanging on the lines. Nuns' habits, petticoats and bloomers which must have covered their knees. As one wit remarked, "Perhaps they don't put so much faith in the Lord after all." What we would have given for those yards of material.'

While conditions at Irenelaan were never good, to begin with at least they were relatively benign and for several months the nurses were able to establish and maintain basic rules for themselves, individually and collectively, within the wider camp. Individual characters and characteristics soon emerged in the group. Veronica Clancy was regarded as one of the great givers, and was frequently the central character in elaborate stories because she had arrived in Muntok wearing nothing more than a navy greatcoat and a corset. Plus she had a wicked sense of humour and an egalitarian attitude. Jess Doyle owned the only working watch among the girls, and was constantly being sought out and asked the time, although no-one was really certain why the time of day was important. For some reason, however, Jenny Greer was probably the most popular of all in those early months, among civilian internees as well as the Australian nurses; it was soon established that she owned the only pair of eyebrow pluckers in the camp.

One of the most threatening confrontations with their Japanese captors was also one of the earliest challenges the girls faced. Their internment camp was run by the Japanese Army, and the commanding officer was a Captain Miachi, an English-speaker who had spent some time in Malaya before the war. Miachi fancied himself as a bit of a 'looker'; he parted his hair in the European style and had a small, pencil-thin moustache. Around a month after the Australians moved into Irenelaan Captain Miachi announced that the staff was establishing an officers' club, which was strange as there were only six Japanese officers at Irenelaan, and that they expected the Australian nurses to help staff the club and also act as 'hostesses'. It was obvious that a great deal of thought had gone into the venture. To begin with there was a movement of housing, with the Dutch houses between the Australians being emptied, and all the Australian girls moving into those from the two they had lived in. Both of the houses they vacated were designated as the 'clubrooms', and local labourers spent several days taking beds, settees and even a piano into the houses, which were also tidied up and made more club-like in their lighting and fittings.

The Japanese had even identified those they wanted to work at the club – Jessie Blanch, Winnie May Davis, Jess Doyle, Pearl Mittelheuser and Nesta James – all small, dark and attractive. It was patently obvious what the Japanese wanted and expected, and the nurses discussed at length what the most appropriate response to their demands might be. When asked directly why those girls had been nominated to work as hostesses, the senior Japanese officer replied equally frankly that they were chosen precisely because they were 'medically clean and free of disease'. In among the discussion over how best to deal with the situation, one of the nurses stated: 'To think of all the times I said "No!" I wish I hadn't now.'

In postwar interviews and in their writings, a number of nurses would later describe how, instead of the requested half dozen, around 20 nurses turned up at the club's opening, all dressed as unattractively as possible, with no make-up and with their hair greased down. Split into two groups with each group assigned to one of the houses, all the girls refused the alcohol they were offered and refused to dance with their Japanese hosts. One nurse who believed she had been touched inappropriately smacked her molester across the face. The evening ended in farce, the Japanese on one side of the club's main lounge, the Australians on the other. The majority of the Australians were sent back to their houses, but four remained. They were not there long, as they made it quite plain there would be a free-for-all if any one of them was touched. They, too, were dismissed.

Afterwards Jean Ashton and Nesta James, the senior Australian nurses, formally complained about the attempt by the Japanese to force the girls into prostitution. Their complaint went through the senior Dutch Red Cross representative in the camp and on to the Japanese commander in chief for all Japanese and auxiliary forces in Sumatra. Four weeks later, and without any further incident, the club was closed down and most of the Japanese camp officers transferred elsewhere. It was the end of what most believed was the most unsavoury incident in their first 12 months of imprisonment. It took a lot longer for the Australians to forgive the Englishwoman who had done all the planning and catering for the club. A young mother, she had shared their experiences aboard the *Vyner Brooke*.

While it could never be described as a time of plenty, compared to what had gone before it and what was to follow, the first 12 months at Irenelaan was a time of comparative fun and happiness. Though a long way from home and with practically no contact with or news from the outside world, the 32 young women had survived the traumas of warfare and shipwreck and were relatively safe and secure in their two little houses. The goodwill and comradeship that had characterised their pre-war service and the dark days of retreat and surrender grew to encompass the nurses from the other units and in a short while the girls grew into what was really just one extended family.

Although it was not and never could be the type of life they would choose to live, the Australians decided, individually and as a group, to try to make the best they could of their circumstances. This group approach, more than anything else, differentiated the nurses from many of the other groups with whom they shared their imprisonment. Their kongsi was all-embracing; it did not depend on unit, state of birth, age or any other factor. Within 12 months they were as solid a team as could be found in a prison camp anywhere. The other prisoners sorted themselves into family groups within language groups within social classes, and suffered needlessly through these sometimes artificial distinctions. Dutch colonial families, in particular, had difficulties accepting a subservient status, and many would later die needlessly as a result.

If nothing else, the Australian nurses proved to be good scroungers and within days of their arrival had 'claimed' an enormous old black cooking pot, which they named Matilda, and an old piano in reasonable condition. It took 14 nurses half an hour to move the piano from a Dutch house next door to one of theirs, and several days to dry it out in the sunlight before it could be tuned and used. It was an immediate success, and a couple of the girls – Shirley Gardam in particular – proved to be competent players. Shirley was a young Tasmanian, recruited for the 2/4th CCS by Tom Hamilton. Her age and relative lack of experience meant she was very much out of the limelight in Malaya and Singapore, but at Irenelaan her musical talents and sweet disposition brought her to the fore.

Within weeks of their arrival at Irenelaan, both Shirley and the piano were put to good use, and there were singalongs in the piano house every Saturday night, events that grew in popularity as the months rolled by. The singalongs were organised primarily by Mina 'Ray' Raymont, and would include sketches and impersonations between songs. Wilma Oram was always popular as Mae West, the tall and blonde Vivian Bullwinkel made an excellent Greta Garbo, Beryl Woodbridge, small and dark, was equally successful as Shirley Temple, while Sylvia Muir, with luxuriant hair down to her waist, was Dorothy Lamour in a sarong. Jean Ashton, who had a background in amateur theatrics, could always be relied upon for a soliloquy. Ray earned herself a reputation for her improvisational songs, one of which would be featured at every singalong. The best loved was the one she would regularly trot out, with her own words to the tune of 'The Quartermaster's Store':

There is rice, rice
Mouldy, rotten rice,
Nothing more, nothing more . . .

These singalongs were always held in the biggest room of the larger of the nurses' two houses. All furniture would be removed from the room and a small stage set up in one corner. The doors and windows would be left open, as the audiences were always far larger than the room's capacity to hold them. The singalongs became more formal and organised affairs as the months passed, and soon became shows and revues in their own right. The more popular of these would be put on several times, and it was not unusual to find Japanese guards in the audience. To vent their frustration, the girls sometimes included parodies in their revues, and Mrs Brown was always a popular figure to poke fun at, sometimes in a way that verged on cruelty. She was normally represented by a figure with pillows for padding, who walked with a distinctive waddle, feet pointing away from each other at 45 degrees.

Growing out of these singalongs was a concert party, a group of nurses who could hold a note and harmonise, and who would turn up at the small parties and morning teas the nurses would put on to mark birthdays and other significant dates. There was some attempt at normality through these. 'Jeff' Jeffrey was a keen bridge player, and to celebrate her birthday in May, a bridge party was held at her house and in her honour. Toasts were offered and drunk using cold tea in scrounged wine glasses, with accompanying comments on the quality of the vintage. Gifts were usually items that had been hoarded or made, often without any intrinsic value beyond the feelings of love they represented. Dot Freeman and Rene Singleton, by now fast friends, made Jessie Simons a small powder puff for her birthday in 1942; it was a gift she would treasure forever.

Val Smith and Mina wrote and performed their own material on these occasions – as they did for the reviews – and also joined Dot Freeman, Rene Singleton, Flo Trotter, Ada 'Mickey' Syer, a hard-working and popular Queenslander from the 2/10th AGH, and Betty Jeffrey in the larger camp concerts that were a regular occurrence. In fact, during 1942, a remarkable Englishwoman named Margaret Dryburgh, a missionary schoolteacher interned by the Japanese, wrote a song she called 'The Captive's Hymn'. First performed in July 1942, its lyrics still have the power to move, and the song became the high point of the camp concerts. Elsewhere, internees produced a weekly magazine, aptly named the *Camp Chronicle*.

Flo Trotter was one of a number of committed Christians who met regularly to pray together and support one another through the trials and tribulations they faced on a daily basis. The group included Chris Oxley, Sylvia Muir, Mitz Mittelheuser, Joyce Tweddell and Mickey Syer, and it was the companionship in this group that helped them cope individually with the circumstances they found themselves in. Others took a more secular approach to coping. Through good fortune and clever trading, the nurses built up a little library of books which they read, passed around, and usually reread at least once or twice. For some reason there was a preponderance of whodunits in their collection. Jessie Simons drolly observed: '. . . we read and reread enough detective novels to be able to spot a criminal on sight.'

As well as the small occasions of birthdays and anniversaries – graduations and enlistment dates were both popular – the Australian nurses also made certain they recognised the larger occasions. On 11 November 1942, Jean Ashton and an English civilian internee organised an impromptu Armistice Day service. The nurses also decided to make the best possible Christmas for themselves. Some weeks before Christmas Day, Chris Oxley and Jenny Greer found a shrub that, viewed from a certain angle, could pass as a Christmas tree. They uprooted it and smuggled it into one of the houses, and dressed it as decoratively as they could. Chris took the idea of Christmas spirit even further and, under a veil of secrecy, devised, brewed and eventually delivered chilli wine to accompany the Christmas luncheon.

On Christmas Day, they all attended an ecumenical and non-denominational church service to start the day, the service featuring the traditional hymns, carols and sermons. For many of the Australians, the high point was the sermon delivered by Sally Oldham, a middle-aged Englishwoman who had worked in China as a missionary for many years. In her sermon, Oldham revealed that 30 years earlier, on that very day, she had been saved from sin. One of the Australian girls later wrote: 'We were fascinated of course, and waited for more, but we didn't get it.' Back at the 'Christmas House', the nurses had the best meal most had eaten in the last 12 months as delicacies that had been hoarded or traded for made an appearance on the table. For a while they almost forgot where they were, but then someone sat at the piano and played one of their old sentimental favourites, and it all came rushing back. Christmas – Irenelaan – prisoners.

During these first few months of imprisonment the individual characters of the girls became more pronounced. From the time Irenelaan was established as an internment camp, it contained women and children from many countries and stations in life. At various times there were Australian, British, Dutch and Chinese nurses imprisoned there, with larger numbers of civilians from at least a dozen different national backgrounds. Interaction among these various nationalities was encouraged by the committee set up internally to run the camp. Quite early in the camp's life, an 'Ashes' cricket match was planned. It was held, too, but was over in record time. Jess Doyle and Iole Harper, from prominent cricketing families in New South Wales and Western Australia, cut a swathe through the opposition with both bat and ball.

Other individuals made their names and their reputations in a dazzlingly wide range of endeavours. Mavis Hannah and Jessie Simons were generally regarded as the two best chook stranglers in the camp. They had formed a close friendship and went into business together, specialising in the production of straw hats. In their first year of operation, they sold several hundred of their distinctive head gear. Sylvia Muir excelled herself in arranging flowers. In an equally refined display, Pat Gunther proved to be a more than competent artist, one whose sketches and drawings were always sought after as gifts. Perhaps the most spectacular of all was 'Shorty', Sister Eileen Short, who was the best woodcutter in the camp. Before chopping wood – dressed in sun top and shorts – Shorty would carefully construct a cigarette from any leaves she could scrounge rolled in half pages from a Bible. With this fag perched in the corner of her mouth, Shorty would start swinging the axe. Within minutes, she would be surrounded by an admiring circle of children.

Other popular pursuits were more cerebral. Within three months of arriving at Irenelaan, the nurses had organised Thursday night lectures, semi-formal occasions when one of the Australian nurses or a guest from elsewhere in the camp would address the occupants and guests in one of the Australian houses. At one of these Thursday night lectures, Shirley Gardam spoke about Tasmania, while at another Iole Harper spoke about growing up on a sheep station, and Shorty was able to complement this with her tales of growing up on a cattle station. Winnie May Davis used to write out any Australian poems she remembered and share them with the other nurses. 'Waratah and Wattle' was especially popular. The Japanese eventually banned the Thursday night lectures, ostensibly because of the size of the crowds they were attracting. It is more likely they suspected the meetings were either poking fun at them or plotting against Japan.

There were also things for the modern girl. Fashion shows were a popular, if occasional, event. Featuring designs by 'Paula of Palembang', one show's highlight was the appearance of models wearing what Paula considered would be the fashion statements of succeeding years: 1943 was represented by 'Ray' Raymont wearing an attractive twin-set comprising sun top and shorts, while 1944 was Mickey Syer wearing another matching outfit, this one a bit more worn and made from blackout material found in one of the Irenelaan houses. Three models were chosen to represent 1945, a year Paula obviously believed might represent the end of fashion in Irenelaan; each of three models was wearing nothing but strategically placed pawpaw leaves.

At this stage of their internment, many of the girls thought that their greatest enemy was boredom, and they would form little discussion groups to break up the tedium of the days and nights. One of the most popular discussions, apparently initiated by Betty Jeffrey, was to design the perfect woman from among their number. To create that woman the group had to choose particular features from its members. Wilma Oram recorded how their perfect woman was made: 'Mitzi's facial bone structure was chosen, Pat Blake's smile, Jenny Greer's complexion and eyes, my hair, Jeff's beautiful long legs, Win Davis's graceful movements, Dot's dimpled knees . . . we amused ourselves for a few hours.'

Stories, rumours and innuendo became mainstays of camp life and were hoarded or passed around depending on what an individual thought of their credibility. A lot of them were brought into Irenelaan by the male prisoners of war who regularly brought firewood to the women's camp. One rumour concerned a ship alleged to have recently arrived at Palembang with a cargo of powdered milk. It was further alleged that only nursing and expectant mothers would be given the milk. When the rumour was passed to one of the Australian nurses collecting the firewood, she responded by saying that the women in the camp would certainly be doing something about that. A male voice from the wood party asked: 'Can I be of any assistance?'

One day, in April or May 1942, they were all cheered when one of the members of the wood party, an Englishman named Mr Tunn, passed on a report that he claimed to have heard on a concealed radio. It said that a party of 65 Australian nurses evacuated from Singapore on 11 February had arrived safely in Australia after some incredible adventures and escapes.* It was news that cheered all the girls considerably.

As 1942 wound down in Irenelaan, the nurses knew they were starting to falter. They were used to the food of the East and could make a better meal from a basic rice issue than many of the locals, but there was simply not enough rice and nor was there enough to add to that rice to halt the slow decline in health that all the girls were beginning to feel. The bonhomie generated by Christmas did not last beyond the first month of the New Year. On 16 February 1943, the Australian nurses at Irenelaan held a memorial service for their sisters who had been lost at sea and on Radji Beach 12 months earlier. They did not know it, but their lives would continue to change for the worse because of decisions made by the Japanese War Cabinet in Tokyo. From February,

---

* Because the six *Wah Sui* nurses and the 59 *Empire Star* survivors arrived in Australia from Java around the same time, they were joined together in media reporting.

prisoners of war would only be given rations if they worked, while internees were expected to become self-sufficient in food. The military administration of the POW and internment camps was to be replaced by a civilian administration, releasing troops for service on any one of the fronts where the Japanese military were coming under increasing Allied pressure. Japanese authorities considered the nurses internees rather than prisoners; they were therefore expected to become self-sufficient in everything.

There was, however, no real way of understanding the Japanese mind when it came to their prisoners. One morning in early January 1943, a senior Japanese official the girls had never seen before appeared at rollcall. Through an interpreter, he explained to the nurses assembled on the parade ground that he had travelled from Singapore with a special message just for them, one that the Japanese government had received personally from Australia's Prime Minister John Curtin. The message to the girls was: 'Keep smiling.' Following the customary bows, the nurses were dismissed, none the wiser for the experience.

While food had never been plentiful, by the middle and later months of 1942 it became a matter of grave concern to the nurses who were more aware than most people of the dangers an unbalanced and insufficient food intake could cause. The girls did whatever they could to improve their diets. At Irenelaan there was a Chinese cemetery to the rear of the Australians' houses. The nurses learned very early that Chinese mourners would leave food on their relatives' graves. This food became an important supplement to their rations. Equally important were the food supplies they developed themselves, with the girls saving and planting any seeds they found in those rations.

The Australians still maintained an extremely high morale and general health, primarily because of the bonds their shared experiences had forged. Not all had fully recovered from injuries received at the time of their evacuation and sinking, and a number of new, relatively serious ailments began to appear as 1942 became 1943. Vivian developed extremely bad tinea on both her feet and was eventually hospitalised at the Charitas Hospital in Palembang; she would spend three periods receiving treatment in hospital for the affliction. Run by a Dutch charity and staffed by nuns, the hospital was the only proper medical facility the prisoners had access to. It was there that Veronica Clancy was diagnosed with myocarditis and Val Smith with neuritis. There was no dental expertise available either, and by this time several of the girls were suffering from dental problems. The camp doctors had one basic solution: they would extract the offending tooth irrespective of its health. While this often solved the problem, it also ensured there were rarely queues for their service.

There were also small and simple pleasures that gave the nurses the occasional fillip. On 16 February 1943, the anniversary of the massacre, all the girls observed two minutes' silence at some stage during the day, but did so by themselves for fear of any formal gathering drawing the attention of the Japanese. On 25 April 1943, the nurses conducted an Anzac Day service early in the morning. The service, led by Jean Ashton, was very powerful and moving. It also stirred up memories of those who were not with them to share the moment, and most of the girls finished the service in tears. Informally, they decided they would not hold such services again until they were free. The nurses also had a secret pet. The Japanese announced early in the New Year that there were too many dogs straying in and out of the camp, and undertook a dog eradication program. While there were rumours that some of the strays were killed by the Japanese tying a brick around their neck and throwing them into a swimming pool, most were simply shot by Japanese guards on patrol.

One dog that survived the purge was a fox terrier which arrived at the back door of one of the houses at the time the strays were being shot. Given the name Toby, he was kept hidden whenever Japanese soldiers were in the vicinity of either of the houses. While generally a quiet dog, he would bark if he spotted a Japanese soldier so the girls made sure he never saw one. Despite their own short rations, they always made sure there was a little bit left over for Toby. He brightened the lives of all who knew him and reminded many of better days at home. Late in the year, Toby fell ill and was obviously wasting away in pain. Jean Ashton made the decision that his suffering was too much for both him and them, and euthanased him with drugs from the hospital. They all felt they had lost another special friend.

In March 1943 they were allowed to write a postcard home. By then, most of the girls expected to spend the duration of the war at Irenelaan, and many of their letters reflected this expectation. The actual cards had only five lines for writing – and some would take up to 18 months to be delivered – but it gave the girls the opportunity to think about and do something practical for their loved ones.* Mavis Hannah somehow managed to write more than 20 lines of tiny print in the five lines on her postcard and, surprisingly, the card was allowed through by the Japanese. Included in Mavis's card were some specific instructions to her

---

* Wilma Oram's card alluded to the fact that Mona Wilton had been killed, and the news was passed to her family. The Wiltons would have been particularly hard hit by the news. On 22 February 1942, an Australian soldier named Corporal Ralph Parkes had forwarded a note to the Wilton family from Mona. It was probably the one she had scribbled and given to a wounded Australian who was being evacuated. In January 1942, Mona sent two telegrams home asking her parents not to worry, and assuring them that she was safe and well. Then came Wilma's news over 12 months later. Official word was much longer in coming. On 9 June 1944, the Wiltons received an official telegram from the Defence Minister which said, in part: '... source, considered reliable, but cannot be made known for security reasons ... [Mona] left Singapore but not reported as prisoner. Now considered missing, believed killed.' On 12 January 1945, a more official-sounding telegram informed the Wiltons that Mona was, 'for official purposes, presumed to be dead'.

family: '... please communicate with the Red Cross and send a letter and parcels and money... washing materials, sewing cotton, serviceable shoes or sandals, size four and a half, toilet requisites, Vitamin B tablets, sunglasses, dried fruits, vegetable seeds, especially carrots, parsnips, lettuce, tomatoes, beans, peas, onions, etc., in fact anything edible or plain useful...'

Around the same time, the girls were given a clothing issue which, although they did not know it at the time, would prove to be the only such issue they would be given. Each girl was given two metres of voile, or enough to make one blouse and two pairs of underpants. They swapped designs and materials, and somehow made the material last a lot longer than it should have.

The 16 months from February 1943 until the middle of 1944 became one of slow decline. Small gardens had always been part of the nurses' accommodation, but as the rations delivered by the Japanese camp authorities were reduced in both quality and quantity, the Australians looked to supplement what they grew themselves with purchases from elsewhere in the camp or from the occasional trader the Japanese allowed inside Irenelaan. To either trade or purchase, the nurses needed either goods to barter or hard currency. As shipwreck survivors, they had very little of either. Many of the Dutch internees were quite wealthy in both comparative and absolute terms, however, and many of the Australians therefore looked to establish businesses to generate the funds they would need for their own and their group's survival.

Some of the approaches were ingenious. Winnie May Davis and Pat Gunther made hats from the woven-reed bags that fish were delivered in to the camp, adding bits and pieces of material to give their creations an Australian holiday feel. Mavis Hannah borrowed a sewing machine from one of the Dutch internees and used it to make new clothes from old garments. Mavis in turn loaned the sewing machine to Winnie May, who managed to make seven pairs of black shorts from a donated nun's habit. Val Smith repaired sandals and 'trompers', a kind of slip-on shoe, using nails she salvaged from old furniture that was being broken up for firewood. Iole Harper worked as a washerwoman and nursemaid to a Dutch family, Cecilia Delforce chopped wood, and Beryl Woodbridge made rag dolls for the camp's many children. Flo Trotter and Betty Jeffrey both set themselves up as hairdressers, while most of the others either did laundry or cleaning in the Dutch civilian area of the camp.

These developments occurred against a background of changing Japanese fortunes and attitudes towards how they should administer the tens of thousands of prisoners and internees under their control. At times there was no clear logic to what the Japanese authorities did. After several months of military administration, a new civilian administration took over the running of Irenelaan until it, too, was again replaced by the military in late 1943. For the nurses, it didn't seem to really matter who was in charge, whether civilian or military. The arbitrary slapping, random rollcalls that lasted for hours, and the continuing reduction in rations was a constant. As 1943 became 1944 the conditions in the camp and the condition of the prisoners went into a slow and inexorable decline.

In the final months of 1943 more internees had been moved into the limited space available at Irenelaan, and non-Australians were pushed into one of the Australian houses, causing increasing tensions and even some physical altercations between a particularly aggressive and obnoxious Irish family and some of the nurses. In January 1944, the Australians lost half their other house to the 'hei-ho's', the name they gave to the Javanese trainee auxiliary guards. The greater numbers in the reduced spaces also threatened the synergy and the energy of the group by forcing it to break into smaller units. Dot Freeman and Rene Singleton voluntarily moved out of their house to relieve the overcrowding, and for the rest of their time at Irenelaan lived in a lean-to they built and furnished in the backyard of the house.

Generally, by early 1944 the nurses were starting to suffer the effects of long incarceration under increasingly difficult circumstances. Gladys Hughes was generally regarded as the best cook in the camp, someone capable of turning out a decent meal from the most unappetising of ingredients. From the beginning of the year, even Gladys was unable to put together anything decent as she did not have enough ingredients to prepare anything beyond token meals. In July 1944, Betty Jeffrey recorded in her diary: 'For the last two months we have lived on three bowls of rice every day, with kang kong (a native vegetable) leaves as a vegetable at midday and their stalks, cut like French beans, for the evening meal.' What made the situation even more bizarre was that, from mid-1944, the Japanese began to regularly weigh the nurses. By September of that year, only five of the girls weighed more than 50 kilograms.*

Food became an all-consuming focus for the girls. The most popular book in the Irenelaan camp library had always been a Dutch recipe book and a popular game had been swapping recipes between different nationalities. By the middle of 1943, food was no longer either a game or a subject of polite discussions; it was *the* only subject of most conversations, polite or otherwise. The

---

* In what was probably the most obvious example of the sheer ineptitude of the Japanese approach to prisoners of war and internees, camp authorities used the combined weight of their inmates to calculate the amount of rations they would issue. Their calculations for average daily calories needed to sustain life were badly under what was actually required, while they also would not provide rations for prisoners who were unable to work. Using a camp's 'weight of prisoners' as their baseline, the Japanese actually *reduced* rations as those prisoners lost weight from overwork on an inadequate diet.

girls talked about it and dreamed about it, to the extent that many would wake in the morning with pillows wet from drool caused by the food of their dreams. It was why they chose to do the extra work and why they chose to take the extra risks involved in black market trading or outright theft. Some girls would sneak into the camp gardens at night to dig up vegetables. For some vegetables, like carrots, they would cut the top third off and replant that, as it would look like the garden had not been disturbed and the carrot tops would take a couple of days to die. For other vegetables, they would simply take the lot and hope they wouldn't get caught.

The nurses and the doctors in the camp knew precisely what was happening. The rations, pitiful as they were, were also unbalanced in their nutritional value. The prisoners were getting all they needed in the way of starch in the rice that was supplied, but both proteins and vitamins were sadly missing, and over time that imbalance would lead to a significant, and perhaps irreversible, decline in health. Those prisoners with a medical background, a number that included all the Australian nurses, knew that deficiency diseases would soon start to strike and that, when they did, there was little if anything that could be provided in the way of effective treatment.

As well, the attitude of the Japanese seemed to reflect their changing fortunes in the Pacific War. While most of the guards were no longer Japanese – they were Koreans or Formosans – they, too, were increasingly angry towards the prisoners, and in some areas even outdid the Japanese in their insistence on respect for everything associated with Japan. From the time the Australian nurses had been first imprisoned on Banka Island, the guards had insisted that all prisoners bow to all Japanese, explaining that Japanese soldiers represented the Japanese emperor, and the prisoners were therefore bowing to him. Failure to bow low enough would result in face-slapping, and all minor misdemeanours were punished. Mina Raymont was punished for one such minor infraction by being made to stand to attention in front of the main guard post at Irenelaan, hatless, during the heat of the day in late 1944. After two hours she collapsed, and although revived, Mina's health noticeably deteriorated from that point.*

The combination of decreased rations and increased punishments was exacerbated by a growing sense of futility as the months passed by in 1944. They had all been prisoners for well over two years, they had had little if any contact with loved ones, and there seemed little possibility that the war would be over for several more years at least. Most of the girls believed they were spending what should have been the best years of their lives wasting away behind barbed wire and, in dozens of conversations, canvassed the possibility that they would never marry and have children. All had stopped menstruating within a month of becoming prisoners. In such circumstances, it was inevitable that their physical and mental health would suffer. For the Australians, this was minor at first; Mina Raymont struggled with physical labour after her collapse while Jessie Blanch slowly went deaf in one ear. Elsewhere in Irenelaan, the outcomes were grimmer. The civilian internees recorded their first death around March 1944 and a second in June when Sally Oldham, saved from sin in 1912, quietly passed away. The nurses wondered when their turn would come.

---

* In her statutory declaration for the International War Crimes Tribunal, Nesta James stated that Mina Raymont was punished because there was a hole in the wall of the hut where she slept, and the Japanese believed that she had made it. Nesta said the hole had been there since the Australians arrived, but that the Japanese had not noticed it because of their poor attention to their prisoners' conditions. At the time, the other nurses believed Mina and Valerie Smith had been punished because they had been outside their hut during an air raid. Two other sisters, Vivian and Wilma, once failed to notice and consequently bow to a Japanese sergeant major. They, too, were made to stand bare-headed in the sun for an hour.

CHAPTER 11

The Song of Death

Had Olive Paschke or Irene Drummond survived the sinking of the *Vyner Brooke*, the subsequent history of their nurses would undoubtedly have followed a significantly different path. Both were outstanding matrons in their own quite different ways, and either or both of them would have provided the girls with strong leadership. But they weren't there, and the nurses were forced to make do without them. In their absence a number of individuals stepped forward. Through a combination of age, experience and strength of character, Jean Ashton and Nesta James assumed leaders' roles and proved worthy successors to Olive and Irene.

Betty Jeffrey, too, provided a range of leadership initiatives. Knowing that it would be a thankless task, she volunteered to be the Australian representative on the camp's rations committee, as well as any other group that needed an Australian representative.

And she was always the source of a good joke, or an even better rumour. While the circumstances of their lives grew increasingly problematic, the nurses continued to use humour as a tonic and looked for ways to boost each other's sometimes flagging spirits. Camp news and rumours, and news of rumours from the wider world provided an endless source of conversation and speculation. In April 1944, Betty Jeffrey recorded that the Australians '. . . were just too popular because the Japs in the submarines lost their lives and their ashes had been sent back to Tokyo. Wilma Oram wished under her breath that they would send our bones back to Australia, with us outside them.'

The first Allied air raids on the Palembang oil installations in 1944 gave the girls a brief thrill. Although the early raids were few and far between and the girls were uncertain about what to read into them, they were an increasingly regular interruption to their lives and welcome, if only for that. The first raid recorded in the secret diaries some of the girls kept occurred on the evening of 11 August. Less than a week later, on 17 August, the first mail from Australia the girls had received since leaving Singapore arrived in the camp. The impact of this second event clearly outweighed that of the first.

This mail from home raised the spirits of all the girls, including those who did not receive any letters. Jessie Doyle and Flo Trotter received several letters each and were more than happy to share their news with all the other Australians. Mail always had the ability to raise the girls' spirits. A letter that Betty Jeffrey received in October 1944 electrified them. The letter was two years old and had been written by one of Betty's friends, a nurse then serving with the 2/7th AGH in the Middle East. In the letter, Betty's friend noted how excited all the AANS nurses had been when sisters Torney and Anderson had been awarded the OBE and George Cross respectively. The Australian nurses knew both, and were aware that their ship, the *Empire Star*, had made it back to Australia. They now knew that at least some of their work in the war had been recognised by the authorities.

For reasons perhaps known only to themselves, the Japanese POW administrators decided to relocate the Irenelaan prisoners midway through 1944. They first emptied the men's camp at Palembang. This was located only a few hundred metres from Irenelaan and the women were able to wave to the men as they were marched away. The Japanese then informed the women that they had an hour to pack their belongings before they, too, would be relocated. Several hours later, they were marched down the road to the men's camp, given a dormitory of their own, and told to establish themselves there. This proved to be a much greater task than originally thought because the men, led to believe the camp would be occupied by elements of the Japanese Army after they left, had wreaked as much destruction as they thought they could get away with.

It was a challenge to the nurses, but it was one they accepted and addressed. No job was considered too menial if it meant putting food on the table for the group. Iole Harper and Betty Jeffrey in one team, with Dot Freeman and Rene Singleton in another, set up bakeries which used every scrap of rice they could beg, borrow or steal to produce little rice savouries that they would either sell or exchange for more substantial foods. An increasingly frail Mina Raymont sewed little handkerchiefs from scraps of material and traded these to Dutch civilians for food. Others worked on latrine duty, emptying the overflowing septic tank with coconut shell cups in return for a small payment from those who were not prepared to do such things. It mightn't have been much of a life, but it was a life.

It was soon after they arrived at the men's camp that the girls found a pet to replace Toby, their much-loved fox terrier. This time it was a cat that found them by simply walking into the nurses' area of the camp. He was big and he was black and they named him 'Hitam', the local word for black. As well as reminding most of the girls of pets they had loved in childhood, Hitam did sterling work in keeping the rat population in the Australians' area within bounds. A few short weeks after he attached himself to the Australians, however, Hitam was cornered and kicked to death by a Japanese guard.

Then, in October 1944, the group that had been brought together two years earlier, on 12 February 1942, was separated on the orders of the Japanese. An initial party was selected and despatched by sea to Banka Island, back to Muntok but to a camp a little further inland than the coolie lines. The camp looked new and relatively attractive, and even contained a crude hospital. It was much larger than either Irenelaan or the men's camp, and the main accommodation consisted of nine huts on a hill, built parallel to one another. Six were for accommodation and the others for a hospital and kitchen and ablution facilities. There was no electricity in the camp, however, and all water was drawn from a well, while the latrines were actually located next to the kitchen. There was a small hut with a thatched roof of palm fronds next to the front gate of the camp. All the camp grounds had been covered with gravel. In case anyone was in any doubt about the new camp, the whole facility was surrounded by a high bamboo fence. It would eventually contain 700 prisoners and internees of whom 150 were children. The adults were all female, as the male internees and prisoners from Palembang were placed in the nurses' original accommodation on Banka, the coolie lines outside Muntok. Both facilities were under the command of a Japanese Army officer who was always called 'Captain Seki'.

All the remaining women at the men's camp in Palembang, civilians and nurses alike, followed the first group within a few weeks, and it was a difficult trip. Not only was the weather changeable, but a considerable swell was running throughout the crossing. Seasickness was an issue for many as soon as their transport cleared the mouth of the Musi River but, from who knew where, one of the women produced an old empty tin which was passed to those who needed it and the tin was then passed to those travelling on deck who tipped it out over the side. More surprisingly, one of their Japanese guards produced a helmet to be used as a chamber pot and it, too, was passed up and across and tipped over the side. The waves were part of the larger problem, as those that crashed over the side of the transport added to the miseries of those already sick and suffering.

Waiting for the second group at the landward end of the Muntok pier was Vi McElnea, regarded by all the women as probably the most compassionate person any had met. She had asked for and been given permission to walk the considerable distance from the camp to the jetty carrying a large bucket. When the second tranche arrived they were met by Vi and her bucket, full of fresh water, which she replenished from the nearby customs house when it was emptied. Her Japanese escort watched this all impassively.*

Nesta James was upbeat about the change of scenery, if not the other conditions: 'We sailed early and arrived at Banka Island at about 5 o'clock. We were then taken to a large camp. The camp was very much nicer than any camp we had been in, but the food was very scarce, particularly vegetables.' It soon became apparent though, that there were health issues at the Banka

---

* What was even more impressive was that Vi did all this, and a host of other selfless acts, either barefoot or wearing a clumsy pair of trompers. Her feet were a tiny size two and a half and she had left her shoes on the *Vyner Brooke*. She spent the rest of the war with an assortment of unsatisfactory substitutes.

Island camp that they had not faced before. Jean Ashton and a Dutch nun had been chosen to run the camp hospital, with Wilma Oram their deputy, and they were soon faced with a situation that involved too many patients and not enough medicine.

Malaria had not really been a problem up until then, but by February 1945 it was endemic. At one stage, 31 of the 32 Australian nurses were suffering from it. In the wider camp, which contained 700 people, at times some 75 per cent of those people were bedridden. The malaria was compounded by an increasing number of people falling victim to beriberi, a disease precipitated by a lack of vitamins in the diet. The disease appeared in both wet and dry forms, both of which left its victims grossly disfigured. Those with the wet form of the disease would begin to bloat. If they pressed a finger into their swollen flesh, the impression left by the finger would take a long time to disappear, while the mark where the finger pressed would often not disappear at all.

The nurses at the little hospital also noted the first cases of what they called 'Banka fever'. Probably a form of cerebral malaria, the illness started cutting a swathe through the already debilitated internees and prisoners. The path it followed with its victims would become frighteningly familiar and predictable. The sufferer would develop a high temperature and accompanying fever, and would gradually lose orientation and slip into unconsciousness, which was followed by a deep coma and death. For those already weakened by other illnesses the disease was always fatal; one of the civilian internees lost four of her five children to the disease in one week.

On 8 February 1945, Betty Jeffrey recorded in her diary: 'Our own Ray, Sister Raymont, dies today after 36 hours of being desperately ill. Ray had an attack of malaria, suddenly became unconscious and didn't recover . . . Val Smith has lost her best friend. Our girls gave Ray a military funeral, all wearing their uniforms.' The brief diary entry tells only part of the story. Tall and fair, but increasingly frail after her punishment at Irenelaan, Mina Raymont had been hospitalised several times in both Palembang and Muntok. Those who nursed her were convinced that the Japanese punishment had either brought on heart problems or had aggravated a pre-existing heart condition. During the afternoon of 7 February, she had collapsed and was carried to the camp hospital by her friends. At times literally raving mad, Mina had slipped into a coma during the early hours of 8 February and died soon afterwards.

Wilhelmina Rosalie 'Ray' Raymont was not the first of the *Vyner Brooke* nurses to die, but she was the first to die as part of the kongsi the group had formed at Irenelaan, the extended family that had been together for just on three years, and that family wanted to farewell her with dignity and respect amid the squalor that their lives had become. During the morning on the day after her death, a group of nurses dug a grave in a small clearing in the jungle outside the camp. Another group made a coffin from rough-hewn timber. Others still dressed Mina for burial. Uniforms – many still stained with oil from the sinking of the *Vyner Brooke* – were retrieved from special storage places. Late in the day the funeral party, all in uniform, came together and lifted Mina's coffin, draped with the flowers she loved, onto their shoulders. As they moved off they may have shuffled, but they shuffled in step, and when they passed the guard post at the camp's entrance gates, the two Japanese soldiers on duty snapped to attention and saluted them. The burial party marched down the short path to the jungle clearing and lowered Mina's coffin into the grave. Val Smith stepped forward and read from the Bible, passages from Revelations 5 and 7: 'They shall hunger no more, neither thirst any more; neither shall the sun light on them, nor any heat.' The nurses gathered in the jungle clearing then sang the second and third verses of 'Jerusalem the Golden'. Mina Raymont, formerly of the 2/4th CCS, was finally at rest.*

Rene Singleton was the next to die. In January 1945 she had been admitted to the camp hospital with advanced beriberi, the dry type that literally consumes the flesh from within as the body seeks sustenance. Always popular with her sister nurses and regarded as the life of their many parties, Rene went steadily downhill and, from mid-February, slipped in and out of consciousness, not really knowing where she was. She died on 20 February, a death that prompted Jessie Simons to record: 'Rene Singleton, 2/10 AGH, a Victorian, will always be remembered for her dry humour. Emaciated, almost beyond recognition except for her deep blue eyes, poor Rene was always hungry. On the day she died, she asked for "more breakfast please".' Late on the same day, another sad little procession made its way to the jungle clearing where Mina had been buried less than two weeks previously, and laid Rene alongside her. Margaret Dryburgh from the civilian internees' quarters delivered the eulogy at the graveside. Rene had died not knowing that her two brothers, the lights of her life, had both predeceased her, killed a few days apart in fighting in North Africa almost two years previously.

Blanche Hempsted, who had become increasingly ill over the previous few weeks, died on 19 March, another victim of beriberi. Blanche was an extremely hard worker, in battle conditions

---

* One of those who observed the scene from afar was an interned Dutch teenager named Helen Colijn. Colijn later wrote a book on her wartime experiences and that book, with additional material from a number of other prisoners, including several of the surviving Australian nurses, was made into a film entitled *Paradise Road*. In the book, Colijn described the scene: 'I had seen them lined up at the gate, standing still and straight, conveying a sense of pride and spunk despite their haggard appearance and the oil stains on their wrinkled grey dresses.'

and in the internment camps, and her final illness was presaged by a harsh cough that many of the nurses thought indicated cancer. At the end, and between the coughs, she apologised to her carers for taking so long to die. She then just slipped into a coma and died within 30 minutes.

Within two further weeks, Shirley Gardam was also dead, a victim of starvation and neglect as much as the dysentery that eventually took her away. She died swiftly and left behind a host of friends who would always remember a tall and fair girl who was loved by all who knew her. During her three years of captivity, Shirley had not received a letter from home and was unaware that her mother had died in 1942. Like Mina Raymont, Shirley had always loved flowers; her coffin was covered in them when it was lowered into the ground in the little jungle clearing.

Pat Gunther later wrote of the funerals they held on Banka Island:

> It took 20 of us to carry out a coffin. Three poles were placed under the coffin. Eighteen people lifted the poles. One person led out, holding her hands behind to steady the coffin, and keep an eye on the track, as we all had a dread of walking on grass. The end of the coffin was supported by the twentieth person to avoid any risk of it slipping. The funeral services were carried out most correctly by the missionaries and nuns, while we ragged remnants of humanity stood with bowed heads. The burials took place any time after 3 p.m. The usual 'Sumatra' — a noisy electric storm — frequently blew up as we finished filling in the graves. On our way back to camp, we spread out to collect wood. As the weeks went by, we had to go further afield.

What Pat didn't mention was that the coffins were rude affairs, merely slats of wood joined with the few nails the girls were able to scrounge. The materials were supplied by the Japanese, and completed coffins were stored at the back of the hut that served for general amenities and acted as a church. All coffins were usually filled with flowers, in part because the wooden slats rarely fitted together and it was thought inappropriate to watch the body moving around within the coffin.

The girls dug the graves themselves, using mattocks provided by the Japanese, and prepared the bodies for burial, ensuring they were dressed as Australian Army nurses, and also making certain that some little keepsake made the journey with their friend. The little jungle clearing became a larger jungle clearing as the weeks went by and more and more civilians and nurses died, ostensibly of Banka fever or one of the tropical diseases, but in reality of simple neglect. While illness was not necessarily the end – both Vivian and Jeff overcame quite serious ailments – Banka fever was inevitably fatal. Those who caught it were fortunately unaware that they were dying, such was the speed of the onset and progress of the disease. Before they died, though, all who contracted the disease made a distinctive noise, a deep sigh almost as if they were giving up life knowingly and going somewhere else. The nurses who heard the noise would forever call it 'The Song of Death'.

The Japanese did not appear to care about their prisoners one way or another. Their only interest seemed to be in following the rules and regulations laid down by authorities somewhere else, and counting their prisoners time and time again. All the Australian girls made wills at the Muntok camp – not because they were convinced they would die there, but because any who died without a will would have their possessions seized by the guards. By all appearances, a written will carried more power than the person who wrote it for their guards. The Japanese also insisted that all their prisoners continue to contribute to the war effort. One of the tasks the nurses were given was sewing bags for the tin mines on the island. All were required to stitch their initials onto the bags so the Japanese authorities would be able to recognise any deliberate attempts to produce inferior products.

It was at the Muntok camp that a tipping point was reached. Before Muntok, the health of both civilian and military prisoners was not good, but few were in danger of death as a direct result of untreated ailments. At Muntok, the dietary deficiencies coupled with the malarial conditions, poor water and hygiene and general neglect created a deadly cocktail. Before Muntok, most of the girls realistically believed they would survive the war; at Muntok, most accepted that they may not live to see peace. It was also at Muntok that the first really terrible incidents occurred. Several of the civilian internees were so emaciated that they collapsed in the latrines and fell through the slats into the pit below. All of those who fell were recovered, but all of them perished soon afterwards.

And it was at Muntok that the girls realised that their kinship alone would no longer guarantee their survival, that they would need an inner strength as well as the ongoing support of their sisters. Most adopted the approach championed by Jessie Blanch, who chose to only think one month ahead at any given time. She felt that living day to day would lead to depression when nothing ever changed, and looking too far ahead would be counterproductive and would simply encourage false hopes and wishes that would weaken them all. Living a month at a time was comfortable; they could tick off a few highlights of the previous month and, come the first of each month, start planning a few for the weeks ahead.

* * *

Shirley Gardam was the last Australian nurse to die on Banka Island. They, and the other internees, were only in the camp for a few months, but 100 of the 700 occupants of the camp died during that time. Then, in one of the increasingly bizarre decisions being made by the Japanese authorities, the entire camp was again put on notice for an imminent move, and in May 1945 they prepared to return to Sumatra, to a camp in the mountains that Captain Seki said would be good for the health of all. Most of the girls were either too sick or too tired to care. When the time for the move came, the Japanese insisted that even patients who were unconscious and near death were to be moved and, realising the inevitable outcome of this decision, made further arrangements for a number of coffins to accompany those who were being relocated. In the event, two of the coffins were filled before the prisoners had left the camp, and several others at points on the road to Muntok pier.

The move from Muntok to the new camp in Sumatra was made in two tranches. The Australian nurses were split between the groups. The girls were told to take rations to last for 24 hours plus all the medical supplies and equipment needed to establish a hospital at their new camp. The reality was they had so little that they would barely be able to stock a first-aid station.

Each of the two parties of nurses would also be responsible for the transportation of their patients, and each group would have a number of stretcher cases in their care. The tone of the relocation was set by the first tranche, a group whose Australian nurses were led by Jean Ashton. The party travelled to Muntok pier on the back of trucks and then marched to the end of the pier where a small craft waited to carry them across to an old and worn coastal freighter anchored offshore. At the end of the pier, and before boarding the boat, all the women were lined up in the sun for the inevitable rollcall. As this was being conducted, one of the stretcher cases died. The death meant the numbers would not tally, and so one of the nurses informed the Japanese of the death. The guards directed a group of nurses to carry the body to the customs house to await burial, and then return. When they did so, the rollcall was recommenced. Finally, some 400 women, including 17 stretcher cases, were crammed aboard the freighter and taken across to Palembang in the steaming heat of the day. Eight died during the crossing. Their bodies were wrapped and weighted and slipped into the sea.

The second group made the crossing to Palembang four days after the first. On this trip, one of the stretcher cases died shortly after the freighter set off from Muntok. The body and the soiled mattress on which it lay were passed over the side and lowered into the sea with as much reverence as the exhausted women aboard could muster. The body on the mattress did not sink however, but simply bobbed in the wake of the freighter until it disappeared from sight. Several others died during the crossing, but their bodies were kept aboard until the ship docked at Palembang. Another two died while the women were counted on the Palembang docks, and still more while the pathetic group waited for a train at the nearby railway sidings.

This time neither group stayed in Palembang but were marched to a railway station, directed into carriages with the blinds permanently shut, and transported through the night to the west, to a small town named Loebok Linggau. After more bodies were removed from the train and laid out on a platform at the train station after both trips – the first took two days and the second three – the survivors were marched about 15 kilometres to a large rubber plantation called 'Belalau'. They did not know that Belalau was the largest rubber plantation in Sumatra, nor did they know they had just completed the last wartime journey they would make.

At Belalau, some three years previously, the Dutch plantation manager had adopted a scorched earth policy, and destroyed or damaged almost everything the plantation contained. When converted to a prison camp, the manager's house and a smaller one nearby were taken over by the Japanese for themselves and their predominantly Javanese guard force. Some newer timber huts, with leaky roofs and earthen floors, were set aside for the British and Dutch civilian internees, while the nurses and nuns were given accommodation in the old coolie lines. While in poor condition, they had the advantage of concrete floors. The civilians' camp was in turn divided into separate men's and women's camps, with male internees expected to work to bring the plantation back into full production. Belalau was probably the most isolated of the major internment camps. It was not one homogenous camp, either, as there were upper and lower camps, with the upper separated from the lower by a steep bank which led down to the river that flowed through the camp. The journey between the two was hellish in wet weather, as the track soon turned to deep mud, as did any steps cut into the bank. Hidden tree roots were an additional impediment. With the exception of Gladys Hughes, who was outposted to the upper camp, all the Australian nurses were housed in the lower camp.

On one side of the river, which was spanned by a small bridge, were the communal kitchen, coolie lines and a number of older buildings, including the hospital. The Australians occupied one of the old coolie buildings on the opposite bank to the hospital and, beyond their building but before the jungle that surrounded the camp, was another house occupied by the three doctors, including Dr Goldberg who actually appeared to have prospered as a prisoner. The hospital itself was two buildings attached to each other, both timber and both with earth floors. They were surrounded by large trees and rarely received any direct sunlight; hardly the ideal circumstances for a hospital. To add insult to injury, the Japanese and Javanese guards lived upriver from the internees and their latrines were wooden boxes set above the river, guaranteeing that diseases and health issues would always be at the forefront of the prisoners' concerns.

On first appearances alone, several of the girls had likened Muntok to a country resort, and their new camp at Belalau could have appeared like the Garden of Eden. Located relatively high up in the mountains that form the backbone of Sumatra, it reminded many of Frazer's Hill in Malaya. It is doubtful any of the Australian girls even gave their new setting much thought, however, because none of the nurses was in anything near good health. When they were weighed in May 1945 Mavis Hannah, one of the fittest, recorded her weight as being 4 stone, 6 pounds. Today, she would have recorded it as 27 kilograms. The nurses found that their weight loss really made them feel the cool of the evenings and the cold of the pre-dawn mists, and they all had to rug up as much as possible to get through the night. They were cheered somewhat by an enormous mail delivery shortly after their arrival; some of the girls received up to 20 postcards, although all had been written in 1942 and 1943.

But beautiful surroundings and letters from home are sustenance for the soul not the body, and the nurses continued their daily struggle to stay alive. On 31 May, Gladys Hughes died. Famous for her cooking abilities, Gladys, like many of the others, had been suffering from malaria and dysentery. Betty Jeffrey, though, thought Gladys had died because she simply gave up her hopes of ever being released and chose to die rather than continue in captivity. She had been living and nursing in the upper camp, and the girls believed that her isolation from them hastened her death. In the tradition they had established at Muntok, Gladys Hughes was carried to a shallow grave in a nearby glade and buried there by her Australian sisters. On 19 July, she was joined there by Winnie May Davis, one of the younger nurses, and one who had been loved and protected by all the other sisters. Winnie was already suffering from beriberi when she was struck down with dysentery in early July. Too weak to look after herself, she was placed in the small, inadequate camp hospital, and simply faded away on 19 July 1945.

By then, the funerals were simple and brief. The cemetery was established a short distance away from the camp on a hillside. Because of the weakness of all the Australians, if a grave had to be dug, it was dug in the morning, for by the afternoon none of them had enough strength to dig. Crosses were made from rough timber and the name and date of death were burnt into the crosses using a heated wire.

It was at Belalau that the realisation set in for many that they were going to die a prisoner of the Japanese, and for the first time in their three and a half years of captivity, some girls felt the cold fingers of despair. They went to bed in the evenings not knowing whether they or their friends would be alive the next day. On each short journey they all made when burying friends, they wondered if that trip would be their last. Each day a team of nurses would assess how many patients they believed were likely to die within the next 24 hours. This information would be passed on to the grave-digging party, who would then dig the required number. They always seemed to have dug too few.

By June, most women had accepted the likelihood of their own deaths, and made arrangements accordingly. The wills they had drawn up at Muntok were simply for form, and to direct their camp possessions to friends rather than have them seized by the Japanese. Now they drew up more formal wills and testaments, documents not only for their friends in camp but for their families far away. Many also wrote last letters to those families. Pat Gunther's read:

> Dear Family, please don't worry about me. I enlisted of my own free will, knowing I could be going into a war zone. We nurses have been interned with a lot of other women. We have always managed to stay together. I have not been raped, bashed or tortured. If I die, it will be due to malnutrition or malaria. I am still me. All my love, Pat.

Like most of the others in the camp, Pat hoped to die in her sleep. She not only hoped to die in her sleep, but actually dreamed about what it would be like. Pat found that it was not a particularly bad dream because the friends and relatives who she met in heaven – for that is where she went – looked both healthy and happy compared to the human misery that characterised her daily life. If her lot was to be death, Pat decided that she would accept it with good grace.

And many felt that death was literally only a heartbeat or two away. As well as sharing one of the few mosquito nets each night, Wilma and Vivian shared their rations and their medications, with the stronger Wilma doing anything and everything to look after her friend. In mid-June, Vivian sunk to her lowest point, and the camp doctors felt that her only chance of overcoming the chronic dysentery she had was a dose of Epsom salts. Wilma found out that Chris Oxley had a small supply of Epsom salts, and convinced her to give them to Vivian, who survived. Pat Blake was so ill that she was not aware that one night a rat actually chewed the end off one of her toes. At around the same time, Jeff was gravely ill with the combination of ailments that afflicted them all. Wilma took no chances; while nursing Jeff with some of her scarce medicines, she also asked that a grave be prepared for her.

Pat Gunther summed up the girls' feelings when she wrote:

> We had reached the stage where we envied those who had been lost at sea, and even the nurses who had been massacred. They had not known the misery and wretchedness of life in a Japanese internment camp. It was all over so quickly for them.

Despite a strange interlude when a Japanese orchestra appeared and played a selection of classical airs for the prisoners, it was just a matter of time before they all perished. Not one of the nurses weighed 40 kilograms by July 1945, and they all knew that those among them who did not succumb to disease would have starved to death by the end of the year. On 8 August, Dot Freeman, another Victorian and Rene Singleton's best friend, died from a combination of malaria, dysentery and beriberi. She, too, had been fading away for some time and simply curled up into the foetal position, closed her eyes, and passed away. On 18 August, another of the best-loved nurses, Pearl Mittelheuser, died. Her best friend, Sylvia Muir, was with her when she passed away, also curled up like a baby, but Sylvia was so dehydrated that she was simply unable to cry. Another friend, Jessie Simons, had also been with Mitz before she slipped into the final coma, and remembered Mitz saying quite conversationally that the one thing she really wanted was to once more hear her family call her by her given name.

The next day, Captain Seki, the Japanese camp commandant, called all the Belalau prisoners and internees together in the rough parade ground and climbed on a bench to address them. The war was over, he told them – it had ended on 15 August – and now they could all be friends. As a gesture recognising that friendship, he ordered the opening of a shed that had served as a combination storage area and guards' quarters. It contained a large amount of both food and medicine, mainly from Red Cross parcels that had accumulated over the years, sufficient to guarantee that no-one in his camp had ever needed to die of starvation or neglect. Between their arrival at the camp and this day, some 96 men and 59 women had died at Belalau.

CHAPTER 12

Homecoming

The girls' responses to the news that the war was finally over were both muted and intensely personal. Captain Seki's announcement had been followed by the spontaneous singing of the Netherlands' national anthem and 'God Save the King', the voices fading away as the parade broke up and small groups and individuals went their own ways to digest the news. While most of the Australians wanted to group together and talk, a few took the opportunity to be alone with their thoughts. Jessie Simons walked away, sat down under a tree, and cried her heart out for 30 minutes, simply overwhelmed by the fact of her survival.

Like Jessie, the Australian girls experienced powerful emotions as they examined the implications of war's end. Alongside a general feeling of relief, there were individual feelings of grief at their loss of both friends and youth, concern at how they would cope in a world they knew little of and fears of what they might find when they returned home. While Seki had not actually mentioned who had won the war, no-one was in any doubt that it had been the Allies, and as the groups formed the girls speculated on what might lie ahead.

For all, it removed the major part of the uncertainty that surrounded them. All had doubted that they would survive the war, and for the last few months had planned and behaved accordingly. They had survived and could now begin to plan for themselves in a future that had seemed unlikely to ever occur. This future was, of necessity, short term and revolved largely around food, and how to send and receive messages from home.

For some, there was an almost immediate physical relief. Like all the others, Chris Oxley was facing certain death from starvation in August 1945. The only thing she still possessed of any slight value was a dental bridge spanning four teeth at the rear of her mouth, and its value was in the small amount of gold it contained. On 20 August, Chris removed the bridge and gave it to a Javanese guard the girls trusted, asking him to sell it on the black market for whatever he could get. Two days after Seki announced the end of the war, the guard approached Chris to apologise and say that he had not yet sold the bridge. The response from the overjoyed Chris was not exactly what he had expected.

But for most, the end of the war was simply something remote, an event that had prompted increased rations, open gates and a free interchange between the men's and women's camps. Their immediate future was in their camp and there they would stay and simply wait to see what fate now had in store for them. After 42 months, they really did know how to sit quietly and wait.

While the nurses were not aware of anyone actually knowing where they were and what had happened to them, the truth of the matter in Australia was slightly different. The Australian public at large, including family and friends, was aware that the *Vyner Brooke* had been sunk with 65 Australian nurses aboard, but the suppositions of what had happened to those nurses was just that – supposition. In 1944, General Gordon Bennett published a book that was part memoir and part apologia, and he made passing mention to the nurses surviving the sinking of their ship and probably being held in a camp in Sumatra. In a way that was almost dismissive, he suggested that they would be all right because, at one time during his command of the 8th Division, he had arranged for them to be evacuated. Other people in Australia and in the camps knew a lot more than this and, with the Pacific War rapidly coming to a climax after the war in Europe had ended successfully, were preparing to find and free those nurses.

On the Allied side, no-one really knew how many nurses there were or where they could be found, but the search for them started in early 1945. Allied reconnaissance flights had identified all the POW and internment camps in southern Sumatra, and from the early months of 1945, teams of Allied commandos – British, Dutch and Australian – were parachuted into Sumatra to identify just who was there, and also to call in assistance if the Japanese appeared to be preparing to massacre their prisoners, then considered a real possibility. A team led by a South African-born Royal Marine commando major named Gideon Jacobs was able to identify and confirm the presence of Australian nurses at the Belalau camp in the final stages of the war, and two Dutch commandos were parachuted into the camp shortly after the surrender. They brought with them a letter telling the nurses not to worry. Jacobs and the remainder of his team followed soon after, and were at Belalau by early September.

Major Jacobs and his team called in support for the survivors they found at Belalau, but at first did not connect the Australians they found there with the almost mythical nurses who had come through the fall of Singapore and the sinking of the *Vyner Brooke*. A brief series of conversations with the nurses established the connection, and the evening after his team arrived at Belalau, Jacobs radioed his headquarters in Ceylon:

> Have encountered among 250 repeat 250 female internees in Lubuklinggau [sic] camp Sister Nesta James and 23 other surviving members of Australian Army Nursing Service remnants of contingent AANS evacuated from Malaya in Vyner Brooke STOP In view their precarious health suggest you endeavour arrange air transport direct to Australia from here soonest STOP Am collecting particulars massacre of AANS at Bangka [sic] Island for later transmission.

The great silence into which the girls had disappeared was now over.

Jacobs' report detailing more than 20 Australians among the 250 women at Belalau (most of them were Dutch civilian internees) was cross-referenced to an Australian team that had been brought together in Singapore to search for the nurses. Its two senior members were an Australian doctor named Harry Windsor and Colonel Annie Sage, Royal Red Cross, Matron in Chief of the Australian Army Nursing Service. Hayden Lennard, the senior Far Eastern war correspondent for both the BBC and the ABC, was attached to the team, and his reports were attracting growing interest in Australia.*

By the second week of September, identification of the *Vyner*

---

* Lennard, aware of the interest in the *Vyner Brooke* nurses, had been pestering Mountbatten's headquarters in Colombo for several weeks, seeking permission to travel to Sumatra where he believed the nurses would be found.

Brooke nurses was completed and confirmed, and plans for their rescue and repatriation were drawn up. There were some potential complications. There were still considerable numbers of Japanese troops in southern Sumatra but not yet enough Allied troops to effectively disarm and control them. Sporadic fighting had also broken out between Indonesian nationalists and returning Dutch troops, and there were fears that these clashes could grow into a large-scale insurrection.

During the afternoon of 10 September, the nurses were informed by Jacobs that they would be evacuated the following day, and that they should be prepared to depart. The move was confirmed when a surprised Nesta James, as the senior Australian nurse, was summoned to the camp telephone and spoke to Ken Brown, an Australian pilot, who informed her that he would be meeting the group at Lahat the next day to accompany them on their journey to Singapore. A number of the girls had been dressing chickens and ducks for a birthday party they had planned for that evening, and it was decided to combine that party with one to farewell the nursing and civilian friends they had made among the English and Dutch women with whom they had shared three years of hell. Not all the girls attended the birthday party; some made their way among the huts to farewell special friends, giving them keepsakes, while others just sat and talked quietly among themselves. Still others sorted and resorted their meagre possessions, knowing they would only be able to take one bag, in which they could fit a change of clothing, a blanket and a pillow. All the nurses spent time trying to make their ragged uniforms as presentable as possible. A long time earlier – months? years? – they had decided that they would wear their uniforms only on certain occasions. One of those was when they transferred from one camp to another, and a second would be when they buried one of their own. The third would be when the uniform would be placed on their body as a shroud, and the final occasion would be when they marched to freedom. That time had come.

The rescue plan was put into action on 11 September when the nurses, wearing what remained of their uniforms and as clean and tidy as they could make themselves, were escorted by Jacobs' team to the railway station at Loebok Linggau. They travelled as a group, all of them together. Iole Harper had been in the camp hospital recovering from an abscess on her hip, but discharged herself so that she could travel with her friends. Similarly, Jenny Greer was very ill and had to be carried between stops on every leg of the journey, but they were together, and that was important. Late the previous evening, a doctor had issued quinine tablets and told them to be ready to depart at 0400 hours; at 0415, the camp cooks, still volunteers, had distributed coffee and sweetened milk. Rain had commenced around midnight, a tropical downpour that was easing when the group assembled.

Leaving the camp at 0600 hours in cool and damp conditions, the nurses were part of a larger group of around 60 – the 24 Australians with the remainder a mix of British civilians and nurses, most of them seriously ill. Two Australian paratroops arrived aboard two army trucks and introduced themselves as 'Bates from Thornbury' and 'Gillam from Perth', and then helped the girls board the trucks. It took the group almost three hours to travel the 15 kilometres to the station, partly because one of the trucks broke down, but mainly because of the state of the roads and the health of those who were travelling.

At the station, the group was met by Hayden Lennard and Flying Officer Ken Brown, an RAAF pilot who had flown to the town of Lahat the previous day to assess the viability of an evacuation by air, and who had driven up to Loebok Linggau overnight, while Lennard had come up on the previous day's train. The expanded group of soldiers and civilians boarded a train that was waiting at the station and, precisely at 1000 hours, headed off.* As they travelled, they pestered Lennard for details on what had taken place elsewhere during their three and a half years of imprisonment. War news was interesting, political developments marginal; fashions, films, music and major sports results were what the girls really wanted to hear. They also asked Bates and Gillam ('Young, with very white teeth') how the war had actually ended. Writing later, Betty recalled how:

> The two boys also told us of a bomb dropped on a Japanese city which killed thousands of people and reduced the place to a shambles. We were horrified to think one bomb could do that. They then said another similar bomb had been dropped on another Japanese city that did the same thing. What amazing progress has been made while we have been Rip Van Winkles.

At Lahat station they waited aboard the train for about an hour before they were disembarked. During this time they were given a meal of bully beef and rice, followed by coffee, served to them by Japanese soldiers from the local garrison. They made a point of not saying thank you to the soldiers. The group was then divided in two, with the 24 AANS nurses and the six sickest

---

* Almost unbelievably, the stationmaster and train driver refused to allow the train to leave when all the ex-prisoners had boarded because it was still a few minutes short of the official departure time. Ken Brown and the commandos worried about the attention the train was receiving from a number of Japanese soldiers, and wanted it to leave as soon as all were on board. Even some pistol waving from Brown was ineffective; the train left at the exact time it was scheduled to. Some Japanese officers aboard the train, variously described as 'unctuous' and 'obsequious' were ordered to serve the ex-prisoners morning tea, but most of those aboard were too excited to eat.

civilians being loaded onto buses with padded seats and driven the short distance to Lahat airfield. The second half of the group, British civilians and nurses, were taken to a local hospital to await their evacuation. Only one aircraft would be available for the group that day, with those left behind to be flown out the following day.

At the airfield, the girls grouped together, guarded by the commandos, and watched and waited. Nothing seemed to be happening and, for the girls, the waiting seemed to last forever. It was a hot day and there were little in the way of amenities at the airfield. The more dangerously ill were placed either in the shade of the trees or under a sun shelter someone had constructed at some earlier time. Mostly, though, the girls sat in groups talking among themselves. There were some Japanese at the airfield, but most were kept away from their former prisoners. One of the Japanese, an officer, had some kind of field telephone and startled the girls by calling something that sounded like *'Banga'* into it at seemingly random intervals.

Finally, after four hours of waiting, a 'speck of silver' appeared in the distant sky, slowly growing in size and becoming more distinct. Within minutes, its engines could be heard and soon afterwards, the shiny transport plane, a Dakota, new to the girls, made a good landing and taxied towards where the group of soldiers, civilians and nurses had gathered. The door opened, the steps dropped down, and a handsome soldier ('I think some of the girls almost swooned'), an officer dressed in the uniform of a major in the Australian Army Medical Corps, emerged and introduced himself as Harry Windsor. Pat Gunther recalled being thrilled to her core. Her brain wanted her legs to move, to run towards the aircraft, but they wouldn't respond. The Australian Army had provided the rescue team with the enlistment photographs of the nurses they were to rescue, and Windsor could see no-one bearing any resemblance to the photographs he had studied for the past few days. He looked at what was obviously a motley group of women and asked, 'Where are the Australian nurses?' A couple of the girls laughed, and Nesta James called out, 'We're here!' Next off the plane were two figures wearing grey safari jackets, pants, gaiters and boots, with badges of rank on their epaulettes. They were obviously women, but they were *wearing trousers!* 'Who are you?' asked one of the nurses. In tears, the older of the two replied, 'I am your mother.'

After a short silence, the older nurse then introduced herself as Colonel Annie Sage, Matron in Chief of the Australian Army Nursing Service, and her companion as Lieutenant Jean Floyd, formerly of the 2/13th AGH. When Sage asked where the other nurses were, she was told they were dead. After another pause, some of the nurses recognised Sage and Floyd as old colleagues, and suddenly everyone wanted to talk at once.* Sage told them that, on becoming Principal Matron of the AANS, she had made a silent vow to solve the mystery of the *Vyner Brooke* nurses, and she felt that she had now fulfilled part of that vow. Most of the girls, Sage and Floyd included, knew and shared mutual friends, and they were suddenly talking and shrieking and laughing as they remembered earlier and happier times. Their reminiscences were interrupted by the pilot of the aircraft, Squadron Leader Fred Madson, who emerged from the aircraft and pointed to the darkening sky. Ten minutes later they were airborne and just over an hour later they had landed in Singapore, not far from where they had left three and a half years earlier.

---

* Jean Floyd was an original member of the 2/10th AGH and had sailed with them to Malaya in February 1941. She had been among the group selected for evacuation aboard the *Empire Star* and was now returning with the 2/14th to see if she could help rescue any of her old friends. A few of the nurses recognised Floyd in that initial meeting, but she did not recognise any of them.

In what was for some an almost mirror image of their escape from Singapore, the aircraft landed at the newly restored RAF Base at Kallang, where there were ambulances waiting on the tarmac. Among those awaiting their arrival were a number of newspaper reporters, who sensed they were on one of the war's great stories, and wrote accordingly:

> It was a sad if thrilling sight as the girls – now older than their years – were helped from the plane. Young Australian Air Force nurses, Red Cross girls and ambulance men were there to meet them. All the nurses were in weak condition. They were somewhat dazed at being among their own folk again. They broke into excited conversation and bravely smiled but behind the smiles was a tale of fortitude during years of terrible trials. When the girls spoke of their dead colleagues, their voices were very low.

The Melbourne *Argus* was no less dramatic:

> As the nurses stepped out of the plane they looked thin and a little shaky, though of comparatively good physique [sic]. Red Cross workers and servicemen took their pathetic little bundles of possessions and steadied an elbow as they walked to the airport cafe, before they were moved to the hospital.

The ambulances took the nurses to St Patrick's School at Katong, once again a hospital and now occupied by the 2/14th AGH, a unit formed specifically to deal with ex-prisoners of war in Singapore. All were admitted immediately. To give some idea of their condition, Jenny Greer – the Wizard of Oz – who had been one of the biggest of the nurses in 1941, now weighed just over 20 kilograms, one-third of her enlistment weight. Specialist doctors at St Patrick's considered that at least five of the nurses would not have survived another week without treatment, with Joyce Tweddell being just hours away from death. There were other newly released Australian prisoners of war at St Patrick's, as well as a number of Japanese sick and wounded. When the Australians saw the condition of the nurses, several had to be physically restrained to prevent them attacking the Japanese patients. The forces' newspaper described: 'Sick Australian POWs in hospital when the nurses were brought in wept at the sight of them and demanded guns to go out to the Japanese concentration area here.' Even the normally objective Dr Harry Windsor could not contain his anger and disgust at the wretchedness he had seen. He wrote a report on the rescue operation, which concluded with a wish that all associated with the mistreatment of the nurses be tracked down, 'and slowly and painfully butchered'.*

The girls, and their story, were not only news in the armed forces' newspaper, they were becoming very big news in Australia, and this had some unforeseen implications. Their rescuer, Gideon Jacobs, had recommended they be airlifted back to Australia as a matter of priority, but there were several considerations if this were to occur. In the first place, some of the nurses were clearly unfit to travel any distance, and it was felt preferable for the survivors to remain together as they went through the difficult process of rehabilitation and re-entry into a world they had been excluded from for three and a half years. There was also a question of appearances. The first Australian prisoners of war from

---

* Major Harry Windsor would go on to an outstanding career in medicine. At St Vincent's Hospital in Sydney in 1968, he performed Australia's first heart transplant and later mentored the career of one of Australia's greatest heart surgeons, Dr Victor Chang.

Changi had been flown to Sydney's Rose Bay aboard Catalina flying boats, and their arrival had been witnessed by a crowd in excess of 50,000 cheering Australians. They looked poorly, but no-one seemed too concerned amidst the euphoria of their return.

The feelings of the Australian soldiers at St Patrick's gave a clue as to the possible reaction of the Australian people to the return of the nurses. Not only were 41 of the 65 who fled Singapore on the *Vyner Brooke* dead, but 21 of those dead had been executed after surrendering to the Japanese. The average weight of the nurses when they arrived at St Patrick's was around 30 kilograms. Authorities quite rightly feared the reactions of the Australians who saw the nurses at first hand in such a condition. If the normally calm Harry Windsor was driven to rage, what might others' responses be like? All in all, it was decided that it would be preferable to keep the nurses where they were until they were fitter, healthier and photogenic enough to be presented to the Australian people.

And those people included the family and friends of all 65 nurses who had left Singapore all those years ago. That group had done it hard during the war years, and now their uncertainty had ended and they could start planning for a future. During the three and a half years since the girls disappeared, families were given only limited details about the fate of their daughters and sisters. In the immediate aftermath of the fall of Singapore, those relatives were all notified that the nurses were 'Missing', but no detail was added to the description. Despite repeated requests by both the prisoners and the Australian government, the Japanese never did succeed in giving details of exactly who their prisoners were to any of the Allied nations.

There was some indication of the nurses' fate as the war years rolled on. Vivian had given details of the Radji Beach massacre to Air Commodore Modin in March 1942, and Modin shared this knowledge with other senior officers when he passed through Singapore en route to another POW camp. Diaries and notes from Changi prisoners indicate that the murder of the nurses was known to many Australians by July 1942. The first indications reached Australia via an unusual channel; in 1944, a POW ship en route to Japan was torpedoed by an American submarine and there were a number of Australians among the survivors. All eventually returned to Australia, where they reported what they knew.

Other indications came from the nurses themselves, when their cards home eventually arrived. For those whose loved ones had written there was both relief and hope, for those who received nothing there was just hope. There was always the possibility that their kin were in another camp, or that they were living in a remote area on one of the thousands of islands that made up the Indonesian archipelago. Perhaps they were in hiding or using another name or had lost their memory. Those who had nothing but hope had that hope dashed when the army officially informed them in mid-September that their daughters would not be coming home. Their dreams were shattered and many never recovered emotionally.

At St Patrick's, the nurses were placed in a specially decorated, light and airy ward, put on high protein diets, given the best medical treatment available and occasionally treated like movie stars. Fresh bowls of flowers were arranged daily, and most also took at least one bath a day. Each was given a sponge bag that contained, among other items, a toothbrush. For most of them it had been years since they were able to clean their teeth properly. They believed their imprisonment had literally made them smell like animals, and all were determined to wash that smell away once and for all. Their imprisonment had also changed them in ways immediately apparent to the nurses who assisted them, some of whom had been their colleagues until February 1942. Phyllis Pugh had specifically requested a transfer to the 2/14th AGH so she could help her former colleagues and friends from the 2/13th, those she had farewelled as she left for the *Empire Star*. Phyllis was there when the ambulances arrived:

> I walked past the hospital's entrance as an ambulance pulled up and its passengers alighted: 'They are coolies and should go to the European hospital.' Looking closer I saw, under the coolie hats, the old grey uniforms worn by our nurses, thongs on their feet and carrying small bundles of their belongings. It's them, thank God.

Phyllis had been good friends with Vivian Bullwinkel and, some days later, the two were catching up with what had been going on in each other's life since they had last spent time together. Out of the blue, Vivian asked Phyllis how she had reacted the other day when all the survivors had been brought to the hospital. Phyllis admitted that it had been extremely harrowing for her and that, after the greetings and the gifts, the hugs and the kisses, she had returned to her quarters, gone into her bathroom and vomited.

The survivors talked and talked and talked, with each other, with their friends in the 2/14th, and with anyone who asked them questions. They had years of catching up to do, and were anxious to learn everything about what they might have missed while they were away. It was like they wanted to talk themselves through and out of their experiences, as they gradually spoke less and less about what had happened and more and more about what was to happen in the future. Old habits also slowly fell away. When they first arrived, they would talk to each other while squatting on their haunches in the middle of an open space; chairs and lounges gradually became their preferred talking spots. For the first few nights, some simply could not fall asleep if they were lying in beds, so they hopped out and slept on the hard tiles underneath. The men at the hospital constantly brought them gifts – makeup and the like, but also foodstuffs, bananas, nuts and eggs. It was not unusual during the first week to see the girls squatting in a circle with cups of tea into which they would break one or two eggs as they chatted among themselves. They crammed so much protein in after their years of deprivation that several became bloated and had to be put on special diets.*

They were visited by Lady Edwina Mountbatten, photographed in and out of bed, and interviewed by dozens of Australian reporters who were, by then, filing daily reports from Singapore. Physically, the nurses' recovery was amazing. After less than a month in hospital they were all judged to be fit for travel, with only six being significantly less than their pre-war weight. They were taken from St Patrick's to Keppel Harbour, and then out to the Australian hospital ship *Manunda*. It was a far cry from their departure from the same point all those years earlier in all but one dimension: the nurses who lined the rails were again crying.

The story of the *Vyner Brooke* nurses captured the hearts and minds of a nation still trying to understand just how the Japanese had come to treat their prisoners in the way they had. Throughout most of September 1945, the front pages of every major Australian newspaper contained stories of Japanese atrocities committed against Australian service personnel, with each story adding meat to the ones that had preceded them. The nurses'

---

* In an interview with the *Argus*, published on 18 September, the medical superintendent of the 2/14th AGH was quoted as saying: 'They will go as soon as we have fattened them up.'

story was central to all that was printed; for two weeks at least, the major dailies contained reference to it in every edition, generally on the front page. The stories were not always accurate, and sometimes they did not even make sense, but they were about survival in extreme circumstances, and that made them newsworthy.

The second theme was that of the girls' honour, and many stories were based around the officers' club incident of March 1942 at Irenelaan. Again, style usually won out over substance. Bill Tebbutt's report on the *Vyner Brooke* nurses, written in Changi at war's end, was published in full in a number of Australian papers, and contained the passage:

> To put it bluntly, the Japanese officers had their eyes on the Australian nurses and a most serious situation was about to happen. Team work won the day or rather the night, when all turned up looking decidedly unattractive – dirty in body and filthy in clothing. The ruse worked for the Japanese were not impressed, thinking they could do much better in a camp of hundreds of women. So the nurses did not end up in brothels; but other women did offer and were accepted. They were often those who could not afford to buy the important 'extras' and who now had light duties in the camp.

The better reporters, though, spoke to those directly involved and asked them for their recollections of the incident. Mavis Hannah:

> We were billeted first in houses in Palembang, and Japanese officers who opened a club invited us to come along. The sisters, however, withstood all inducements, and eventually they left us alone when they realised that we did not desire to become geisha

girls. But whenever the Japanese were annoyed, they slapped the girls on the face. Gosh, I would have liked to slap them back.

And, finally, the senior surviving nurse, Nesta James:

. . . we were invited to the Officers' Club . . . the Japanese senior officer sent for and told me that it was our duty to work for the Japanese officers, clearly indicating what type of work. He added, 'How would you like to die?' I replied, 'We would prefer that.' Thenceforth, we were forced to hoe fields, carry water for Japanese baths and generally act as slaves with the barest of food. But we were much happier that way.

And so, honour was maintained.

The girls boarded the *Manunda* on Friday, 5 October and were escorted through the Malacca Straits by a Japanese minesweeper – the straits had been mined and, until the mines could be neutralised, the Allies relied on Japanese charts and seamanship to successfully navigate the seas around Singapore. The physical and psychological recuperation continued as they crossed the Indian Ocean, as did preparations for their arrival. In Perth, the local newspapers and radio had reported that there was a possibility that the nurses might have to spend a few days at a local hospital recuperating from their long voyage home. When Matron Eileen Joubert, the matron of that hospital, appealed via Perth radio for flowers to brighten up the nurses' rooms, the hospital was overwhelmed by the response. As well as providing enough flowers for every room in the complex, the entire forecourt of the hospital was covered in posies and tributes and single blooms, some of which had been brought hundreds of kilometres. In the end they weren't needed; the nurses' health had recovered enough in the six weeks since their rescue that, physically at least, they were able to resume a normal life in a country now at peace.

On 18 October, they arrived in Fremantle, with the inveterate diarist Betty Jeffrey recording:

> We saw our first little piece of Australia at about 3 p.m . . . the deck rails were lined with hundreds of soldiers and us twenty four nurses. We were terribly excited at first, but as it got nearer silence reigned. For an hour we watched Fremantle getting closer and still there was silence everywhere.

The *Manunda* anchored in Gage Roads and waited for something to happen. They had to wait a while as they had arrived home during a transport workers' strike. Pat Gunther observed: 'We then knew we were back in Australia.'

When the *Manunda* eventually docked at Fremantle, the nurses were allowed ashore to attend a reception held in their honour. Wearing borrowed uniforms, they mingled with the dignitaries and with the relatives of the Western Australian nurses who wouldn't be coming home. Mavis Hannah, a native of that state and the only survivor from the nursing staff of the 2/4th CCS, made it a point to speak to all the relatives of the dead girls who attended the reception, saying a few words to them individually about their daughters and sisters. After more tearful dockside farewells, the *Manunda* continued its voyage east. Arriving at Melbourne on 24 October, it discharged its Victorian, Tasmanian and South Australian nurses before sailing north to arrive in Sydney on 26 October. There, the nurses from New South Wales and Queensland departed, each to make her way home to whatever awaited her. They were feted in the state capitals, with official receptions in each, then admitted overnight to a repatriation hospital, and finally were given 28 days' leave to think about what they wanted to do.

It was just as well that the public showed its appreciation, as it became apparent that the army was uncertain of the best way to cope with its ex-prisoners, whatever their service or their gender. During their voyage home, the girls had all been given copies of a booklet entitled *While You Were Away* to read. Prepared by journalists at one of the country's major newspapers, the booklet detailed what had taken place in Australia and the wider world during the three and a half years they had been in captivity. As well as charting the course of the war, the booklet contained a hodgepodge of sports results, political, social and economic milestones, and pointers to changes in fashion and entertainment. When first rescued, the nurses were amazed at meeting women in trousers, and were also surprised by the size of those women's bosoms and bottoms. *While You Were Away* described a world they looked towards with some trepidation.

The army neither understood nor acknowledged the real price paid by prisoners of war of the Japanese. Vivian Bullwinkel and Nesta James were given somewhat different treatment from the others because they were to be part of the broader Allied effort to bring Japanese war criminals to account. The others were given a medical, some leave and a choice – stay or go. Welcome home, heroes. You are now free to return to the family and friends you left a lifetime ago.

Army psychologists had determined that reliving their POW experiences would probably not be a good thing for anyone who had gone through them, and so any relatives and friends of all the girls, if they asked about the most appropriate responses and approaches, were told that it would be best to pretend that the whole thing had never happened. In hindsight, it is difficult to think of worse advice. Vivian Bullwinkel would suffer nightmares and flashbacks for the rest of her life, but had to wait almost 30 years to find someone who she could share those stark memories with. Others buried them deeply, refusing to talk about their experiences to anyone but those with whom they had been shared.

In the weeks and months after their return to Australia, many of the nurses felt that something was missing from their lives. They had lost the love and companionship they had shared with their fellow nurses, fellow Australians who had gone through the living hell that was Irenelaan, Muntok and then Belalau. Flo Trotter later recalled that she found most people in Australia when she returned to be light, superficial and frivolous. Families and friends, they all felt, could not understand what they had been through and how they had changed, and they especially no longer seemed to have a lot of interests in common. Jenny Greer also recalled her early days at home as being bittersweet: 'It seemed a very lonely time. So much so that we used to try to meet the others from camp for lunch or for drinks after duty every day until we got used to being among civilians.'

Such emotions were almost universal among the girls. Mavis Hannah: 'We missed our companions who had sustained us for so long and who understood how we felt. Our people nearly killed us with kindness and couldn't see through our eyes at all.' Jessie Blanch: 'We got out of uniforms as soon as we could. It was fairly easy adjusting back to civilian life – as everyone was so kind – but I did miss my POW friends, and saw them as often as I could.'

Following their recuperation leave, the nurses reported back to the various army headquarters around Australia. Most of them indicated a desire to be discharged, and the separations commenced early in 1946. 'Del', Cecilia Delforce, was the first to leave, being discharged with the rank of lieutenant on 9 January 1946, and by the end of that year, only three of the girls remained in the AANS. Many of those discharged walked comfortably into civilian life and spent the rest of their lives in relative anonymity, their stories known only to family, close friends, and 'the girls' who they caught up with whenever they could.

As 1946 rolled on, the separations increased apace. 'Woodie', Beryl Woodbridge, left as a lieutenant in March and was followed soon afterwards by Chris Oxley, who also held the army rank of lieutenant by war's end. Jessie Blanch was demobilised on the same day as Chris Oxley, and had a double celebration; she had turned 36 a few days earlier. 'Shorty', Eileen Short, and Violet McElnea were both discharged on the same day in early April, both lieutenants, and were followed into civilian life the following day by Captain Jess Doyle. As April ended, Lieutenant Valerie Smith and Captain Jessie Simons ended their army nursing careers. In May 1946 lieutenants Sylvia Muir and Iole Harper were discharged and in June, Joyce 'Tweedie' Tweddell left the service. Captain Kathleen (Pat) Blake departed in July and Captain Jenny Greer was discharged in September, hopefully singing 'We're Off to See the Wizard' as she left. Captain Nesta James became a civilian in October 1946, while the year closed with the separations of Lieutenant Veronica Clancy and Captain Mavis Hannah. Captain Pat Gunther stayed only a little while longer, leaving the AANS in February 1947 after 12 months' service with the 113th AGH at Concord in Sydney. With the discharge of both Betty Jeffrey and Vivian Bullwinkel in late 1947, a major chapter in the history of Australian military nursing was closed.

CHAPTER 13

All Their Tomorrows

Most of 'the girls', as they would refer to themselves for the rest of their lives, simply wanted to pick up the pieces where they had left off when they volunteered for the AANS. Many had all but given up on the possibility of having a normal courtship followed by marriage and a family after all that they had experienced, fearing that what they had lived with and through had probably made them unsuitable, both physically and mentally, for the roles of wife and mother. Sixteen of the 24 *Vyner Brooke* girls would eventually marry, and eight of them had children. Some of those who married did so later in life, after they had completed a long and mostly distinguished career in nursing. Those who married within a year or two of war's end started – or tried to start – a family almost immediately. Those who didn't marry, as far as I have been able to determine, continued in nursing. Those who had already given so much simply continued to give, either to their family or to the larger community.

Flo Trotter went from the AANS to Allen and Stark Limited, at the time one of Brisbane's leading department stores, where she was appointed to an internal staff nursing position – basically a first-aid nurse. Flo was able to convince company management of the benefits of professional nursing care being available at the store for more than headache tablets and bandaids, and she was appointed the company's – and one of Australia's – first industrial nurses in late 1946. She married Mickey Syer's brother, Frank, and they had two daughters. Flo continued her nursing career in increasingly senior positions, until she retired in 1976.

Mavis Hannah returned to Malaya after the war. During her time there previously, both before and after the Japanese attack in December 1941, she had met and befriended an English expatriate plantation manager, Joe Allgrove, and his wife, a Red Cross volunteer nurse who had performed outstanding work during the last few days before Singapore fell. Joe's wife was among a group of English civilians evacuated aboard the *Gian Bee*, and was killed when that vessel was sunk by Japanese naval craft. Joe had become a prisoner of war after surrendering as part of the Malay Volunteer Forces, and survived both the Burma-Siam Railway and the war. Joe wrote to Mavis after the war, and she travelled to Malaya to see if their friendship had survived the tragedies the war had brought down upon them. It had. That friendship blossomed into romance and they married in late 1946.

Joe and Mavis – who he always called Nell – returned to the upcountry Malayan rubber plantation Joe had managed before the war. There, Mavis ran the plantation's medical clinic, but was only able to do so on a part-time basis after she and Joe started a family. They raised three children in Malaya, children born when Mavis was 38, 40 and 42 years old and believed she was beyond child-bearing age. When their children were still young, a communist insurgency broke out, the Malayan Emergency, and the Allgroves' isolation made them vulnerable. Although they both loved Malaya, Joe and Mavis made the hard decision to leave, and returned to Joe's native England. Every Anzac Day, Mavis would travel from their home in the English countryside to the Cenotaph in London, where she would lay a wreath in memory of her AANS sisters, the girls who did not survive the war.

Others who married also moved overseas with their husbands. Jenny Greer married a Scotsman, Duncan Pemberton, whom she'd met in Sydney in December 1940, shortly before being called up for service. Their brief pre-war friendship, sparked by a chance encounter on the street while Duncan was holidaying on leave from his job in Singapore, grew into something special and they married in Singapore in 1947. The Pembertons later moved to Chichester in England. Jess Doyle married another ex-prisoner of war, Norman Macauley, an officer in the 8th Division's 2/30th Battalion. In Changi, Macauley had been an aide de camp to Black Jack Galleghan. The Macauleys moved to New Zealand for Norman's work, and there raised a family of two daughters and a son. They subsequently returned to Australia, where Norman died in 1968. Sylvia Muir, too, married an Australian soldier and ex-prisoner, Colin McGregor, whom she had first met when he was admitted to her hospital in Malaya in 1941. After their marriage in Brisbane, the McGregors moved to a dairy farm near Bega in southern New South Wales. Sylvia helped Colin on the farm and raised three sons at Bega. After Colin's sudden and unexpected death, Sylvia returned to her home town of Brisbane.

Jessie Simons also returned to her home town, Launceston, at war's end and there reintroduced herself to her now extended family; several new in-laws had joined the family while Jessie was a prisoner. After her discharge from the AANS in 1946,

Jessie returned to nursing at the Launceston General Hospital. She retired from nursing to look after her elderly parents, and married later in life, in 1970. The love of Jessie's life was Hayman Hookway. The couple lived out their remaining years together in the little village of Boat Harbour on Tasmania's northwest coast. In 1954, Jessie had written a book about her wartime experiences. Entitled *While History Passed*, it was reprinted several times and was republished in 1985 as *In Japanese Hands: Australian Nurses as POWs*.* Throughout her working life and in retirement, Jessie remained active in nurses' and related associations.

Pat Gunther also continued in nursing until 1957 when she married Colin Darling, a widower with four children. The family made their home at Mount Keira outside Wollongong. In 2001, Pat also published her memoirs in a book entitled *Portrait of a Nurse*.

Joyce Tweddell continued her medical studies, eventually becoming a radiographer and a leader in the use of radiotherapy in treating cancers. Wilma Oram, too, continued her nursing. Like several of the others, Wilma married an ex-prisoner of war, Alan Young, albeit one captured by the Germans. They raised four sons in South Gippsland in Victoria and, following Alan's premature death in 1991, Wilma became very involved in local and state Returned Services' League activities.

The best known of the surviving *Vyner Brooke* nurses was and always will be Vivian Bullwinkel, who was to devote the rest of her life to the profession of nursing. Upon her separation from the AANS in November 1947, Vivian returned to civilian

---

* Jessie's book was written less than a decade after the war ended while she was in northeast Tasmania, about as far from Banka Island as you could get. In it Jessie wrote, quite wistfully: 'Even now, surrounded by my friends and relatives, I still long for my old pals.'

nursing, accepting a position at the Heidelberg Repatriation Hospital in Melbourne. She was later appointed Matron and Director of Nursing at the Fairfield Infectious Diseases Hospital, also in Melbourne. Vivian steadfastly maintained an interest in the wider issues affecting nursing in general and military nursing in particular.

Vivian was appointed Matron of the Army Nurses' Training Unit in 1955, a part-time position which allowed her to work closely with the regular army nursing staff in the training of recruits in all aspects of military nursing. While matron at Fairfield, Vivian organised a reserve nurses' mission to evacuate Vietnamese war orphans from Saigon. When the orphans were successfully brought to Australia, she supervised their convalescence before they were adopted by Australian families. She was later to become patron of the National Service Nurses' Memorial. Between 1964 and 1969, Vivian served as the first female trustee of the Australian War Memorial, and was also appointed to the governing body of the Royal Humane Society of Australia. Finally, Vivian became a council member and later president of the Australian College of Nursing.

In among all these achievements were two that Vivian always thought were her most valuable. One was meeting and marrying, in 1977, the love of her life, an ex-army colonel named Frank Statham. After their marriage, the couple set up house in Perth. The second was working with her wartime friend, Betty Jeffrey, to establish a Nurses' Memorial Centre in Melbourne to both recognise and commemorate the work of their fallen colleagues. Vivian, Betty Jeffrey, Jean Ashton and Beryl Woodbridge had thrown some ideas around when they were having one of their regular chinwags at Irenelaan in 1943, thinking about and looking at ways to remember all the sisters who had gone since the evacuation of Singapore. The girls agreed any memorial should be something 'living' rather than a cold piece of granite because, when they thought of the girls, it was of their liveliness and vitality. Any memorial should have similar qualities. It was an idea that never really went away.

When Betty Jeffrey was discharged from hospital in 1947, she and Vivian discussed their plans to create a living bequest, remembering the dreams they had formed and shared those years before at Irenelaan. They wanted to build a centre that would house all things associated with nursing – education, recreation and the likes – as well as providing residential accommodation for the nurses and trainers. Utilising all their spare time, including their weekends and holidays, Betty and Vivian drew up a plan and crisscrossed Victoria and most of southeastern Australia, addressing any public meeting that would have them. At every town that contained a hospital of 20 or more beds, they would address the nurses about their dreams for a centre to recognise another group of nurses just like them, and ask those nurses to support the idea in any way they could.

One of the first meetings they addressed was in the Victorian regional centre of Ballarat, and it was a meeting they felt had gone well. At the reception afterwards, Betty and Vivian were approached by an older man who thanked them for what they had said and what they hoped to do and presented them with a cheque for five guineas. He introduced himself as Mr Cuthbertson, and said his daughter Mary had died on Radji Beach. In Albury, they took time out of their schedule to visit a house in Wilson Street, the home of a Mrs Calnan, a widow whose daughter Ellenor had died in the sinking of the *Vyner Brooke*. Both found that, after a while, telling their stories became easier, and they were no longer upset at recalling some of the things they had seen. It was almost as if they were talking about a stranger on the beach at Radji or in the jungle at Belalau.

At the end of those 12 months, they had raised the total of 123,000 pounds, several million dollars in today's terms, and an enormous amount in the constrained postwar economy. It was enough to purchase a property, a century-old mansion at 431 St Kilda Road, Melbourne. By 1949, the sisters' dreams were a reality.

Betty Jeffrey served as the centre's administrator when it was finally operational. The qualities that stood her in good stead as a prisoner of war – compassion and a willingness to undertake any job necessary for the benefit of the group – also underpinned her capacity to guide the early development of the Nurses' Centre. Betty also found time to write a book based on the diary and notes she had kept, at considerable risk, throughout her years of imprisonment. She called the book *White Coolies*, to reflect how the Japanese perceived the nurses and even, perhaps, how they had sometimes perceived themselves. It became one of Australia's top-selling books of all time.

The survivors of the 8th Division proper, the formation of which the three nurses' units were a part, also decided to establish some form of living memorial to the men and women from the unit who perished in battle or as prisoners. On 27 August 1945, before the nurses had been liberated, a meeting of senior officers of the division was held at the Changi POW camp. At that meeting, the idea of a nursing scholarship was put forward by Major John Cade of the 2/9th Field Ambulance. The proposal was presented to Colonel Annie Sage in Singapore in September, and gained her approval and support. The first scholarships awarded under the scheme were for Chinese nurses only, but this was later expanded to include all Malaysians and, after their breakaway from Malaysia, all Singaporeans. The first nurses to be awarded scholarships for postgraduate studies arrived in Australia in 1947, and the scheme continues to this day. One of its long-serving board members was Vivian Bullwinkel.

In the immediate postwar period, the Australian government also recognised individual contributions within the greater service that was provided to the Australian soldier by the members of the Australian Army Nursing Service. Fifty-five members of that nursing service were decorated for various meritorious acts, 80 others were Mentioned in Despatches, and two were awarded the George Medal, the highest decoration that could be bestowed upon them. The *Vyner Brooke* nurses were well represented in this Roll of Honour. Jean Ashton, Nesta James and Cecilia Delforce were all Mentioned in Despatches, James for her work before the surrender in Malaya and Singapore; Ashton and Delforce for the leadership they provided as prisoners of war.

Their own profession also recognised the nurses' war service. At war's end, Jessie Blanch, Nesta James and Vivian Bullwinkel were all awarded the Associate Red Cross. The awards recognised the work of the three under fire and in prisoner of war camps. Part of Nesta James' citation outlined why the award was made, noting: '. . . the disregard she had for personal danger and the quality of the leadership she exhibited in the performance of her duties.' It was a description that could have been applied to most of the girls.

The ongoing work of Betty Jeffrey and Vivian Bullwinkel was also recognised by the wider community they served. In 1987, Betty was awarded the Medal of the Order of Australia for her services to ex-service personnel. Vivian was made a member of the Order of the British Empire, and was later awarded the Florence Nightingale Medal, the highest award the Red Cross can give.

* * *

While the nurses who survived were welcomed back by their families and friends, and eventually found some kind of 'normal' life, those who did not return were never forgotten, by either those that survived when they perished, their families or by the communities they had served. In the months and years after August 1945, the names of all those who had perished in the sinking of the *Vyner Brooke*, on Radji Beach, or in the camps at Muntok or Belalau were recorded on Rolls of Honour at the Australian War Memorial at Canberra. Some who were recorded there were mourned in private by their loved ones only, while others were given more public recognition.

In July 1947, in the town of Maffra in Gippsland in eastern Victoria, a service was held in the Maffra Memorial Hall to dedicate another memorial, a stained glass window, and to honour the memory of Rene Singleton. Sharing the event with her father Robert, who had given up two sons and a daughter to the gods of war, were several local dignitaries and a number of women in army nursing uniforms. Led by Colonel Annie Sage, Matron in Chief of the AANS, was a number of Rene's sisters and friends: Vivian Bullwinkel, Betty Jeffrey, Mickey Syer and Flo Trotter.

Alma Beard is commemorated by the community she served in Toodyay by the Alma Beard Community Health Centre, while to commemorate Flo Casson's sacrifice, after the war the Pinnaroo Soldiers Memorial Hospital named one of its health promotion facilities after her. Lavinia Russell is the subject of one of the local history projects which are part of the 'St George District and the War' promotion by her local government area in Sydney. Marjorie Schuman's service and death are commemorated on the 8th Division's War Memorial at Gunnedah in New South Wales, a memorial opened by that division's commanding officer, General Gordon Bennett, on 8 December 1957, 15 years to the day after the Japanese invaded Malaya. Her name also appears on the war memorial at Manly in Sydney.

In 2003 a street in Port Hughes, near Moonta in South Australia, was renamed Trenerry Place to recognise that family's contribution to the area as well as Merle Trenerry's sacrifice. Merle was also commemorated at the 2001 Kernewek Lowander, held each May to recognise and celebrate the region's Cornish heritage. Minnie Hodgson is commemorated on the Lake Yearlering Memorial Gates at the local primary school, while on 11 November 1984, a memorial to Lainie Balfour-Ogilvy was unveiled at the Children's Library in Renmark, South Australia. Lainie's old school, Woodlands, in Adelaide, each year awards the Elaine Balfour-Ogilvy to a Year 11 student, maintaining the memory of the young woman who must have been one of that school's greatest students. In 1942, before news of Lainie's fate was known in Australia, her older sister Audrey had a baby, a girl she named Elaine.

In Yanaina, Western Australia, the sub-branch of the Returned Services' League used its February 2007 email newssheet to publish photographs of Louvinia Bates, Ellenor Calnan and Mary Cuthbertson as well as a brief note about their fate. Mary McGlade is commemorated on the war memorial at Wallalong, Florence Salmon on the war memorial at Punchbowl and Kathleen Neuss on Inverell's Roll of Honour. Jenny Kerr is commemorated on the Roll of Honour at Woodstock, near Young in New South Wales, where there is also a beautiful memorial to her in the town's main street. The memorial was unveiled by the Governor of New South Wales in 1984.

Mona Tait, the nurse who trained at Royal Canberra Hospital and who was shot dead on Radji Beach, is remembered along with another Canberra-trained nurse named May Hayman, through the Returned Services' League Tait/Hayman Fund, established to honour the two nurses' memory. Income from the fund's investments is donated to the University of Canberra to purchase books for its Nurses' Library. May Hayman was not an army nurse, but joined the Anglican Mission to New Guinea where she worked in several remote villages. May was posted to Gona shortly before the Japanese invaded and, when they did, May and another nursing sister attempted to escape to Australian lines. Captured by Japanese soldiers, both were bayoneted to death, as was May's fiancée, a missionary doctor. Mona Tait is also commemorated on a wall plaque at Canberra Hospital.

William Sydney (Bill) Sedgeman, of the town of Fishguard, Pembrokeshire, was 27 years of age when he died on Radji Beach near the nurses he had tried so hard to succour and protect. His friend and fellow officer, James William (Jimmy) Miller was 29 when he, too, was killed on Radji Beach. The two sailors are commemorated on the Liverpool Naval Memorial.

There is a children's playground in the grounds of the Broken Hill Hospital. Within it is a memorial to Irene Drummond. Its beauty and simplicity are paralleled by the memorial to Olive Paschke in her home town of Dimboola.

The clamour for revenge that accompanied each new revelation about Japanese war crimes was not a call that appealed to most of the girls, who simply wanted to go home to get on with their lives. The extent of those Japanese war crimes was such, however, that all the Allies established war crimes investigation units, and all Allies cooperated with the system of criminal justice designed specifically to deal with what had happened to those who were abused by the Japanese. Only two of the *Vyner Brooke* nurses were directly involved in those legal processes – Nesta James and Vivian Bullwinkel. In Australia, Vivian gave evidence before the Australian War Crimes Commission of Inquiry on 29 October 1945 and was followed into the witness box three days later by Nesta James. While the bulk of Vivian's evidence was based around the events on Radji Beach, she also offered some testimony about conditions in the various camps in which the Australian nurses had been confined. Her evidence was complemented by that of Nesta James. As the senior Australian nurse in those camps, Nesta was able to talk about the fruitless, indeed pointless, negotiations with successive military and civilian administrations and how her nurses, like the civilians, weakened and died even though both food and medicine were available. Such was the power of their evidence that the Australian government decided to send both women to Tokyo in 1946 to make depositions before the International Military Tribunal there.

The nurses travelled to Japan aboard HMAS *Kanimbla*. Vivian in particular was quite deeply moved by what she saw in Japan. The extent of the destruction wreaked by American bombers was a sobering surprise and, after seeing how Japanese women were treated in the factories and the fields, she felt that she understood at least a little of the thinking that led to the Radji Beach massacre. When she saw Japanese soldiers in uniform being led into and out of the courtroom, however, Vivian struggled with her emotions. Despite those feelings of unease and dread, she was determined to present the events of Radji Beach in a clinical and objective manner. Before her appearance, she wrote out her deposition on small index cards, arranged in sequence. Several times a day, she would take the cards out and go through them until she was able to make her statement word for word and without hesitation. When called to the witness box, she gave a bravura performance.

The wheels of justice moved slowly and there were some

elements that reported on every creak, every movement of those wheels. In October, a number of Australian newspapers reported on Vivian and Nesta's appearances before the War Crimes Tribunal. Most concluded with the statement: 'Investigators are closing in on those believed responsible for the murders.'

Most of the surviving *Vyner Brooke* nurses stayed in touch with one another through visits and letters, and through attendance at the annual AANS reunion, an event commenced in the late 1940s. These reunions survived longer than the AANS itself; in 1949, the service became part of the regular army rather than a volunteer reserve, and is now known as the Royal Australian Army Nursing Service. The nurses' reunions were rotated among the Australian capital cities with the 1988 reunion being held at the Nurses' Memorial Centre in Melbourne. The *Vyner Brooke* nurses always made every effort to attend these reunions, with Mavis Hannah (Nell Allgrove) travelling from England to attend the event in 1990.

As well as providing an opportunity for old friends to catch up, the reunions allowed the nurses to plan for their profession's future and to lobby the politicians who inevitably attend such events. The reunions also provided the occasional opportunity to put those plans into practice through involving a wider public audience. Responding to concerns raised by the surviving nurses, several years after the war the Commonwealth War Graves Commission recovered the remains of the girls who died in captivity and reinterred them in the Jakarta War Cemetery in Mentong Poewtow.

February 1992 marked the fiftieth anniversary of the fall of Singapore and a large party of Australians, including several former AANS nurses, travelled there as part of the celebrations.

The tourists visited Changi Prison and the Changi Museum, then Selarang Barracks, the main hospital for Australian POWs in Changi. On the second day of their organised trip, Joyce Tweddell and Wilma Oram (Young) made a special trip to the Methodist Girls' School to present the students with some books on Australia. The larger group then attended a service at St Andrew's Cathedral. The next day, their last one in Singapore, the party visited the Kranji War Cemetery, where the names of the sisters whose bodies were never recovered are engraved in marble.

Later that year, Vivian and Frank Statham travelled to Banka Island to select a site for a memorial to the slain nurses. Vivian found that the beach had changed considerably in the 50 plus years since her ordeal. While she was able to locate the freshwater spring, she could not be certain of the exact spot where so many of her sisters had died. On 2 March 1993, a group of increasingly frail survivors, accompanied by relatives and Australian officials, attended the dedication of a memorial to honour all 65 of the nurses evacuated from Singapore aboard the *Vyner Brooke*. A stone from one of their POW camps is embedded in the memorial, which is located not too far from where the massacre occurred. One of those younger people who witnessed the ceremony described it as: 'A quiet, dignified ceremony, marked by the individual contributions of each of those women, some reading from the Bible, others offering prayers from the heart.'

Following the war and the return of thousands of ex-prisoners of war of the Japanese to Australia, army and repatriation department doctors undertook a number of medical surveys of those ex-prisoners. The results suggested that three and a half years as a prisoner of the Japanese would reduce a person's life expectancy from five to 15 years. Time would inevitably finish what years of ill-treatment had started.

By 1984, Violet McElnea, Eileen Short and Nesta James had all passed away. Vi was the first to go, dead of a heart attack in the late 1950s. Nesta did marry, becoming Nesta Joy; she passed away in 1984. Betty Woodbridge never married; her health began to fail in the early 1980s and she died in 1986. Mickey Syer passed away in April 1991. In 1999, her sister-in-law Flo Trotter (Syer) would be honoured for her services to nursing when the Flo Syer Ward was dedicated and opened at the Repatriation/Greenslopes Private Hospital in Brisbane. In October 1994, Mavis Hannah (Nell Allgrove) passed away in the United Kingdom. With her death, Australia lost a great nurse and the world lost a great heart. Tweedie (Joyce Tweddell) died in Caloundra in November 1995, aged 79 years. In the early 1970s, Tweedie had refused a nomination for the award of an MBE as she believed all surviving POWs deserved one. The Oncology Building at the Royal Brisbane Hospital was subsequently renamed in her honour. Veronica Clancy died in October 1997 some time after writing what may be the best memoirs of a prisoner of war and Australian nurse ever written, and in 1999 both Iole Harper and Sylvia Muir (McGregor) passed away.

Frank and Vivian Statham were guests of honour at the unveiling of a memorial to the *Vyner Brooke* nurses in their home town of Perth in April 1999. Frank died in December of that year, and most of the light went out of Vivian's life. Vivian Statham passed away in Perth in July 2000 following a massive heart attack. Monash University in Victoria subsequently established a Chair of Palliative Care in her honour. Three months after Vivian's death, her good friend Betty Jeffrey passed away in Melbourne. In 2001, Wilma Oram (Young) died in Victoria, still grieving for her friend Mona Wilton but always recalling the life they led in pre-war Malaya as one of the highlights in a long and rich career. Jenny Greer (Pemberton) passed away at Chichester in the United Kingdom also in 2001, 59 years after she raised the spirits of all who heard her singing as she floated away on a plank from a sinking ship. Hopefully, this time she did get to meet the Wizard. Flo Trotter (Syer) in August and Sister Carrie Jean Ashton, in December and aged 97 years, both died in 2002. When Pat Gunther (Darling) passed away quietly at her home in December 2007, aged 94 years, the last of the *Vyner Brooke* nurses was gone; the sisterhood had ended.

In the only postcard the Japanese ever allowed her to send to Australia while she was a prisoner, Vivian wrote to her mother and brother in March 1943 that: 'My roving spirit has been somewhat checked.' For Vivian and her sisters from the *Vyner Brooke*, the checks that war and imprisonment inflicted on them were only ever regarded as temporary ones. They had served and survived in the past and they would serve and survive in the future. They were friends and they were family, a kongsi forged in pain and suffering, but a kongsi that would survive whatever fate threw at them. It did until December 2007, when it was reformed in a different way and at a different place.

In her tiny handwriting, the woman who was, perhaps, the strongest of them all, Mavis Hannah, hand-wrote a speech she would give at a Sisters' Dinner at an RSL in Adelaide on 14 February 1988 – Banka Day:

> Recently I went to Kranji War cemetery and I found the names of our sisters, who have no known graves, on the marble arches. I thought of them as I knew them, young and beautiful, and of all the love, laughter and courage. All they have now, except the love that is theirs, from relatives and friends who knew them, is a name on a piece of marble.

Looking back, I think of all the sisters who didn't come home. I think of them as young and beautiful, not growing old but eternally young. 'Tis them I think of particularly when I say, 'They shall not grow old, as we who are left grow old.'

I would like to close with the epitaph on the Kohima Memorial in Burma, which says: 'When you go home, tell them of us and say, "For your tomorrow, we gave our today."'

POSTSCRIPT
CANBERRA 2010

The story of the murder of 21 Australian nurses on Radji Beach, Banka Island, on the morning of Monday, 16 February 1942 is just a small part of the much wider story of the Pacific War. Like so many incidents that occur within a broader context, it is also a story of what might otherwise have been. If the British had prepared their Malayan and Singaporean defences better than they did, the incident may not have occurred, but it is at the micro rather than the macro level that the seemingly random nature of fate is thrown into stark relief.

Statistically, almost one in six of the AANS nurses who served in the Malayan campaign was executed on Radji Beach on 16 February 1942. While not exactly the result of mere chance, those who were on the beach when the Japanese patrol arrived were there as a direct result of the actions of time and tide. More indirectly, they were there because of commission or omission by their superior officers.

With the exception of Vivian Bullwinkel, all the nurses who

eventually made it to Radji Beach and the welcoming bonfire that had been lit there died. Vivian was second from the left end of the line of nurses as they started to walk down the beach and into the water at the direction of the Japanese soldiers. Those on the right end of the line were shot before they entered the water, and any not killed outright were despatched by bayonets shortly afterwards. By the time the spray of bullets reached Vivian, the water reached almost to her knees. She was not shot a second time or bayoneted because she was in a blood-stained dress in a blood-stained sea, and no Japanese was prepared to enter the water to ascertain otherwise.

Those survivors who gathered at Radji had the misfortune of being surrendered to soldiers of the 229th Regiment of the 38th Division of the Imperial Japanese Army. While soldiers of that regiment and that division were regarded within the army as being particularly tough, they were also capable of being exceptionally cruel. It was probably the attitude and actions of their captain, Orita Masaru, that were most responsible for what happened. It seems likely that Orita had been directly in charge of the soldiers who raped and murdered their way through St Stephen's Hospital in Hong Kong, and it was certainly Orita who issued the orders for all the killings at Radji Beach.

Orita's reasons for ordering the killings will never be known, although it is possible to speculate on them. In Japanese eyes, the surrender of soldiers, civilians and nurses by First Officer Sedgeman was viewed as an act of failure and cowardice, and those who surrendered had no honour and were therefore unworthy of any consideration. Their disposal was also therefore a matter of no great weight. Captain Orita Masaru had been given clear orders to seize and hold the town of Muntok and the tin-mining facilities in the area; however, the two companies he had at his disposal were rapidly being overwhelmed by the sheer number

POSTSCRIPT

of prisoners they were expected to house, feed and guard. The news that another hundred or so, including many wounded, were waiting to surrender at Radji Beach – and also both required and expected assistance – would not have been welcome. The fact that Orita himself accompanied the patrol he despatched is also significant for, as the senior Japanese officer at Muntok, his place was probably at the headquarters he established in the police station. Sergeant Major Taro Kato could easily have handled bringing the prisoners back in. Orita's accompanying the patrol suggests he wanted to see the prisoners in situ before determining their fate.

It appears that no Japanese troops were killed in the process of occupying Muntok, but that the Japanese did suffer casualties in the following days. When Betty Jeffrey and Iole Harper were brought into Muntok, they were taken to a room at the police station where a number of Japanese wounded were being treated by other soldiers. It is likely these casualties were the result of air raids undertaken by aircraft of the Dutch Army Air Force, for several of the contemporary accounts mention air attacks on shipping in Muntok harbour on 15, 16 and 23 February. If there were soldiers wounded, there may have been soldiers killed, something which may have predisposed their fellow soldiers to take revenge on those they held responsible.

It also seems probable that the Radji Beach killings occurred because the senior Japanese commander on Banka Island decided it was going to be too much of an effort to look after an additional hundred or so prisoners, especially as some of them were wounded and there were no Japanese medical facilities available for them. While other killings were carried out by Japanese soldiers on Banka Island, most of these seem to have been spontaneous; Vivian Bowden, for instance, or the execution of native troops that one of the nurses witnessed. What happened at Radji Beach was the result of a premeditated decision by Orita Masaru, who took what he saw as the easy option. The shame of surrendering seems to have been a one-way street for Orita, as his surrender at the end of the war does not seem to have weighed too heavily on his heart. Orita was a prisoner of war in the Soviet Union for almost three years before his extradition to Tokyo. It was only on the eve of being tried as a war criminal that he rediscovered his warrior spirit and committed suicide.

There were persistent rumours both during and after the war that the nurses at Radji Beach had been raped before they were murdered. Although he did not witness the crime, an English soldier named Robert Seddon survived an attack by Japanese soldiers not far from Radji Beach and, recovering, traversed the site of the killings some time later on the day of their occurrence. He saw the bodies and believed that some of them appeared to have been 'interfered with'. Ernest Lloyd also said that the clothing on the bodies of the nurses on the beach appeared to have been disturbed, but he thought the disturbance may have been caused by the actions of bullets, bayonets and waves. Vivian Bullwinkel never mentioned any form of sexual assault before the shooting commenced, and all the rumours appear to have been started by people not associated directly with the nurses.

The possible sexual abuse of the nurses was a source of ongoing interest to the newspaper reading population of Australia, as well as to military authorities. In response to a question from Army Headquarters in Melbourne, the commanding officer of the No. 2 Prisoner of War Repatriation group reported back to Australia that none of the nurses had been 'molested' in captivity. In general, Japanese soldiers' sexual violence was directed more towards Asian women than it was towards European women – both military and civilian – in part perhaps because of the 'otherness' and apparent unattractiveness of European women.

In the immediate postwar years, several of the nurses published books about their wartime experiences – Betty Jeffrey, Jessie Simons and Pat Darling – while Jean Ashton's daughter edited and published her mother's wartime diary. Biographies were also written about Vivian Bullwinkel and Wilma Oram. Many of the nurses also gave interviews to local journalists and to authors researching books on the POW experience and archivists from the National Library of Australia. Several were involved in contributing to a fictionalised account of the experiences of women prisoners of the Japanese, the critically acclaimed film *Paradise Road*. One story that was recounted regularly in all these reminiscences concerned the opening of the Japanese officers' club at Irenelaan just a few weeks after the Australian nurses arrived there from the coolie lines at Muntok.

With slight variations, they all spoke of how the Japanese camp commandant announced that an officers' club was to be opened in one of the Irenelaan houses and how the Australian nurses would be required to provide a number of 'hostesses' for the club. The commandant even identified who those hostesses should be – a number of the younger nurses, all small, dark and attractive. On the evening the club was to open, almost 20 of the nurses turned up at the clubhouse. They wore their oldest clothes, were without makeup and had oiled their hair so that it sat tightly against their skulls. One of the girls later claimed that she had even splashed her own urine on her clothes. At the club, they refused all invitations to drink alcohol or to dance with the Japanese officers who assembled there, and who produced a gramophone and records. A Japanese officer led one of the girls outside and tried to kiss her. She escaped his grasp and fled back inside. The party broke up soon afterwards. The next day, the Australians lodged a formal complaint with the senior Dutch Red Cross official at the camp. Nothing more was heard of the officers' club or of its need for 'hostesses'. So the story was passed down.

During the mid-1990s, one of the surviving nurses was diagnosed with breast cancer, and was told that the cancer was inoperable and that she had only a short time to live. A postgraduate student from a local university had been seeing the elderly woman regularly, gathering information on the history of Australian nursing for a thesis she was writing. With only a short time to live, the elderly nurse told the young student another story about the officers' club at Irenelaan. The club's opening night had gone pretty much as all the nurses had described, but the Japanese response was far different to what had become the accepted history.

The day after the farce of the opening night, the Japanese camp commandant was still furious about the behaviour of the nurses, and called for the two senior Australian nurses to report to his office. He told them that the attitude and behaviour of the Australian nurses was an insult to the Emperor and the Japanese Army and would not be tolerated. No rations would be issued to either of the Australian houses until they had supplied four hostesses to the club. When the Australians mentioned the Dutch Red Cross, his response was to laugh and to ask them precisely what the Red Cross was in a position to do. If there were a Dutch Red Cross, the commandant observed, they were now a very long way away and besides, compared to the Imperial Japanese Army, exactly what kind of power did the Red Cross wield? The choice they had was a simple one, he continued: provide the hostesses or starve to death.

Back at one of the Australians' houses, a meeting of all the

POSTSCRIPT

nurses was held. The Japanese demand was explained to them and the meeting was thrown open to suggestions and discussion. No-one present doubted that the Japanese were perfectly capable of acts of cruelty – Radji Beach was too recent – and the senior nurses were convinced that the Japanese commandant was serious and would carry out the threats he had delivered if his demands were not met. There was a lot of discussion and a decision was eventually taken: the Australian nurses would provide four hostesses for the club, knowing those hostesses would be required to provide sexual services for the Japanese officers. However, the nurses provided would not be the young women already identified by the Japanese but four volunteer nurses, older women who said they were prepared to work at the club because they knew their profession was their life, and they would probably never marry or raise a family.

A Bible was produced and all nurses present swore an oath upon it. No-one would ever reveal the names of the four nurses who volunteered to become comfort women to save their sisters from that fate. This decision was conveyed to the Japanese and for several weeks, four Australian nurses worked as hostesses at the officers' club. After that time, the camp was handed over to civilian administrators and the officers' club was closed. The nurses themselves, in their memoirs and in interviews given after their repatriation, were scornful of those Eurasians and Europeans who voluntarily entered into sexual relationships with Japanese soldiers in return for preferential treatment. They referred to them contemptuously as 'the girlfriends' or the 'satin sheet brigade'. There was some sympathy, however, for the well-documented cases of mothers in internment camps offering themselves as comfort women rather than allowing their adolescent daughters to be put at risk.

Three years after the postgraduate student heard the true

story of the officers' club at Irenelaan, an American university professor visiting Australia interviewed a wide range of Australians as part of his research into the factors that contributed to the distinctive Australian character. While looking at the religious aspects of Australian life, he interviewed another one of the *Vyner Brooke* nurses, three years and several thousand kilometres from the woman interviewed by the student. Independently, his interviewee confirmed the earlier story of the officers' club and the comfort women. She, too, did not reveal who the four volunteers were, and they have never been publicly identified. The sisters honoured the oath they swore, and took their secret with them to the graves.

Primarily through the internet, it was possible to partially close some of the loops and links that contributed to the story of the *Vyner Brooke* nurses. Little June Bourhill, who lost her mother and part of a finger when the *Vyner Brooke* went down, survived the war and was returned to her father in Australia who had never really known her. Misha Warman, orphaned in the same incident, also survived the war and at its conclusion was returned to relatives who had stayed behind in Shanghai. Misha's was not a straightforward journey though, as he travelled to Shanghai via Scotland accompanying a Miss Cullen, one of the Christian missionaries from the camp, and the woman who finally located his relatives. Rumour has it that Misha, and his adoptive parents, fled China after the communist takeover and settled in the United States. There the adult Misha found success in business and eventually retired as a millionaire.

The captain of the *Vyner Brooke*, Richard 'Tubby' Borton, spent 18 hours alone in the water after his ship was sunk, and was eventually washed ashore near the Tanjung Kelian lighthouse.

POSTSCRIPT

After time in the men's section of the coolie lines at Muntok, Borton was transferred to Changi Prison in Singapore where he spent the rest of the war. While imprisoned, he did not reveal to his captors that he had been the last captain of the *Vyner Brooke*. Postwar, he returned to the sea, and was later awarded an Order of the British Empire for his wartime services. Borton retired to Bradford in northern England and died there in 1965, aged 75 years. One of his daughters now lives just outside Melbourne.

Colonel Douglas Pigdon, Commanding Officer of the 2/13th AGH, was one of a group of senior officers, including Colonel Albert Coates of the 2/10th AGH, who were sent from Changi to different POW camps in mid-1942, presumably to prevent them having any influence on their soldiers. Pigdon was firstly imprisoned in Taiwan and later transferred to Mukden in Manchuria where he died of disease in July 1945. All other medical officers, including Bruce Hunt and Tom Hamilton, survived the war and returned to Australia and to private practice, where many of them achieved great success.

Colonel Annie Sage retired as Matron in Chief of Army nurses in August 1952. The recipient of many Commonwealth honours and international nursing awards, the mother of the *Vyner Brooke* nurses passed away in 1969, aged 73 years.

The *Vyner Brooke* itself was named after the third, and last, White Rajah of Sarawak. In 1946, Sir Charles Vyner Brooke ceded Sarawak to Great Britain. It now forms part of Malaysia.

Researching and writing this story was something of a journey for me. The *Vyner Brooke* nurses were contemporaries of my parents and while I knew the bare bones of their story, all I really understood was that they were killed by the Japanese somewhere in what my father always referred to as 'the islands'. I had no real knowledge of those who had died, how they had died or even really understood how they came to be in harm's way in the first place. I came to writing their story later in life and did not have the opportunity to speak to the survivors, to hear their stories in their own words and to ask the questions I really wanted answers to: How did it feel? What were you thinking at this point? What did it look like?

I have read their books and these now sit proudly on my bookshelves at home. I have listened to some of their voices on audiotapes and thought how much like my aunties they sounded. I have read their letters and diaries and postcards at the Australian War Memorial, but I still do not *know* them. I know what many of them did before, during and after the war, and have thought about what those who did not return may have been able to do given the chance. War really is the tragedy of what might have been. Each and every one of the *Vyner Brooke* nurses, those who survived and those who did not, had and has a story of her own, of youth and adulthood, of Australia and elsewhere – of dreams and hopes, and pains and fear. I often visit Vivian Bullwinkel's corner in the war memorial because I find it inspirational. It hints at lives cut short, of sacrifice and self-sacrifice. It makes me proud of who I am and where I come from, and helps me understand my parents, now long gone, a little more, and it puts a feeling of comfort in a tiny corner of my heart. Seeing the girls as they were, and then seeing what those who survived made of their lives, has been always fascinating, always somehow comforting. It does, though, highlight just what the families of those who did not return actually lost in Banka Strait, on Radji Beach and in the camps of Muntok and Sumatra.

We will never know what contributions Olive Paschke and Irene Drummond would have made to their profession in a postwar world, but I believe those contributions would have been mighty. I feel Olive in particular was a woman of unlimited vision and energy. But, equally, we can never know just what that superb letter-writer Buddy Elmes may have done for her beloved Tripehounds or just where the multi-talented Lainie Balfour-Ogilvy would ultimately have finished. For me, one of the enduring images of the story is what Jeff and Iole saw as they drifted away from their raft in Banka Strait. Olive Paschke, ever organised, with her team about her on the raft and in the water, with Caroline Ennis cuddling two small children. None would ever be seen again, but their image, for me, sums up all that was special about the AANS, and all that their families and their country have lost.

ENDNOTES

Prologue
Page
5. 'But the voice faltered . . .': Pat Darling, *Portrait of a Nurse*, ch. 6.

Chapter 1: Elbow Force
Page
13. 'The nurses were calling her . . .': Pat Darling, *Portrait of a Nurse*, ch. 1.
13. 'Curly haired girl . . .': Biography of Marjorie Henderson at www.pabooks.libraries.psu.edu

Chapter 2: 'The Land of Stinks, Chinks and Drinks'
Page
27. 'The Malayans . . .': Pat Darling, *Portrait of a Nurse*, ch. 2.
28. 'Each block consisted of . . .': letter of Dorothy Elmes, Australian War Memorial PR 88/108.
28. 'Four of us in a cubicle . . .': Elmes letter.
31. 'The local residents . . .': Elmes letter.

329

ENDNOTES

32. '. . . we went over . . .': Elmes letter.
32. 'To reach Frazer's . . .': Elmes letter.
33. 'A delightful small city . . .': Darling, ch. 3.
33. 'It was said . . .': Darling, ch. 3.
33. 'The Botanical Gardens . . .': Darling, ch. 3.
34. 'One sign in front . . .': Elmes letter.
34. '. . . the narrow, smelly streets . . .': Ann Synan, 'Rene Died on Banka Island', p. 4.
34. 'We had many long . . .': letter of Wilma Oram, AWM PR 84/345.
35. 'The army, in the early . . .': Private soldier in 2/30th Battalion, contained in a letter of Betty Jeffrey, AWM PR 01780.
36. 'We didn't think . . .': Mavis Hannah, AWM MSS 1486.
39. 'The people of Malaya . . .': *Australian Women's Weekly*, 3 May 1941.
40. '. . . you will think . . .': Elmes letter.
41. 'Uncertain about her ability . . .': diary of Betty Jeffrey, AWM PR 01780.

Chapter 3: Reinforcements
Page

46. 'Post the Army': Wilma Young, *Victorians at War Oral History Project*, Tape 1, 4 December 2000.
46. 'You'll never guess . . .': letter of Mona Wilton, Australian War Memorial PR 89/092.
46. 'Mona and I are together . . .': letter of Wilma Oram, AWM PR 84/345.
48. '. . . you are going to nurse . . .': Veronica Clancy, AWM MSS 1086.
48. 'No written messages . . .': Lex Arthurson, *The Story of the 13th Australian General Hospital*, p. 6.
50. 'At night . . . the reflections on the water . . .': Clancy, AWM MSS 1086.
50. '. . . he was encouraging them . . .': Arthurson, p. 116.
53. 'I was most impressed . . .': Arthurson, p. 117.
54. 'I shall never forget . . .': Arthurson, p. 116.

55. 'It was a surprise to me . . .': Jessie Simons, *While History Passed*, p. 2.
56. '. . . very formal affairs . . .': Clancy, AWM MSS 1086.
57. 'I'll never forget . . .': Simons, p. 3.
57. '"We" means Wilma and me . . .': Wilton letter.
58. 'There will be a war . . .': Arthurson, p. 118.
58. '. . . hibiscus, bouvardia . . .': Clancy, AWM MSS 1086.
60. '. . . an Oriental gentleman . . .': Folklore.
61. 'The two Australian girls . . .': Oram letter.
61. 'What a night we had . . .': Oram letter.
62. 'Below our tent lines . . .': Thomas Hamilton, *Soldier Surgeon in Malaya*, p. 4.

Chapter 4: The Balloon Goes Up
Page

66. '. . . my old one was getting very pongy . . .': letter of Dorothy Elmes, Australian War Memorial PR 88/108.
66. 'I would get plenty of voile underwear . . .': Elmes letter.
67. 'Pigdon added . . .': Lex Arthurson, *The Story of the 13th Australian General Hospital*, p. 118.
69. '. . . your parcel of books arrived . . .': letter of Irene Drummond, AWM PR 87/187.
69. '. . . the blackouts are the bane of my existence . . .': Drummond letter.
69. 'The thoroughfare was christened "Kinsella Avenue" . . .': Thomas Hamilton, *Soldier Surgeon in Malaya*, p. 15.
70. 'We went dancing . . .': letter of Mona Wilton, AWM PR 89/092.
71. 'They took us to the nicest place . . .': Wilton letter.
71. '. . . I gave my tea planter a little bit of cake . . .': Wilton letter.
72. 'On that day, the password was "Coolabah" . . .': Hamilton, p. 25.
76. 'If twenty strong, healthy women . . .': Hamilton, p. 35.
77. 'The Army Signals Corps . . .': Arthurson, p. 118.

ENDNOTES

79. '. . . we have hurricane lamps . . .': Drummond letter.
79. 'I heard a good story the other day . . .': Drummond letter.
80. 'Each night we have . . .': letter of Nell Keats, quoted in Hannah, AWM MSS 1486.
81. 'Matron Paschke has . . .': Official Award Transcript, AWM website, Awards and Honours.
83. 'We commandeered big brass trays . . .': Roy Mills, *Doctor's Diary and Memoirs*, p. 33.
86. '. . . [Lainie] won the hearts of all the men . . .': in the papers of Betty Jeffrey, AWM PR 01780.
88. 'I rang General Percival . . .': H. Gordon Bennett, *Why Singapore Fell*, p. 172.

Chapter 5: The Curtain Comes Down
Page

90. '. . . but the invasion . . .': *The Bulletin*, 31 December 1941.
92. '. . . possessed of a splendid nursing technique . . .': Thomas Hamilton, *Soldier Surgeon in Malaya*.
92. 'He also said that he would be recommending . . .': Hamilton, p. 44.
93. 'Our morale had never fallen . . .': Veronica Clancy, Australian War Memorial MSS 1086.
93. 'Our hospital grows bigger daily . . .': letter of Irene Drummond, AWM PR 87/187.
94. 'Deviating from the entrance . . .': Hamilton, p. 163.
96. 'Later in the week . . .': Betty Jeffrey, *White Coolies*, p. 2.
97. 'The blood bank . . .': Lex Arthurson, *The Story of the 13th Australian General Hospital*, p. 119.
98. '. . . I knelt beside a stretcher . . .': Arthurson, p. 120.
98. 'I shall never forget seeing . . .': Clancy, AWM MSS 1086.
101. '. . . You must have guessed by my letters . . .': letter of Mona Wilton, AWM PR 89/092.
101. 'Our quarters are only a flat . . .': letter of Dorothy Elmes, AWM PR 88/108.

ENDNOTES

101. 'The nurses' quarters are excellent . . .': letter of Nell Keats, quoted in Hannah, AWM MSS 1486.
101. 'Darlings, in a terrible hurry . . .': Wilton letter.
102. 'There is nothing to write about . . .': Drummond letter.
102. 'No news. Cheerio . . .': Elmes letter.
104. 'We were conscious of the danger . . .': Barbara Angell, *A Woman's War*, p. 45.
105. 'The girls who had to go . . .': Clancy, AWM MSS 1086.
108. 'At the time we felt ghastly . . .': in the papers of Helen Jacobs, AWM PR 02064.
108. 'When we were told to leave . . .': Arthurson, p. 118.
109. 'The situation we met . . .': Jacobs papers, AWM PR 02064.
109. 'There was a big crate . . .': Jacobs papers.
110. 'We were to travel in the hold . . .': Jacobs papers.
110. 'Most of us were in the hold . . .': Jacobs papers.
114. 'When the all clear sounded . . .': Jeffrey, p. 4.
116. 'The incident that stands out most . . .': Geoffrey Brooke, *Singapore's Dunkirk*, p. 19.
116. 'Oh no, you're not . . .': Mavis Hannah (Allgrove), AWM MSS 1486.
116. '. . . small, sinister-looking dark grey ship . . .': [Source unknown.]
117. 'From the lawn that night . . .': Hamilton, p. 193.

Chapter 6: The Last Voyage of the *Vyner Brooke*
Page
121. 'The ship's crew were tired out . . .': in the papers of Betty Jeffrey, Australian War Memorial PR 01780.
123. 'It was a never to be forgotten scene . . .': Betty Jeffrey, *White Coolies*, p. 4.
123. 'In the distance, Singapore appeared . . .': Veronica Clancy, AWM MSS 1086.
124. 'As we sailed out of Singapore . . .': diary of Jean Ashton, AWM PR 87/80, p. 3.

333

ENDNOTES

128. 'Friday was the most beautiful . . .': in the papers of Vivian Bullwinkel, AWM PR 01216.
129. 'It was like an unexpected holiday . . .': Jessie Simons, *While History Passed*, p. 10.
134. 'I felt very sorry for the many children . . .': Simons, p. 8.
135. 'Health issues, y'know . . .': From the combined recollections of several who experienced Mary Brown's excuses for not helping.
136. 'For many years a semi-invalid . . .': Simons, p. 24.
136. '. . . Leave for unknown ship . . .': Geoffrey Brooke, *Singapore's Dunkirk*, p. 136.
138. 'Very little food . . .': Brooke, p. 136.

Chapter 7: Banka Strait
Page
150. 'I felt certain that the bombs would miss . . .': Betty Jeffrey, *White Coolies*, p. 5.
153. 'Back came the planes . . .': Jeffrey, p. 5.
153. 'Sylvia Muir was quite close . . .': Lex Arthurson, *The Story of the 13th Australian General Hospital*, p. 100.
156. 'Everybody stand still!': Jeffrey, p. 6.
161. 'Many of the civilian women were hysterical . . .': Veronica Clancy, Australian War Memorial MSS 1086.

Chapter 8: Adrift
Page
168. 'Shut up, Chris . . .': Mavis Hannah (Allgrove), Australian War Memorial MSS 1486.
169. 'Lainie called to Mavis . . .': Hannah, AWM MSS 1486.
171. 'terribly pleased': Betty Jeffrey, *White Coolies*, p. 8.
176. 'I'm a mother of three . . .': Veronica Clancy, AWM MSS 1086.
178. 'Jessie Simons had very short hair . . .' Jessie Simons, *While History Passed*, p. 22.
179. 'Congratulations . . .': my quote, based on Bill Tebbutt's recollections.

180. '... we were practically naked ...': Clancy, AWM MSS 1086.
183. 'In a dream, Mavis heard ...': Hannah, AWM MSS 1486.
187. 'As the raft was swept away ...': Jeffrey, p. 11.
194. 'You know, Sister, the real tragedy ...': Clancy, AWM MSS 1086.

Chapter 9: On Radji Beach
As Vivian Bullwinkel was the only nursing survivor of the events on Radji Beach, the majority of this chapter is based on her recollections as recorded in a number of places, including newspaper interviews she gave after liberation and the deposition she made for the International War Crimes Tribunal. Not all the accounts Vivian gave are identical, and I have given greater weight to those details that are repeated across accounts. I have also given added weight to details she recalled immediately after the event to the other nurses rather than those that appear in much later accounts. The other survivors, Eric German and Ernest Lloyd, also provided material to journalists and, where this doesn't clash with Vivian's account, I have used it to support hers.

Chapter 10: Sumatra
Page
234. 'Matron didn't arrive ...': angellpro.com.au, 'Jessie Blanch'.
242. 'A weird assortment of clothes ...': Veronica Clancy, Australian War Memorial MSS 1086.
244. 'To think of all the times I said "No!" ...': Clancy, AWM MSS 1086.
247. 'There is rice, rice ...': Betty Jeffrey, *White Coolies*, p. 39.
248. '... we read and reread ...': Jessie Simons, *While History Passed*, p. 53.
249. 'We were fascinated of course ...': Clancy, AWM MSS 1086.
251. 'Mitzi's facial bone structure ...': Pat Darling, *Portrait of a Nurse*, ch. 13.
252. 'Can I be of any assistance?': Clancy, AWM MSS 1086.
256. '... please communicate with the Red Cross ...': Mavis Hannah (Allgrove), AWM MSS 1486.
258. 'For the last two months ...': Jeffrey, p. 104.

ENDNOTES

Chapter 11: The Song of Death
Page
262. '... were just too popular ...': Betty Jeffrey, *White Coolies*, p. 95.
265. 'We sailed early ...': Nesta James, War Crimes Deposition, Australian War Memorial 54/1010/4/78.
266. 'Our own Ray, Sister Raymont ...': Jeffrey, p. 149.
267. 'They shall hunger no more ...': Veronica Clancy, AWM MSS 1086.
268. 'Rene Singleton, 2/10 AGH, a Victorian ...': Jessie Simons, *While History Passed*, p. 89.
269. 'It took 20 of us to carry out a coffin ...': Pat Darling, *Portrait of a Nurse*, ch. 21.
277. 'Dear Family, please don't worry about me ...': Darling, ch. 24.
278. 'We had reached the stage ...': Darling, ch. 22.

Chapter 12: Homecoming
Page
280. 'Jessie Simons walked away ...': Jessie Simons, *In Japanese Hands*, p. 111.
281. 'Chris Oxley was facing certain death ...': Betty Jeffrey, *White Coolies*, p. 186.
283. 'Have encountered among 250, repeat 250 ...': Norman Manners, *Bullwinkel*, p. 174.
286. 'Young, with very white teeth': Jeffrey, p. 191.
286. 'The two boys also told us ...': Jeffrey, p. 192.
287. 'I think some of the girls ...': Clancy, MSS 1086.
288. 'Where are the Australian nurses?': Barbara Angell, *A Woman's War*, p. 173.
288. 'Who are you?': Pat Darling, *Portrait of a Nurse*, ch. 25.
289. 'It was a sad if thrilling sight ...': Adelaide *Advertiser*, 18 September 1945, p. 1.
289. 'As the nurses stepped out ...': Melbourne *Argus*, 18 September 1945, p. 1.

ENDNOTES

290. 'Sick Australian POWs in hospital...': South East Asian Command Bulletin, Singapore edition, No. 11, 19 September 1945.
290. '...and slowly and painfully...': in Bullwinkel Papers, AWM PR 01216.
293. 'I walked past the hospital's entrance...': Lex Arthurson, *The Story of the 13th Australian General Hospital*, p. 119.
295. 'To put it bluntly...': Adelaide *Advertiser*, 18 September 1945, p. 3.
295. 'We were billeted first...': Mavis Hannah (Allgrove), Australian War Memorial MSS 1486.
296. '...we were invited to the Officer's Club...': Nesta James, War Crimes Deposition, AWM 54/1010/4/78.
297. 'We saw our first little piece of Australia...': Jeffrey, p. 203.
297. 'We then knew we were back in Australia...': Darling, ch. 26.
299. 'It seemed a very lonely time...': Lavinia Warner and John Sandilands, *Women Beyond the Wire*, p. 267.
299. 'We missed our companions...': Hannah, AWM MSS 1486.
299. We got out of uniforms...': angellpro.com.au, 'Jessie Blanch'.

Chapter 13: All Their Tomorrows
Page
308. '...the disregard she had for personal danger...': Official citation, Australian War Memorial website, Honours and Awards.
309. 'In July 1947, in the town of Maffra...': Ann Synan, 'Rene Died on Banka Island', p. 6.
314. 'A quiet, dignified ceremony...' Judith Spence, *Bangka* [sic] *Island*, anzacday.org.au/history.

SOURCES

AUSTRALIAN WAR MEMORIAL RESEARCH CENTRE
As well as being a wonderful and wonderfully moving place to visit, the Australian War Memorial in Canberra has a research centre which contains an extremely rich variety of resources for the historian, whether amateur or professional. The holdings are categorised broadly into personal records (PR), which are the items donated to the memorial by ex-service personnel, their family or friends, that are of a nature to contribute something to our understanding of the personal experience of conflict. These personal records can be just about anything, and requesting them can be a bit like a lucky dip. Sometimes the folders will contain a single letter or photograph, but at other times there may be hundreds of pages of tiny notes, a Bible or a series of illustrated letters. I can remember handling, with reverence, a tiny diary that an Australian POW had kept while working on the Burma-Siam railway, recording in his minuscule writing his thoughts and experience. I was turning the pages carefully, and peering

SOURCES

closely at his writing when I read the sentence about how he kept the diary concealed from his Japanese captors. Each day, he would carefully insert the book between the bottoms of his bum cheeks under his loincloth. I read the rest of it at a considerably further distance from my face.

A second category is the manuscripts (MSS), which can range from four pages to in excess of 400. Many of the veterans chose to write down their experiences, sometimes at the urging of family or friends, and at other times as a way of recollecting and recognising the extraordinary times they lived through. Some are poorly written while others are of almost publishable quality with just a modicum of editing. All are worthy of reading.

Finally, there is a wealth of material in the official documents held by the memorial, which are given the prefix AWM. These also range across quite a large territory, and include all manner of official documents from individual units' War Diaries, to individual depositions for war crimes investigations. The research centre may not be an Aladdin's cave for historical researchers, but it is very close:

PR 84/345	Wilma Oram (Young)
PR 84/357	Sylvia Muir
PR 86/129	Shirley Gardam
PR 87/80	Carrie Jean Ashton
PR 87/187	Irene Drummond
PR 88/003	Wilhelmina Raymont
PR 88/108	Dorothy (Buddy) Elmes
PR 89/092	Mona Wilton
PR 01141	Jean Stewart
PR 01216	Vivian Bullwinkel
PR 01780	Betty Jeffrey
PR 01989	Pat Darling (Gunther)

SOURCES

PR 02064   Helen Jacobs
PR 03126   Mary McGlade
MSS 1086   Veronica Clancy
MSS 1486   Mavis Allgrove (Hannah)
AWM 54/1010/4/78   Nesta James Deposition

There was also a wealth of other materials to support the story I was trying to tell in this book. The National Library of Australia remains the first port of call for anyone researching social history, and its newspaper and maps' collections are basically traps; they catch you and won't let you go. As well, there is the internet, the starting point for anyone who wants to *know*. Finally, Dr Madonna at the Nurses' Memorial Centre pointed to many sources not available elsewhere.

Using a search engine and any person's name, any event, or any circumstance or ship mentioned in the book will take you away to the world of the *Vyner Brooke* nurses, and it is a world that retains an attraction for those of us born to parents who were part of it. More specifically, websites dedicated to Australian nurses (Barbara Angell's sets the standard) or the prisoners of war (Children of Prisoners of Eastern Prisoners of War, COFEPOW), or even the various official websites like the Australian War Memorial, the Commonwealth War Graves Commission, Department of Veterans' Affairs, and the like in Australia and elsewhere give flesh to the sometimes dry bones of history; no pun intended.

BIBLIOGRAPHY

BOOKS

Adam-Smith, Patsy, *Australian Women at War*, Penguin, Ringwood, 1996.

——*Prisoners of War*, Ken Fin, Collingwood, 1998.

Angell, Barbara, *A Woman's War*, New Holland, Sydney, 2005.

Armstrong, Ralph, *Short Cruise on the Vyner Brooke*, George Mann Books, Maidstone (UK), 2003.

Arthurson, Lex, *The Story of the 13th Australian General Hospital*, self-published, no date.

Ashton, Jill, *Jean's Diary: A POW's Diary, 1942–45*, self-published, Adelaide, 2003.

Barber, Noel, *Sinister Twilight*, Arrow Books, London, 1958.

Bassett, Jan, *Guns and Brooches*, Oxford University Press, Melbourne, 1997.

Bayly, Christopher and Harper, Timothy, *Forgotten Armies: The Fall of British Asia 1941–45*, Harvard University Press, Boston, 2006.

Bennett, H. Gordon, *Why Singapore Fell*, Angus & Robertson, Sydney, 1944.

BIBLIOGRAPHY

Black, Airlie, *Elaine Balfour-Ogilvy*, Woodlands Old Scholars' Association, 2008.

Brooke, Geoffrey, *Singapore's Dunkirk*, Leo Cooper, London, 1989.

Burchill, Elizabeth, *Australian Nurses since Nightingale*, Spectrum Publications, Richmond, 1992.

Burfitt, James, *Against All Odds: The History of the 2/18th Battalion, AIF*, self-published, 1991.

Caffrey, Kate, *Out in the Midday Sun: Singapore 1941–45*, Andre Deutsch, London, 1974.

Chapman, Ivan, *Tokyo Calling: The Charles Cousens Case*, Hale and Iremonger, Sydney, 1990.

Coates, Albert and Rosenthal, Newman, *The Albert Coates Story*, Hyland House, Melbourne, 1977.

Cody, Les, *Ghosts in Khaki*, Hesperian Press, Perth, 1997.

Colijn, Helen, *Song of Survival*, Headline, London, 1995.

Connolly, Ray and Wilson, Bob (eds.), *Medical Soldiers*, 2/10 Field Ambulance Association, Kingsgrove, 1985.

Cooper, Bryan, *Decade of Change: Malaya and the Straits Settlements, 1936–45*, Graeme Brash P/L, Singapore, 2001.

Crouch, Joan, *One Life is Ours: the Story of Ada Joyce Bridge*, St Luke's Hospital, Darlinghurst, 1989.

Darling, Pat, *Portrait of a Nurse*, Don Wall Publishing, Mona Vale, 2001.

Daws, Gavan, *Prisoners of the Japanese*, Scribe, Melbourne, 2004.

De Vries, Susan, *Heroic Australian Women at War*, HarperCollins, Sydney, 2005.

Dodkin, Marilyn, *Goodnight Bobby: One Family's War*, UNSW Press, Sydney, 2006.

Dower, John, *War Without Mercy: Race and Power in the Pacific War*, Pantheon Books, New York, 1986.

Edgerton, Robert, *Warriors of the Rising Sun*, Westview Press, Boulder, 1997.

Gibson, Walter, *Singapore Escape: The Boat*, Monsoon Books, Singapore, 2007.

BIBLIOGRAPHY

Goodman, Rupert, *Our War Nurses: The History of the Royal Australian Army Nursing Corps, 1902–88*, Boolarong Publications, Brisbane, 1988.

Goodwin, Bob, and Dixon, Jim, *Medicos and Memories*, 2/10 Field Regiment Association, Brisbane, 2000.

Guthrie, Stella, and Clark, Jill, *Lighter Shades of Grey and Scarlet*, self-published, Adelaide, 1985.

Hamilton, Thomas, *Soldier Surgeon in Malaya*, Angus & Robertson, Sydney, 1987.

Harries, Meirion and Susie, *Soldiers of the Sun*, Random House, New York, 1991.

Harrison, Ada (ed.), *Grey and Scarlet – Letters from War Areas by Army Sisters on Active Service*, Hodder & Stoughton, London, 1944.

Hodder, Ralph, *The Singapore Chinese Massacre*, Horizon Books, Singapore, 2004.

Jeffrey, Betty, *White Coolies*, Angus & Robertson, Melbourne, 1954.

Kenny, Catherine, *Captives: Australian Army Nurses in Japanese Prison Camps*, UQP, St Lucia, 1986.

Lindner, Robert, *Christianity and the Australian Character*, Monograph, Kansas State University, 2006.

Lodge, A.B., *The Fall of General Gordon Bennett*, Allen & Unwin, 1986.

McBryde, Brenda, *Quiet Heroines*, Cakebread Publications, Essex, 1989.

McKernan, Michael, *This War Never Ends*, UQP, St Lucia, 2001.

McLeod, Ian, *I Will Sing to the End*, Horizon Books, Singapore, 2005.

Manners, Norman, *Bullwinkel*, Hesperian Press, Victoria Park, 1999.

Mant, Gilbert, *The Singapore Surrender*, Kangaroo Press, Sydney, 1992.

Mills, Roy, *Doctor's Diary and Memoirs*, self-published, Newcastle, 1994.

Monahan, Evelyn, and Neidel-Greenlea, Rosemary, *All This Hell, American Nurses in Japanese Hands*, University of Kentucky Press, Lexington, 2000.

BIBLIOGRAPHY

Nelson, Hank, *Prisoners of War*, ABC Enterprises, Sydney, 1985.
Poole, Philippa, *Of Love and War*, Lansdowne Press, Sydney, 1982.
Rees, Laurence, *Horror in the East*, BBC Books, London, 2001.
Reid, Richard, *Just Wanted to be There: Australian Service Nurses 1899–1999*, Department of Veterans' Affairs, Canberra, 1999.
Richards, Rowley, *A Doctor's War*, HarperCollins, Sydney, 2006.
Russell of Liverpool, Lord, *The Knights of Bushido*, Corgi, London, 1960.
Simons, Jessie, *While History Passed*, William Heinemann Limited, Melbourne, 1954. Reprinted as *In Japanese Hands*, 1985.
Smith, Colin, *Singapore Burning*, Penguin Books, London, 2006.
Tanaka, Yuki, *Hidden Horrors: Japanese War Crimes in World War Two*, Westview Press, Boulder, 1996.
Thompson, Peter, *The Battle for Singapore*, Portrait Books, London, 2005.
Twomey, Christina, *Australia's Forgotten Prisoners*, Cambridge University Press, Melbourne, 2007.
VFX47777, *A Brief Record of the Australian Army Nursing Service, 1939–45*, self-published, no date. [This army number belonged to Captain Barbara Haynes, AANS.]
Warner, Lavinia and Sandilands, John, *Women Beyond the Wire*, Michael Joseph, London, 1982.
Warren, Alan, *Singapore, 1942*, Talisman, London, 2007.
Waterford, Van, *Prisoners of the Japanese in World War Two*, MacFarland and Company, North Carolina, 1994.
Wigmore, Lionel, *The Japanese Thrust*, Australian War Memorial, Canberra, 1957.
Williams, Jennifer, *Victoria's Living Memorial: History of the Nurses' Memorial Centre, 1948–90*, Nurses Memorial Centre, Melbourne, 1991.

ARTICLES

—— *A Bitter Fate*, Department of Veterans' Affairs, Canberra, 2002.
—— *Lest We Forget*, Australian Army Pamphlet, 1944.

——*Listening Post*, Journal of the Western Australian Returned Services League, Vol. 28, No. 11, December 2005.

Henning, Peter, 'Some Tasmanian Nurses: An Anzac Story', TasmanianTimes.com, 25 April 2009.

Synan, Ann, 'Rene Died on Banka Island', *Gippsland Heritage Journal*, No. 27, 2003.

Tebbutt, William A., Official Report, Adelaide *Advertiser*, 18 September 1945.

United States Army, Military Intelligence, *Order of Battle of the Japanese Armed Forces*, Washington DC, 1945.

Victorians at War Oral History Project, www.victoriansatwar.net.

ACKNOWLEDGEMENTS

If you've made it this far, you may as well stay around for the final credits. The first of these is to Sophie Hamley at the Cameron Creswell Agency, who believed that Radji was a story worth telling, and to Alex Craig at Pan Macmillan who took the idea and ran with it, and in doing so, made the telling of the story a little bit better than it might otherwise have been. Her colleague, Brianne Collins, put the icing on the cake. To all the people who I have again bored to death with tellings and retellings of the Australians in the Pacific War, I would like to say thank you for your indulgence. To Sean Brawley, historian par excellence; to a small group of friends, the Wilfred 'Chicken' Smallhorn Country Football Appreciation Society, thank you for many decades of forbearance, and to those on the peninsula, hugs and kisses.

While looking at and for another project I dreamed of writing, I had the pleasure of spending time with a soldier, a sailor and an airman who had all done time in the theatre of operations in which all these events took place. The soldier was Jim Kennedy,

ACKNOWLEDGEMENTS

the sailor was John Wood and the airman was 'Spud' Spurgeon. All three had stories of conflict and long years of imprisonment in vile circumstances. All three noted that they were the lucky ones, and that men much better than themselves had not survived the war. I'm just not certain of that, as each impressed me as being living examples of whatever it is that has made Australia what we all like to believe it is. Thank you, gentlemen.

Finally, to my family, thank you again for your humour and also for your passion. The book is partly for my mother, who would have loved it, and for my sister Laraine, who already believes it deserves a shelf of its own at her bookshop. It is for my mother-in-law, Marnie, and my sisters-in-law, Debra and Jill. It is for my daughters-in-law, Julie and Cassie, and for my granddaughters, the princesses Hannah, Clementine and Violet. But mostly it's for the two women who fill my life with love and laughter – my wife Pam and my daughter Amy. So many of the good things I saw in the *Vyner Brooke* girls reminded me of you.

INDEX

Adelphi Hotel 33, 108
Alexandra Hospital 91, 119
Allgrove, Joe 302–3
Allgrove, Mrs 97, 302
Allgrove, Nell *see* Hannah, Mavis
America *see* United States of America
Anderson, Sister 262
Argyll and Sutherland Highlanders 89
Armistice Day 248
Armstrong, Ralph 135, 226
Ashton, (Carrie) Jean 87, 124, 130, 160, 174, 179, 194, 233, 240, 242, 244, 246, 248, 254, 255, 261, 266, 272, 305, 316, 322
 Mentioned in Dispatches 308
Australian Armed Forces
 deserters 109–10, 111
 Malayan Campaign 5, 119

RAAF 47, 54, 70, 180
tropical diseases 29–30, 55, 78, 93, 98, 266, 270, 271
Australian Army Nursing Service (AANS) 4, 11, 13
 allowances 36, 46–7
 ambulance units 91
 Australian College of Nursing 305
 awards and decorations 308
 Belalau, at *see* Belalau POW camp
 Casualty Clearing Station *see* Casualty Clearing Station (CCS)
 deaths in prisoner of war camps 266–70, 272, 275–6, 278–9
 discharge from 300
 eligibility for 11
 emergency kits 67–8

INDEX

Australian Army Nursing Service
    (AANS) (cont'd)
  evacuation of Singapore 103–19
  Frazer's Hill 32–3, 34, 275
  Irenelaan, at see Irenelaan POW
    camp
  leadership of 98–9, 261
  Mentioned in Dispatches 308
  Nurses' Memorial Centre
    305–7, 313
  nursing as a career choice 11–12
  113th Australian General
    Hospital see 113th AGH
  Queen Mary, on 10–12, 14–23,
    102
  Radji Beach, massacre at
    214–18, 291, 318–21
  recreational leave 32–4
  reinforcement nurses, arrival of
    40–1
  request for evacuation 89, 103
  reunions 313
  Rolls of Honour 308, 309
  searches for 282–3
  2/7th Australian General
    Hospital see 2/7th AGH
  2/10th Australian General
    Hospital see 2/10th AGH
  2/12th Australian General
    Hospital see 2/12th AGH
  2/13th Australian General
    Hospital see 2/13th AGH
  2/14th Australian General
    Hospital see 2/14th AGH
  service men, interaction with 35
  Singapore, in 22–3, 24–7, 33–4
  social life 31–4, 56–8, 71–3
  tropical diseases and infections,
    treatment of 29–30, 50, 55,
    78, 93, 98, 266, 270, 271,
    275–8
  uniforms 11, 16, 35, 36, 135,
    141, 199, 238, 267, 284–5,
    299
  venereal diseases, patients with
    37
  Vyner Brooke, casualties on 166
    see also *Vyner Brooke*
Australian College of Nursing 305
Australian General Hospital (AGH)
  see Australian Army Nursing
  Service (AANS)
Australian Imperial Force (AIF)
  (1st) 10
Australian Imperial Force (AIF)
  (2nd)
  cemetery at Malacca 30
  designation of units 10
  8th Division 10, 11, 35, 38, 43,
    54, 89, 282, 307, 309–10
  Japanese forces, battles with
    82–3
  practical jokes in 80
  2/4th Brigade 117
  2/9th Field Ambulance 10, 118,
    307
  2/10th Regiment 35, 75
  2/13th Brigade 117
  2/18th Brigade 10
  2/19th Brigade 10
  2/20th Brigade 10
  2/22nd Brigade 10
  2/27th Infantry 43, 52
  2/30th Battalion 82, 86, 92, 303
  Tobruk, at 93
Australian War Crimes Commission
  of Inquiry 311–12 see also war
  crimes

350

INDEX

Australian War Memorial 305, 309
Australian Women's Weekly 37–40, 60

Balfour-Ogilvy, Elaine (Lainie) 19–20, 86, 100, 138, 169, 173, 214–18, 310, 328
Balfour-Ogilvy, Harry 19
Ball, Harold 118
'Banka fever' 266, 270 *see also* tropical diseases and infections
'The Song of Death' 270
Banka Island 142, 168, 170, 173, 259, 264
    coolie lines 195–6, 232–3, 234–8, 264
    memorial 314
    Muntok, history of 191–2
    psychological damage to prisoners 298–9
    survivors arrival on 176–7, 180–1, 182–4, 187–91, 194–5, 198–9, 235
    transfer to Palembang 238–40
Banka Strait 130, 139, 142, 164, 169, 176, 187, 192, 207, 239
Bates, Louvinia 157, 162, 165, 172, 310
Beard, Alma 216, 309
Belalau POW camp 274–5, 306 *see also* prisoner of war camps
    coolie lines 274
    deaths at 275–6, 278–9
    evacuation of 284–90
    letters from home 275
    psychological damage to prisoners 298–9
    searches for nurses 282–3
    wills made in 276–7

Bennett, Major General H. Gordon 29, 43, 52, 67, 71–2, 81, 85, 88, 89, 102, 164, 282, 309
beriberi 266, 268, 276, 278 *see also* tropical diseases and infections
Blake, Kathleen Constance (Pat) 121, 127, 143, 147, 237, 251, 277, 300
Blanch, Jessie (Blanchie) 96, 98, 163–4, 169–70, 182–3, 234, 244, 260, 271, 299, 300
    Associate Red Cross award 308
'Bomb Alley' *see* Banka Strait
Borton, R.E (Tubby) 2–5, 120, 122, 123, 125, 126–7, 128, 130, 137, 138–9, 140, 142, 152, 325–6
    Japanese attack, tactics during 147, 148–50
Bourhill, June 135, 165, 325
Bowden, Vivian 193–4, 320
Breaker Morant 19
Bridge, Ada 218
British Armed Forces 4, 51, 89
    public denigration of Japanese 43, 51
Brown, Flying Officer Ken 285
Brown, Mary 3, 135–6, 174, 239, 247
Brown, Shelagh 3, 135–6, 138, 174
Bukit Panjang 91–2, 93
Bull, Hazel 174–5
Bull, Mrs 174
The Bulletin 90–1
Bullwinkel, Vivian 45, 47, 117, 124, 128–9, 141–2, 157, 163, 172, 176–7, 196, 199–200, 203–4, 211, 214–18, 234–8, 240, 244, 254, 277–8, 291, 293, 298–9, 300, 304–6, 309, 314, 315–16, 321, 322, 327

INDEX

Bullwinkel, Vivian (cont'd)
   Associate Red Cross award 308
   Australian College of Nursing president 305
   Australian War Crimes Commission of Inquiry, at 311–12
   Australian War Memorial trustee 305
   Florence Nightingale Medal 308
   International War Crimes Tribunal, at 226, 312–13
   National Service Nurses' Memorial patron 305
   Nurses' Memorial Centre 305–7, 313
   Order of the British Empire 308
   Royal Humane Society of Australia appointment 305
   surrender to Japanese 231–33
   survival of Radji Beach massacre 220–7, 318–19

Cade, Major John 307
Calnan, Ellenor 166, 306, 310
Camp Chronicle 248
Campbell, Molly 105
Capon, Captain Selwyn 109–10, 111
The Captive's Hymn 248
Carey, Private John 86
Casson, Flo 153, 182–3, 199–200, 214–18, 309
Casualty Clearing Station (CCS) 4, 11, 13, 69, 91 *see also* Australian Army Nursing Service (AANS)
   2/2nd *see* 2/2nd CCS
   2/4th *see* 2/4th CCS
Cathay Building 57, 112
Chambers, Norah 136

Chang, Dr Victor 290
Changi POW camp 111, 291, 292, 303, 307, 314, 326 *see also* prisoner of war camps
Charitas Hospital 254
Churchill, Winston 19, 38, 43, 51
Clancy, Veronica 105, 138, 148, 156–7, 161, 174, 176, 179–80, 181, 194, 242–3, 254, 300, 315
Clarke, Mary 148, 172, 187, 234
Coates, Colonel Albert 75
Colonial Service Hospital 27, 28–9, 41, 59, 68, 69, 73, 75–6
Commonwealth War Graves Commission 313
Curtin, Prime Minister John 42, 43, 253
Cuthbertson, Mary 96, 157, 218, 306, 310

Darling, Colin 304
Darling, Pat *see* Gunther, Pat
'Dashing Dot' *see* Paschke, Matron Olive
Davis, Winnie May 54, 96, 121, 127, 148, 163, 170, 171, 173, 174, 237, 244, 250, 251, 256, 257, 276
Delforce, Cecilia 172, 189, 257, 300
   Mentioned in Dispatches 308
Derham, Colonel Alfred 89, 103, 104, 107, 108
'Dhobi Itch' 29–30
diseases *see* tropical diseases and infections
Dorsch, Jess 92, 187, 234
Doyle, Jess 121, 127–8, 237, 243, 244, 250, 262, 300, 303

INDEX

Dreverman, Captain (Dracula) 97
drinking culture 26
Drummond, Matron Irene 4, 13–14, 16, 19, 21, 35, 37, 47, 54, 59, 69, 72, 79–80, 93, 98, 102, 107, 108, 122, 130–1, 133, 137, 140, 157, 159, 168, 169, 173, 196, 197–9, 201–3, 205, 208–16, 261, 311, 327–8
Dryburgh, Margaret 248, 268
dysentery 269, 275–8 *see also* tropical diseases and infections

'Elbow Force' 10
Elmes, Dorothy Gwendoline Howard (Buddy) 17–18, 166, 218, 328
 letters to 'Old Smithy' 28, 32, 34, 40, 66, 101, 102
Empire Star 107–12, 252, 293
 attack on 110–11
 sinking of 112
Ennis, Caroline 153, 156, 171, 184–7, 234, 328
European social clubs 31–2, 33

Fairweather, Lorna 141–2, 218
Farmaner, Peggy 169, 218
Florence Nightingale Medal 308
Floyd, Lieutenant Jean 108, 288
Fort Canning 100, 137
Frazer's Hill 32–3, 34, 275
Freeman, Dot 95, 96, 247–8, 251, 258, 263, 278

Galleghan, Lieutenant Colonel Frederick (Black Jack) 92
Gardam, Shirley 92, 113, 174, 179, 246, 250, 269, 272

George Cross 262, 308
German, Eric 219, 220
Giang Bee 126, 302
Gibson, Dorothy 170, 188, 194
Gillman Hospital 91
Goldberg, Dr 134–5, 176, 179, 181, 236, 274
Great East Asia Co-Prosperity Sphere 63
Greer, Jenny 5, 35, 123, 163, 169–70, 171, 182–3, 194, 243, 249, 251, 289, 299, 300, 303, 315
Gregory, Jack 128
Gunther, Pat 27, 33, 54, 104, 121, 127, 148, 159, 163, 170, 171, 173, 177, 237, 250, 256, 269, 277–8, 287, 297, 300, 304, 315, 322
 Portrait of a Nurse 304

Halligan, Clare (Clarice) 96, 153, 159, 177, 199, 214–18
Hamilton, Colonel Tom 18–19, 37, 62–3, 72, 76, 92, 94, 96, 100, 113, 117, 169, 246, 326
Hannah, Mavis 36, 92, 97, 113, 116, 121, 137, 151, 168, 169, 173, 183–4, 233, 250, 255–6, 257, 275, 295–6, 297, 299, 300, 302–3, 315, 316–17
Harper, Iole 49, 157, 162, 171, 184–7, 190–1, 195, 234, 235, 250, 257, 263, 300, 315, 320, 328
Harris, Nancy 86, 117, 124, 141, 214–18
Hayman, May 310–11
Hempsted, Blanche 93, 176, 179–80, 194, 268–9
HMAHS *Wanganella* 44–5, 48–50, 104

INDEX

HMAS *Kanimbla* 312
HMS *Jarak* 126–7
Hodgeson, Minnie 218, 310
Hong Kong 21, 74–5, 104
    Japanese attack on 67
Hookway, Hayman 304
Hughes, Gladys 148, 174, 179–80, 258, 274, 275–6
Hunt, Major Bruce 55, 58, 87, 326

In Japanese Hands: Australian Nurses as POWs 304
Indochina 43, 65
International War Crimes Tribunal 225, 226, 260, 312–13 *see also* war crimes
internment camps *see* Banka Island, Belalau POW camp, Changi POW camp, Irenelaan POW camp, Palembang, prisoner of war camps
Irenelaan POW camp 241–3, 305 *see also* prisoner of war camps
    Camp Chronicle 248
    Christmas at 249
    clothing issue 256
    decline of conditions 252–3, 256–60
    deficiency diseases 259, 271
    Dutch internees at 241–2
    letters from home 262–3
    Maichi, Captain 243
    officers' club at 243–5, 295–6, 322–5
    prayer groups 248
    psychological damage to prisoners 298–9
    punishments issued by officers 259–60
    rations 253, 258–60, 261
    relocation 264–5, 272–3
    social activities in 246–7

Jacobs, Major Gideon 282–3, 290
    rescue led by 284–90
Jakarta War Cemetery 313
James, Maudie 137
James, Nesta 17, 130, 172, 188–9, 233, 240, 242, 244, 260, 261, 265, 283, 284, 288, 296, 298, 300, 315
    Associate Red Cross award 308
    Australian War Crimes Commission of Inquiry, at 311–12
    International War Crimes Tribunal, at 312–13
    Mentioned in Dispatches 308
Japanese Imperial Forces
    atrocities committed by 74–5, 118–19, 193–4, 294 *see also* prisoner of war camps; Radji Beach
    Australian forces, battles with 82–3
    bomber flights 81–2
    'comfort women', abuse of 324–5
    Great East Asia Co-Prosperity Sphere 63
    Hong Kong, attack on 67, 75–5
    Indochina, in 43
    Kato, Sergeant Major Taro 320
    Masaru, Captain Orita 211, 215, 217–18, 319–21
    prisoner of war camps, administration of 252–3, 257–60, 263, 270–1, 272

INDEX

public denigration of 43, 51
punishments issued by 259–60
Radji Beach massacre 212–18, 291, 318–21
Seki, Captain 264, 272, 278–9, 280–1
Singapore, advance into 3, 103
South East Asia, expansion into 63–4
229th Regiment of 38th Division 319
Unites States of America, negotiations with 64, 66
Vyner Brooke, attacks on 141–2, 148–52, 155–8
Yamashita, General 119, 192
Jeffery, Agnes Betty (Jeff) 41, 95–6, 99–100, 107, 108, 114, 121–2, 123–4, 143, 147, 150, 152–3, 155–7, 158, 171, 172, 184–7, 190–1, 195, 234, 235, 237, 247–8, 250, 257, 258, 261–2, 263, 266–7, 275, 277–8, 286, 297, 300, 305–7, 309, 315, 320, 322, 328
   Medal of the Order of Australia 308
   Nurses' Memorial Centre 305–7, 313
   White Coolies 307
Joubert, Matron Eileen 296

Kajang High School hospital 37
Kato, Sergeant Major Taro 320
Keats, Nell 80, 101, 218
Kent-Hughes, Colonel Wilfred 52–3
Keppel Harbour 1–5, 22, 41, 52, 104, 106, 107, 109, 117, 294
   Vyner Brooke departure from 120–1, 123, 126

Kerr, Jenny 214–18, 310
Kingsley, Pat 207, 222–7, 238
   surrender to Japanese 231–3
   survival of Radji Beach massacre 222–7
Kinsella, Katherine (Kit) 46, 54, 59, 91, 98, 100, 130, 165
   Royal Red Cross recommendation 92
'Kinsella Avenue' 69–70
Kluang hospital 62–3, 69, 76, 81, 83, 84
Kranji 118, 314

Lennard, Hayden 283, 285–6
Li Wo 126
Linggo Island 129
Lloyd, Ernest 213–14, 219–20, 238, 321

Macauley, Norman 303
McDonald, Gladys 171–2, 187, 234
McDowell, Dr Jean 236
McEachern, Thelma 105
McElnea, Violet (Vi) 140, 173, 265, 300, 315
McGlade, Mary Eleanor (Ellie) 44–5, 218, 310
McGregor, Colin 303
McGregor, Sylvia *see* Muir, Sylvia
McGuire, Major General 48
Maddern, Mrs 175, 181
Madson, Squadron Leader Fred 288
Maichi, Captain 243
Malacca
   AIF cemetery 30
   Colonial Service Hospital, at 27, 28–9, 41, 59, 68, 69, 73, 75–6

INDEX

Malacca (cont'd)
  evacuation of 76
  social life in 31–2
malaria 98, 266, 271, 275, 277, 278 *see also* tropical diseases and infections
Malay Peninsula 25, 27, 28
  Japanese attack on 67
Malayan Campaign 5, 119
Malayan Emergency 303
Mann, Lieutenant A.J. 126, 137
Manunda 294, 296–7
Masaru, Captain Orita 211, 215, 217–18, 319–21
masseuses 109
Mata Hari 126
media
  Australian Women's Weekly 37–40, 60
  The Bulletin 90–1
  International War Crimes Tribunal, coverage of 313
  Vyner Brooke nurses, coverage of return 283, 289–90, 294–6
  While You Were Away booklet 298
medical treatment *see also* Australian Army Nursing Service (AANS)
  front line, on 83–5
  World War I, differences between 85
Mentioned in Dispatches 308
Menzies, Prime Minister 38, 42
Miller, Second Officer Jimmy 2, 120, 125–6, 131, 163, 172, 176–7, 199–200, 201–3, 205, 208–9, 212, 311
Mittelheuser, Pearl (Mitz) 105, 171, 174, 242, 244, 248, 251, 278

Modin, Air Commodore 240, 291–2
morphia 83, 104, 141, 155, 157, 174
Mountbatten, Lady Edwina 294
Muir, Sylvia 153–4, 170–1, 174, 179, 246, 248, 250, 278, 300, 303, 315
Muntok *see* Banka Island

National Service Nurses' Memorial 305
Neubrunner, Olga 3, 136, 175, 180–1, 235
Neuss, Kathleen 121, 127, 148, 154, 159, 218, 310
No 1 Malayan General Hospital 91
Nurses' Memorial Centre 305–7, 313
nursing *see also* Australian Army Nursing Service (AANS)
  Australian College of Nursing 305
  career choice for girls 11–12
  Nurses' Memorial Centre 305–7, 313
  scholarships 307–8
  training regime 12

Oldham, Sally 249, 260
Oldham Hall Mission Boarding House hospital 78–9, 87–8, 105–6
  bombing of 94–5
  evacuation of 107–8, 113
113th AGH 300
Oram, Wilma 45–7, 54, 56–8, 60–2, 68, 70–1, 73, 100, 104, 121, 140, 152, 154, 159–61, 165, 170, 188,

INDEX

194, 233, 234, 246, 251, 255, 260, 262, 266, 277–8, 304, 314, 315, 322
Orcades 106
Oxley, Christian Sarah (Chris) 168, 248–9, 277, 281, 300

Pacific War 43, 64, 67, 69–70, 89
   end of 279–81
Palembang 238
   Banka Island, transfer from 239–40
   Bukit Besar POW camp 239–40 *see also* prisoner of war camps
   Charitas Hospital 254
   oil installations, air raids on 262
Paradise Road 322
Paris, Brigadier General Archie 164
Parit Sulong massacre 118
Park, Captain John 118
Parkes, Corporal Ralph 255
Paschke, Matron Olive 4, 12–14, 16, 21, 29, 35, 36, 39, 41, 47, 76, 79, 95–6, 98, 105, 107–8, 112, 114, 120, 121–3, 130, 132–3, 137–8, 140–1, 155, 157, 158–9, 161–2, 168, 171, 174, 184–7, 193, 195, 234, 235, 261, 311, 327–8
   'Dashing Dot' 13
   Royal Red Cross award 81
Pearl Harbour, attack on 67
Pemberton, Duncan 35, 303
Pemberton, Jenny *see* Greer, Jenny
Percival, General Arthur 85, 88, 102, 119, 192
Philippines, attack on 67
Pigdon, Colonel 54, 67, 72, 326
Pitts, Zaza 138

Port Dickson 27, 102
Portrait of a Nurse 304
POW *see* prisoner of war camps
Prince of Wales 1, 125, 174, 203
prisoner of war camps *see also* Banka Island; Belalau POW camp; Changi POW camp; Irenelaan POW camp; Palembang
   Camp Chronicle 248
   'comfort women', abuse of 324–5
   deaths in 266–70, 272, 275–6, 278–9
   decline of camp conditions 252–3, 256–60
   deficiency diseases 259, 271
   funerals held 266–70, 276
   Japanese administration of 252–3, 257–60, 263, 270–1, 272
   letters from home 262–3, 275
   life expectancy of survivors 314–15
   payments 242
   psychological damage to prisoners 298–9
   recovery of remains post-war 313
   searches for prisoners 282–3
   'The Song of Death' 270
   tropical diseases in 266, 270, 271, 275–8 *see also* tropical diseases and infections
   While You Were Away booklet 298
   wills made in 276–7
Pugh, Phyllis 53–4, 55, 98, 108, 293

INDEX

Queen Mary 9–10, 10–12, 102
   facilities onboard 15
   Singapore, arrival in 22–3, 24–7
   voyage from Sydney 14–23
   X-Press newspaper 16
QX see Queen Mary

Radji Beach 196, 306
   Japanese soldiers, arrival of 211
   massacre 212–18, 291, 318–21
   memorial 314
   rape speculation 321–2
   shipwreck survivors arrival on 198–9, 207–8
Rajah Brooke 124
Rajah of Sarawak 124
Raymont, Mina (Ray) 92, 174, 179, 246, 248, 251, 260, 263, 266–8, 269
Red Cross 31, 97, 240, 244, 256, 279, 283, 289, 323
   armbands 67, 68, 113, 114, 123, 141
   Florence Nightingale Medal 308
   Royal Red Cross award 81, 92
Reith, Lieutenant David 126, 165
Repulse 1
Returned Services' League 304, 310
Royal Humane Society of Australia 305
Royal Navy Singapore Island naval base 22, 51
Royal Red Cross award 81, 92
Russell, Lavinia 148, 166, 309

Sage, Colonel Annie 283, 288, 307, 309, 326
St Andrew's Cathedral 112, 113–14

St Patrick's School hospital 52–3, 55, 86, 96–7, 101, 108, 112, 113
   bombing of 91
   return of prisoners of war survivors 289–90, 292–3
St Stephen's massacre 74–5, 319
Salmon, Florence 218, 310
Salvation Army 26
Schuman, Marjorie (Shuie) 17–18, 66, 166, 309
2/2nd CCS 106
2/4th CCS 4, 11, 14, 16, 18, 54, 85–6, 91, 92, 97, 100, 107, 113, 169, 175, 233, 241, 297
   Bukit Panjang, at 91–2, 93, 96
   Kajang High School, at 37
   Kluang, at 62–3, 69, 76, 81, 83, 84
   Port Dickson, at 27, 36–7
   The Swiss Club, at 93–4
2/7th AGH 262
2/10th AGH 4, 11, 13, 16, 17, 18, 37, 41, 54, 55, 76, 78, 93, 105, 107, 112, 127, 172, 233, 241, 288
   Colonial Service Hospital, at 27, 28–9, 41, 59, 68, 69, 73, 75–6
   evacuation of Singapore 105–12
   Oldham Hall Mission Boarding House, at 78–9, 87–8, 94–5, 107–8, 113
2/12th AGH 78
2/13th AGH 4, 43, 45, 48, 54, 55, 58, 63, 76, 85, 86–7, 93, 107, 172, 199, 233, 241, 288, 293, 326
   St Patrick's School, at 52–3, 55, 86, 91, 96–7, 101, 108, 113, 289–90, 292–3

INDEX

Tampoi Hill, at 59–60, 62, 67–8, 69, 73, 76, 78, 81, 84, 85, 86–7
2/14th AGH 293, 294
Seddon, Robert 321
Sedgeman, Lieutenant Bill 2, 125, 159, 197–9, 201–7, 212, 311, 319
Seki, Captain 264, 278–9, 280–1
Selatar naval base 26
17th Combined General Hospital 91
shipwreck survivors 236 *see also* Banka Island; Radji Beach; *Vyner Brooke*
Short, Eileen 194, 250, 300, 315
Simons, Jessie 54–5, 57, 129, 134, 136, 142, 154, 157, 162, 170, 173, 174, 177–9, 247, 248, 250, 268, 278, 280, 300, 303–4, 322
  In Japanese Hands: Australian Nurses as POWs 304
  While History Passed 304
Singapore 21–3
  ambulance units on 91
  destruction of causeway 89, 90
  ethnic groups 25–6
  evacuation of nurses 103–19
  fall of 2–5, 119, 192, 291
  nursing scholarship 307–8
'Singapore Ear' 29–30
Singleton, Irene (Rene) 34, 99, 247–8, 258, 263, 268, 278, 309
Smith, Adele Shelton 37–40
Smith, Dr 236
Smith, Val 100, 173, 248, 254, 257, 260, 266, 267, 300
Smithenbecker, Claire (Old Smithy) 18, 28, 32, 40, 66
'The Song of Death' 270

Statham, Frank 305, 315
Statham, Vivian *see* Bullwinkel, Vivian
Stewart, Jean 218
Straits of Jahore
  destruction of causeway 89, 90
Straits Settlements 26, 135, 192
  Govenor Thomas 52, 119
  Volunteer Naval Reserve 2
Sultan of Jahore (Sir Ibrahim) 60–2, 72
Syer, Ada (Mickey) 248, 251, 302, 309, 315
Syer, Flo *see* Trotter, Flo

Tait, Mona 218, 310–11
Tampoi Hill hospital 59–60, 62, 67–8, 84, 85
  evacuation of 86–7
  expansion of 76–7
Tangjung Priok 106
Tebbutt, Major Bill 4, 128, 130, 142, 158, 161
Thomas, Lady Daisy 26
Thomas, Sir Shenton 52, 119
Tobruk 38
Tojou Island 139
Tokyo War Crimes Tribunal hearings 225, 226, 260, 312–13 *see also* war crimes
Torney, Sister 262
Trenerry, Merle 171, 187, 234, 310
'Tripehounds' 18, 32, 66
tropical diseases and infections 29–30, 50, 55, 78, 93, 98, 266, 270, 271, 275–8
Trotter, Flo 169–70, 248, 257, 262, 299, 302, 309, 315, 316
Tunbridge, Phyllis 137, 188–9

359

INDEX

Tunn, Mr 252
Tweddell, Joyce (Tweedie) 168, 169–71, 182–3, 248, 290, 300, 304, 314, 315
Tyersall Park Hospital 102–3

uniforms 11, 16, 35, 36, 135, 141, 199, 238, 267, 284–5, 299
   emergency kits 67–8
United States of America
   Japan, negotiations with 64, 66

Vyner Brooke 1–5, 116–7, 282, 326
   bombing of 151
   departure from Singapore 123, 126
   evacuation of 159–64
   food supplies 122
   history 124–5
   Japanese attacks on 141–2, 148–52, 155–8
   last voyage 120–43
   passengers on 126, 133–4, 137–8
   shipwreck survivors 176–7, 180–1, 182–4, 187–91, 194–5, 198–9, 235, 283
   sinking 164–6

Wah Sui 78, 104–6, 252
war crimes
   Allied investigation units 311–12
   atrocities committed by Japanese forces 74–5, 118–19, 193–4, 294 *see also* prisoner of war camps; Radji Beach
   Australian War Crimes Commission of Inquiry 311–12
   International War Crimes Tribunal 225, 226, 260, 312–13
Warman, Mischa 3, 134, 152, 157, 165, 235, 325
Warman, Mr 3, 134, 152, 165
Warman, Mrs 3, 134, 157, 165
Weston, Lieutenant 119
While History Passed 304
While You Were Away booklet 298
White Coolies 307
'The White Elephant' *see* Colonial Service Hospital
White, Colonel Glyn (Ted) 95, 108, 114, 116
White, Commander J.C.S. 201
White Rajah of Sarawak 1, 117, 326
Wight, Rosetta 153, 159, 177, 199–200, 214–8
Wilmot, Peggy 169, 218
Wilton, Mona 45–7, 54, 56–8, 60–2, 68, 70–1, 73, 100, 101–2, 105, 121, 154, 159–61, 165, 234, 255, 315
Windsor, Major Harry 283, 287, 290, 291
Woodbridge, Beryl (Woodie) 169–70, 182–3, 246, 257, 300, 305, 315

X-Press newspaper 16

Yamashita, General 119, 192
Young, Alan 304
Young, Wilma *see* Oram, Wilma

Zealandia 41